W0112565

Islam in the West

'This book makes a significant contribution to one of the most important issues facing our world. No two civilizations have been as closely intertwined in history as Islam and the West, but in recent times Islamic extremism and Western Islamophobias threaten to polarize our world. Abe and Ali's work is multi-disciplinary and multi-perspective, and it gives us a constructive exchange of ideas that helps us unpack the misperceptions, distrust, and prejudices that stand in the way of good dialogue and understanding. It presents a vision of intercultural relations that affirms the importance of resilience, tolerance, respect, and trust.'

Jane den Hollander AO, president and vice-chancellor Deakin University, Australia

'Doctors Abe Ata and Jan Ali are to be congratulated on bringing together an expert and balanced collection of analyses of Islam within the context both of its character and history and the tensions and prejudices against it in current attitudes by others. That Islam is a complex and widely misunderstood religion is only just being recognized in societies like Australia, which have otherwise seen it only through mass media descriptions of various terrorist episodes or civil wars. Their well chosen and informative contributors go a long way to present a much better understanding of the realities than such typical comments.'

James Jupp, AM, FASSA, visiting scholar at the Australian National University, Canberra, Australia, and general editor, *Bicentennial Encyclopaedia of the Australian People*

'The picture of the West reacting to the perceived threat of Islam provides a clear example of standing over against another group as a way of sustaining an identity. Being over against a "wicked" other justifies extreme positions and then the merry-go-round begins and the "wicked" other plays the victim card and bringing their colleagues onboard. It seems that so many of these "wicked" others are the alienated and nihilistic youth and the fact that so many of them are Islamic is incidental. As Olivier Roy claims, these youths are using Islam and in fact their violent radicalism is really the "Islamization of radicalism" to provide the context within which their nihilistic revolt can make sense. There is, therefore, a need for books such as this to provide information that will enable people to situate moderate Islam in a context that enables others, particularly Westerners, to gain a deeper knowledge of Muslims and to appreciate, accept, and benefit from their participation in a multicultural society.'

Peter Bray, FSC, EdD, vice-chancellor, Bethlehem University (Palestine), West Bank of Jordan

Islam in the West
Perceptions and Reactions

edited by
Abe W. Ata
Jan A. Ali

OXFORD
UNIVERSITY PRESS

OXFORD
UNIVERSITY PRESS

Oxford University Press is a department of the University of Oxford.
It furthers the University's objective of excellence in research, scholarship,
and education by publishing worldwide. Oxford is a registered trademark of
Oxford University Press in the UK and in certain other countries.

Published in India by
Oxford University Press
2/11 Ground Floor, Ansari Road, Daryaganj, New Delhi 110 002, India

© Oxford University Press 2018

The moral rights of the authors have been asserted.

First Edition published in 2018

All rights reserved. No part of this publication may be reproduced, stored in
a retrieval system, or transmitted, in any form or by any means, without the
prior permission in writing of Oxford University Press, or as expressly permitted
by law, by licence, or under terms agreed with the appropriate reprographics
rights organization. Enquiries concerning reproduction outside the scope of the
above should be sent to the Rights Department, Oxford University Press, at the
address above

You must not circulate this work in any other form
and you must impose this same condition on any acquirer.

ISBN-13 (print edition): 978-0-19-948711-0
ISBN-10 (print edition): 0-19-948711-1

ISBN-13 (eBook): 978-0-19-909366-3
ISBN-10 (eBook): 0-19-909366-0

Typeset in Dante MT Std 10.5/13
by The Graphics Solution, New Delhi 110 092
Printed in India by Rakmo Press, New Delhi 110 020

Contents

List of Tables and Figures   vii

Foreword by Garry W. Trompf   ix

Acknowledgements   xiii

Introduction: Understanding Islam–West Relations and
Muslim and Non-Muslim Mutual Perceptions   1
Abe W. Ata and Jan A. Ali

I Perceptions and Attitudes

1. Attitudes of School-Age Muslim Australians towards
   Australia: Gender and Religious Discrepancies—
   A National Survey   15
   Abe W. Ata

2. How Mainstream Australian Students Perceive Muslims
   and Islam: A National Survey   38
   Abe W. Ata

3. Framing, Branding, and Explaining: A Survey of
   Perceptions of Islam and Muslims in the Canadian Polls,
   Government, and Academia   68
   Ali Ghanbarpour-Dizboni and Christian Leuprecht

II Inclusion and Exclusion

4. Integrated Acculturation and Contact Strategies to
   Improve Anglo-Muslim Relations in Australia   91
   Hisham M. Abu-Rayya

5. Australian Muslims as Radicalized 'Other' and Their
   Experiences of Social Exclusion   108
   Jan A. Ali

6. Young Muslims' Identity in Australia and the US: The Focus
   on the 'Muslim Question'   129
   Nahid A. Kabir

7. Islam–West Relations and the Rise of Muslim Radicalism
   and Global Jihadism   156
   Jan A. Ali and Drew Cottle

8. Engaging with Islam, Engaging with Society: The
   Participation of Muslims in Dutch Society   176
   Thijl Sunier

III Faith and Identity

9. 'Muslims in the Modern Sense': Kabyles Negotiating
   Religious Identity in the Czech Republic   197
   Tereza Hyánková

10. Faith, Identity, and Ideology: Experiences of Australian
    Male Converts to Islam   215
    Paul Mitchell and Halim Rane

11. Muslim Communities in a Catholic Country: The Case
    of Italy   237
    Enzo Pace and Mohammed Khalid Rhazzali

Index   256
About the Editors and Contributors   261

Tables and Figures

Tables

I.1 Negative views of Muslims and Jews in Europe   3

1.1 Participant characteristics   20

2.1 Participant characteristics by gender   44

4.1 Differences between the acculturation orientations within the Anglo-Australian and Australian-Muslim samples   97

4.2. Bivariate correlations (r's) between acculturation orientations and intergroup measures within the Anglo-Australian and Australian-Muslim samples   97

11.1 Changes in the relationships between the State, the Catholic Church, and religious minorities   251

Figures

1.1 Responses to select statements reflecting attitudes towards Australia and Australians   21

1.2 Response to 'What are the first words that come to your mind when you hear the word "Australian"?'   24

1.3 Response to 'What do you like most about non-Muslim Australians?'   25

1.4 Response to 'What do you like least about non-Muslim Australians?'   27

1.5 Proportion of correct and incorrect responses   30

1.6 The relationship between knowledge and select attitudinal statements   32

2.1 Response to 'What are the first words that come into your mind when "Muslim" is mentioned?'   45

2.2 Response to 'What do you like most about Muslims?'   46

2.3 Response to 'What do you like least about Muslims?'   48

2.4 Mean attitude scores by gender   52

2.5 Mean attitude scores by religion   54

2.6 Proportion of correct and incorrect responses   57

2.7 Proportion of respondents by social distance of self from Muslims   59

2.8 Proportion of positive responses to attributes of selected religious groups   61

4.1 Effects of social contact strategies on intergroup measures via acculturation strategies   100

6.1 Contestation over the Cronulla Beach space between Anglo-Australians and Lebanese Australians, December 2005   140

6.2 Homegrown terror   145

Foreword

A t this point in time, no two subjects are more pressing for social theorists to understand and explain than the relationship between the two largest religious blocs on the planet and the encounter between Islam and modernity. Considering the upheavals of recent times—with many unpredictable acts of terror by Islamic extremists and the mass exodus of refugees from the war in Syria—other related and now even more pressing matters for research concern what happens to Muslim populations, including many newcomers ripped from their traditional contexts, in ultra-modern Western contexts, and how Islamic-Western relations in these contexts are being affected by crises over the last quarter century. Solid research on these latter issues is unfurled in this valuable volume, and the editors, who make significant contributions of their own, have done well in involving an impressive international cast of scholarly investigators for its making.

Interestingly, this is not a book about high-level dialogue between Christians and Muslims, which usually involves those who are well versed in their traditions; nor is it about how representatives of religious traditions encounter one another and enunciate their 'standard positions'. Questions of inner conflicts within the great Christian and Muslim configurations (Catholic/Orthodox/Protestant/sectarian and Sunni/Shia/sectarian) are not to the forefront either. And the book is not strictly speaking just about unofficial or popular versions of the two faiths brushing up against each other. These are crucial enough matters for the sociology of consciousness in our time, but they are somewhat easier to handle than the agenda set for the authors here. For, the volume concerns Islam and the West; and already the Western world has been affected by 'post-Christian' and secularizing energies, and immigration policies have produced multi-ethnic societies and religious pluralities. How Islam is experienced in the West, then, and how it experiences itself, is not just an inter-religious issue, but involves a complex mesh, even though there will be common projections by Muslims in the West that they are living in a Christian world (often seen as an inadequate one) and many Westerners, Christian, or otherwise, will see Islam as a threat to the Christian values under which their countries were established. On top of this, members of the Islamic fold themselves have not been impervious to modernizing shifts and many will be more 'cultural Muslims' than practising ones, so that perceptions between 'Muslims and others' in the West may be more positive in workplace relations or in secular activities than when religious differences get exposed.

Working out relations between 'Muslims in the West' and 'the realities of Western life' may be one thing, but sorting out Islamic-Western relations in terms of modernity and globalization is another. Modernization and globalism have been connected to Western capitalist hegemony and technological advantage, yet in fact there are now many features of global modernization that have been readily appropriated by Muslims, especially for going about their everyday business. What most draws the attention of the participants in this volume, though, is the plain difficulty of Muslims and non-Muslim Westerners (often in 'host nations') living together when publicization of terrorism and scenes of violence in the Middle East give grounds for mutual antipathy and thus for the noticeable emergence of intra-national divisiveness. The efficient media of the global village exacerbates weaknesses in an already fragile 'multicultural peace'.

This book, then, renders a signal service for concentrating on perceptions, on how Muslims and non-Muslims react to each other in contemporary Western societies, on Muslim feelings of social exclusion, on the relative degrees of Muslims' social participation in secular Western life, on questions of self-identity, government constructions of groups and cultures in policy, and on the phenomena of Westerners converting to Islam. These are all matters of immediate concern, but one suspects also of long-term significance, making this collection both timely and of potential endurance. Indeed, how multicultural societies can manage to hold together, how deeply prejudices can run (over religious matters often cutting more deeply in anti-religious quarters than anywhere else), how undercurrent internal hostilities change the way people feel about their own nationhood and social stability, and how governments often find themselves without the expertise to forge the best policies to cover socio-religious sensitivities, will be perennial issues to address in the West for generations to come. Already Western political struggles have yielded populist parties that speak openly about reducing the intake of migrants from Muslim countries, affecting voters that range from those with plain xenophobic attitudes to anxious Western souls who receive filtered news that Middle Eastern Christians are under threat of extinction.

Thus, in the light of its high intellectual standards and its obvious relevance to today's problems, I commend this volume highly. I salute its editors Abe W. Ata, a veteran publisher on multicultural issues in Australia, and Jan A. Ali, an accomplished sociologist of Islamic revivalism, for their achievement in seeing through this very helpful academic creation.

Garry W. Trompf, professor emeritus in the history of
ideas and adjunct professor in peace and conflict studies,
University of Sydney, Australia

24 October 2017

Acknowledgements

M y deepest appreciation for the ongoing support and encourage-ment for this book, and other recent projects, are reserved to my colleague and co-editor, Dr Jan Ali, and also to Professor Jane den Hollander, Brother Peter Bray, Dr Debra Houghton, Nigel Rovkliffe, and the William Angliss Charitable Fund.

Abe Ata
21 June 2018

ABE W. ATA

JAN A. ALI

Introduction

Understanding Islam–West Relations and Muslim and Non-Muslim Mutual Perceptions

The current Islam–West relations have a long and rich history of subjugation, cooperation, suspicions, and misunderstandings. Islam as a religion and cultural tradition has been at the doorsteps of Europe since its early days, and contrary to common assumption Islam in the West is an old phenomenon. In the first Islamic century, Muslims successfully penetrated North Africa, Spain, and briefly France. The mounting of a crusading effort by Pope Urban II, in an attempt to regain Christian Jerusalem, formed the basis for 'Crusader and anti-Crusader' temperament; this has shaped attitudes of the Christendom and Islamicate towards each other for centuries.

Islamic sciences, medicine, philosophy, and the arts found their way into Spain between tenth and fifteenth centuries, laying the foundation for Western modernity. By nineteenth and twentieth centuries, the West had achieved great success in essentially all spheres of life and became powerful enough not only to exercise tremendous influence over the Muslim world but practically dismantle it into colonial outposts. The consequences of colonialism continue to be felt by Muslim masses in Muslim-majority countries and in diaspora communities, and heavily impacts on Islam–West relations.

In the last several decades of the twentieth century the relations between Islam and the West somewhat turned tense impacted by, for instance, the Iranian Revolution of 1978–9, the Lockerbie bombing in 1988, and the Gulf War of 1990–1. Islam was problematized and Islamic threat accentuated with a clash of civilizations thesis engineered by Samuel Huntington in his 1993 seminal article and the best-selling book entitled *The Clash of Civilizations* in 1996. Islam–West relations reached a new turning point in 2001 with the bombings of the Twin Towers of the World Trade Centre in New York and the Pentagon in Washington and subsequent terrorist attacks in different countries of the West. Islam has been depicted as a global threat on three levels: political, civilizational, and demographic. The global 'War on Terror' has reinforced and fuelled an irrational fear of the religion of Islam and its adherents.

Based on this and the negative portrayal of Islam and threatening Muslim 'other' in the Western media, many in the West have come to understand Islam as a religion that inspires terrorism and Muslims as terrorists who are bent on destroying the West in whichever way possible. Many countries of the West such as the USA, United Kingdom, France, Germany, and Australia have developed a suite of tough policies, laws, and security measures, including targeting Muslims for discriminatory investigation and treatment under their securitization regimes.

The reactions of Muslims to these developments have been diverse but overall a feeling of anger towards those responsible for perpetrating violence in the society and despair over contradictory and self-serving conduct of the West. From Muslim perspective the West says one thing and does another and whilst it claims to be the beacon of moral virtue, rationality, and humanity Muslims find themselves in their own countries and in diasporas victims of discrimination, prejudice, inequality, marginalization, injustice, and mistreatment.

Ethnocentric attitudes are on the rise in Europe and elsewhere with varying degree of intensity. There are more people harbouring ethnocentric attitudes arguably in several major European countries than they were several years ago. The recent data obtained by Pew Research Center[1] has revealed that the numbers of people with unfavourable

---

[1] Pew Research Center (2008).

opinions of both Jews and Muslims have been on the rise with the latter attracting more negative attitudes.

Opinions about Muslims in almost all of these countries are considerably more negative than are views towards Jews (see Table I.1). Fully half of Spanish (52 per cent) and German respondents (50 per cent) rate Muslims unfavourably. Opinions about Muslims are somewhat less negative in Poland (46 per cent) and considerably less negative in France (38 per cent). About one-in-four in Britain and the United States (23 per cent each) also voice unfavourable views towards Muslims. Overall,

TABLE I.1   Negative views of Muslims and Jews in Europe

| | Jews | Muslims |

Percent unfavourable

	Jews	Muslims
Under 50	25	41
50+	30	52
No college	31	50
College	20	37
Political ideology		
Left	28	42
Centre	26	45
Right	34	56

Questions 10e and 10g.
Combined data from France, Germany, and Spain.

Source: Pew Research Center (July 2008).

there is a clear relationship between anti-Jewish and anti-Muslim attitudes: public that views Jews unfavourably also tend to see Muslims in a negative light.

The trend in negative views towards Muslims in Europe has occurred over a longer period of time than growing anti-Jewish sentiments. Most of the upswing took place between 2004 and 2006, and there has even been a slight decrease in some countries since 2006.

Negative attitudes towards Christians in Europe are less common than negative ratings of Muslims or Jews. And views about Christians have remained largely stable in recent years, although anti-Christian sentiments have been on the rise in Spain—about one in four Spanish (24 per cent) now rate Christians negatively, up from 10 per cent in 2005. Similarly, in France 17 per cent now hold an unfavourable view towards Christians, compared with 9 per cent in 2004. There is little data available about attitudes towards Muslim societies at large than towards Christians and other minority citizens resident in Muslim countries.

A notable parallel between anti-Muslim and anti-Jewish opinion in Western Europe is that both sentiments are most prevalent among the same groups of people. Older people and those with less education are more anti-Semitic and anti-Muslim than are younger people or those with more education. Looking at combined data from France, Germany, and Spain—the three Western European countries where unfavourable opinions of Jews are most common—people aged 50 and older express more negative views of both Jews and Muslims than do those younger than 50. Similarly, Europeans who have not attended college are consistently more likely than those who have to hold unfavourable opinions of both groups.

Negative attitudes towards Christians have been on the rise in a few countries over the last several years, most dramatically in Turkey. The trend in Turkish opinions about Christians has been very similar to the trend regarding Jews. In 2004, about half (52 per cent) of Turks gave Christians an unfavourable rating; today roughly three in four (74 per cent) hold this view.

The Indian public has become somewhat more negative towards Christians. In 2005, 19 per cent of Indians had a negative opinion of Christians; now 37 per cent do. Unfavourable views of Christians are also up in Indonesia, rising from 32 per cent in 2006 to 41 per cent today.

That said, significant differences in the teaching and attitudes between the two religions are not to be side-stepped due to a false sense of security. Differences of interpretation towards social values and way of life, individual accountability, consensual decision-making, and attitudes towards implementing moral imperatives do exist. It is feasible that we should be able to acknowledge them, respect them, and address them without aiming at a fine compromise. Not because we no longer need a dialogue, but because 'these different approaches have concrete implications to both communities living together in a shared place'.[2] Professor Robert Manne has referred to this capacity of accommodating many cultural and religious expressions—within a single language, law, and polity—as multiculturalism.

Moderate Muslims who keep their faith on a personal level, avoid bringing political issues out of it, and feel embarrassed at actions made under the banner of their religion are in particular need of such an endorsement. Absence of religious hierarchy has prompted many moderate Muslims to take matters into their own hands and become more organized. For a self-serving minority it may be politically convenient to demonize others on the basis of race or religion, but it never defeats their own phobias.

This book is a collection of international and interdisciplinary essays providing multi-perspectival contributions to the current debate on Islam-West relations. Each chapter will bring to surface recent findings and data and consider the cumulative impact in which Muslims find themselves in the West; how they are at time caught in the middle of two cultural traditions; the dilemma and perception of being accepted by the mainstream society which directly touches the daily life of a growing community, and predictors of what may constitute negatives attitudes towards Muslims that we may predict from the scale of 'our' knowledge, fashionable or well worn.

What Makes This Work Different from Other Publications on This Subject?

Undertaking to cover all aspects of an important subject such as this is a formidable task. The diversity of issues in this book makes it difficult

---

[2] Ata (2009: 15).

to go into the ultimate depth and breadth in any one subject area. For example, the complexity of covering all ethnic Muslim communities and associated variables, dynamics, and reactions by various non-Muslims including secular communities in one project makes it impossible to give it complete justice.

Even conclusions made in this book can only arguably be viewed as tentative—more research is variously needed. It would also have been gratifying to have incorporated several other facets such as women prisoners, secular Muslims, generational difference, Jewish–Muslim dialogue, Middle Eastern Christian–Muslim encounters, and the persecuted and marginalized.

And yet, the broad and diverse topics and perspectives covered in this project are unique, topical, intimate, and have not been broached before in a published form. They are written by contributors who are members of Muslim community and outsiders. This, in many ways widens the frame of reference, effectiveness of argumentation, and style of criticism.

The analysis and understanding of what it means to be a Muslim and its consequences in growing multicultural, multi-religious, technologically advanced contemporary West presents a difficult and sensitive task. This collection provides a stepping stone on that journey and we commend it to those who wish to develop a better broader understanding of Muslims within the broader Western cultural and religious traditions.

Clearly this project was not carried out to garner consent or to be meant to be read by those who agree with its findings. Like all other literary undertakings, it provides a meaningful forum for those who habitually resort to the church hierarchy for authoritative meaning, or as a final frame of reference. It is due to the keen interest, perseverance and dedication, and encouraging gestures expressed by authors of the chapters herewith that brought this project to fruition. Words of tribute to their contribution to contemporary literature will not be sufficient to fully communicate our gratitude and indebtedness.

This publication is different from others in two major areas. Firstly, Muslims are not defined solely by province of their faith, but as an emerging group with dual identities—one which is soul searching, self-critical, reflective, and is redefined by Islam. The second posits the premise that Westerners who are more knowledgeable about Muslims would express more favourable opinions of Muslims and Islam and that through knowledge, greater levels of awareness come from equal status interaction between the learner and individuals of Muslim background. It is thus argued that the scale of our knowledge, fashionable or well worn, and negative attitudes are interrelated.

Islam in the West: Perceptions and Reactions is a multidisciplinary and multiperspective treatise. The collection of essays focuses on several themes including cultural pluralism, the media, religious education, civil engagement, spiritualism and interfaith dialogue, role of women, asylum seekers, sex abuse, mental health, mixed marriages, identity, social services and institutions, conversion to and from Islam, tolerance and factionalism, apologists and the faithful, schools and universities, challenges and future directions. A variety of methodologies, disciplines, and issues constitute the building blocks of this book, including theoretical elucidations, empirical case studies, and historical, political, and sociological analyses and more as summarized.

In Chapter 1, 'Attitudes of School-Age Muslim Australians towards Gender and Religious Discrepancies: A National Survey' by Abe W. Ata, the results of another national survey are outlined. The survey investigated the knowledge, values, and attitudes of 430 Years 11 and 12 Muslim students in 10 Muslim High schools towards the mainstream Australian society. The general picture that emerges is daunting and yet provides information that is relevant to ongoing debates and public concerns such as social integration, cultural harmony, religious tectonics, and fragmentation of values. Importantly the survey found that students were equally divided on statements related to the degree to which Muslim students feel that their school is appropriately educating pupils about Australia and that Australians were an important predictor of certain levels of tolerance.

The second chapter, 'How Mainstream Australian Students Perceive Muslims and Islam: A National Survey' by Abe W. Ata, reports the results from a six-year long national survey of attitudes amongst Australian secondary students towards Islam and Muslims and analyses the results of a six-year long national survey. A total of 3,340 students from Years 10–11 in 90 secondary schools around Australia took part in this survey. This survey revealed a trajectory of unexpected findings of attitudes, feelings, and knowledge towards Muslims in Australia. The themes addressed and the cultural and historical differences between Christian and Muslim communities in our society are too wide to make a definitive statement.

Widespread negative stereotypes and the relatively new presence of the Muslim community in Australia tend to suggest that non-Muslim students may not be well informed, while the long-standing multicultural posture of educational policy suggests otherwise. While non-Muslim students agree that acceptance of Muslims do not come easily in Australia, the school does not emerge as a site for change.

In the next chapter by Ali Dizboni and Christian Leuprecht, 'Framing, Branding, and Explaining: A Survey of Perceptions of Islam and Muslims in the Canadian Polls, Government, and Academia' the focus is on the branding and framing of Islam and Muslims in Canada. A key finding reveals that while the new government's rhetoric records a significant shift compared to the previous Conservative one, the dominant trends in public polls and academia acknowledge some significant degree of association between Islam and security concerns. The authors reveal that Canada's exceptional success in immigration is mitigated by the fact that Muslims and Islam are perceived and conceived as objects of securitization by the public and in academic research. On the bright side, the current government discourse in Ottawa breaks away from these positions and rejects *essentialist* or sweeping statements towards securitizing Islam and Muslims.

Hisham M. Abu-Rayya examines key relational strategies including the extent to which the acculturation orientations of cultural minority members and mainstream majority members play a role in differentiating the levels of positive and negative attitudes they hold towards each other in Chapter 4 'Integrated Acculturation and Contact Strategies to Improve Anglo-Muslim Relations in Australia' in this volume. Another one is related to the viability of Anglo-Australians' acculturation orientations in the way it plays a significant role in differentiating the levels of positive and negative attitudes that Anglo-Australians hold towards Australian-Muslims.

Jan A. Ali takes up the issue of radicalization of Muslims and their experience of social exclusion in Chapter 5, 'Australian Muslims as Radicalized "Other" and Their Experiences of Social Exclusion', which examines how radicalization of Muslims as the 'other' in Australia has turned them into a transnational category. Ali analyses how Islam and Muslims in Australia have become objects of securitization as a preventative measure to secure the 'home' and have been rendered a risky and dangerous 'Other' with serious consequences of their social exclusion.

In Chapter 6,'Young Muslims' Identity in Australia and the US: The Focus on the "Muslim Question"' by Nahid A. Kabir focuses on how some members of the wider Australian and American societies view Muslims as the 'Other'? This is a comparative study of young Muslims in Victoria, Australia (2006–07) and Michigan, USA (2009–11). In this study the author particularly looks at the young Muslims' identity and their sense of belonging in the context of 'Muslim question'. Examining the life stories of the participants the author arrives at the conclusion that the 'Muslim question' can be addressed through dialogue and the promotion of young Muslims' bicultural skills.

Jan A. Ali and Drew Cottle in Chapter 7, 'Islam-West Relations and the Rise of Muslim Radicalism and Global Jihadism', examine how European colonialism and imperialism transformed the Muslim world and brought about monumental institutional and social changes much of which was unproductive and detrimental to Muslim societies. They posit that colonial subjugation of the Muslim world left generations of Muslims with enhanced feeling of despair and sociocultural up-rootedness. European colonialism and imperialism have forced the Muslim world into a deepening state of crisis from which rose Muslim radicalism and global jihadism. They are the results of past European colonial rule and expressions of the crisis of modernity.

Thijl Sunier in the next chapter of this volume, 'Engaging with Islam, Engaging with Society: The Participation of Muslims in Dutch Society', points to a newly emerged reality with the increased migration of Muslims to Europe, namely that they, Muslim communities, have become increasingly concerned with the examination of their primarily loyalties. There is a gradual shift among Muslims from a multiculturalist demand for equal rights to the more sophisticated idea that there are multiple ways of being a Dutch citizen and of engaging with different sections of the population. Thijl argues that the current organizational landscape among Muslims in Europe constitutes the basis for newly emerging forms of engagement. A gradual shift can be witnessed among young Muslims from a 'politics of cultural and religious recognition' to one that advocates a new mode of inclusion and focuses on the multiplicity of ways in which citizens relate to the common good. He concludes that this is an important stage in the process of rooting in society and can be observed not just in the type of activities Muslims engage in, but also in the ways Muslim identity is being reformulated and reshaped.

Tereza Hyánková in Chapter 9 of this volume, "'Muslims in the Modern Sense": Kabyles Negotiating Religious Identity in the Czech Republic' examines the dynamics of de-territorilized identities of Kabyle immigrants to the Czech Republic focusing on the interconnection between ethnicity (that is, Kabyle), national identity (that is, Algerian), and religious identity (that is, Muslim). Unlike other Muslim communities Kabyles in the Czech Republic do not use their religious identity as a boundary marker and as a symbol of unification and exclusion. Kabyle immigrants associate 'kabylity' with secular principles, modernity, individualism, and freedom. Tereza believes that their ideas about 'kabylity' and the specific character of their migration shape their religious practice. Her interpretation of meaning of these declarations and how this attitude serves as an efficient strategy for integration into an Islamophobic Czechsociety complementsthe key premise of her thesis.

In Chapter 10 of this volume 'Faith, Identity, and Ideology: Experiences of Australian Male Converts to Islam', Paul Mitchell and Halim Rane explores the conversion process in Australia in exploring this process particularly concentrates on converts' motivations for embracing Islam, the impact of conversion on their existing relationships and social identities, and how converts incorporate their new faith into their everyday living. The authors' findings reveal varying motivational factors for conversion, converts' identification with different forms of Islam, and different levels of manifestation of Islam in converts' everyday lives.

Enzo Pace and Khalid Rhazzali in the final chapter, 'Muslim Communities in a Catholic Country: The Case of Italy', note that Catholicism is the matrix that is the backbone of Italian identity. Italians continue to believe that Catholicism facilitates a unified perception of a situation that is increasingly differentiated in religious, ethical, and moral terms. The presence of the *other*, identified as the *Muslim* has contributed, in at least a part of the Italian population, to reinforcing the sense of shared cultural roots springing from Catholicism. Italian people continue to consider their country a relatively homogenous society in a religious sense. This is reflected in them being relatively faithful to the ritual forms prescribed by the Catholic Church and social and linguistic customs marking Italian life to continue to mirror a reflection of this collective self-awareness.

References

Ata, Abe. 2009. *Us & Them: Muslim-Christian Relations and Cultural Harmony in Australia*, p. 15. Bowen Hills: Australian Academic Press.

Pew Research Center. 2008. 'Unfavorable Views of Jews and Muslims on the Increase in Europe'. Available at: http://www.pewglobal.org/files/pdf/262.pdf. Accessed on 2 August 2017.

PART ONE

PERCEPTIONS AND ATTITUDES

1

ABE W. ATA

Attitudes of School-Age Muslim Australians towards Australia: Gender and Religious Discrepancies

A National Survey

This chapter assesses how Muslim students perceive their dual Islamic and 'Australian' identities. The results of this five year long investigation are based on a field research questionnaire involving 430 students in 10 Muslim High schools. The primary aim of the study was to examine how compatible the dual identities are, as Muslims and Australians, in the view of these students. A major finding revealed that the percentage of female participants (57 per cent) recognized that the two identities were harmonious. This was slightly higher than male students (43 per cent). Combined, the two groups however (93 per cent) declared themselves to be first and foremost Muslim. The findings also reflect a wide spectrum of nuanced responses with room for further analysis regarding their ultimate adjustment, well being and ease of living in both cultures. Crucially, the survey found that students were equally divided on statements related to the degree to which Muslim students feel integrated in various aspects of the host society in which they have grown.

Islam is the third largest religion in Australia after the Christian denominations and Buddhism, and the Muslim community is one of the fastest growing, having nearly doubled in size between 1996 and 2001. According to the 2016 Australian Census, the combined number of people who self-identified as Muslims in Australia, from all forms of Islam, constituted 604,200 people, or 2.6 per cent of the total Australian population. Many are school students, and of these, many are at Islamic schools. This is advantageous for the purposes of the study. It affords us ready access to respondents (it would be invidious to seek out only Muslim students in a religiously mixed setting) and it presents both a challenge and an opportunity for reaching a target audience.

The overwhelming majority of Muslim schools in Australia are new-comers on the national scene, most having been in existence for only the last 15 years. In Victoria alone they employ about 400 teachers, the majority of whom are Muslim; and obtain more than 42 million dollars a year from state and federal governments. In 2007, there were 3,900 students enrolled in five Islamic schools, however their number has more than doubled in eight years to 2015, with almost 8,000 kids now attending the 10 or so religious schools. This represents a 103 per cent increase; equivalent to 17 per cent overall contribution to the overall enrolments in independent schools.

Of interest, Irene Clyne of Melbourne University found that although these schools may promote a moral outlook, cultural identity, retention of the mother tongue, and religious practice, many parents expressed concern that they might not be a wholesome alternative to secular education (2000, 2001).

An investigative report filed in the database of a national newspaper, *The Age* (31 July 2005), found that education departments have little knowledge of the curriculum content in Muslim schools for junior grades, the quality of education on offer, or religious views propagated. It stated that

> ... there are concerns among former teachers and members of Melbourne's Islamic community about the overall quality of educa-tion the 600-plus students receive.... Muslim extremists were posing a problem for 'vulnerable and impressionable youth' ... [a prominent Muslim leader says that] the proliferation of Islamic schools is causing concern in the Muslim community.... They are accountable to nobody but themselves.

Pew Research Centre released a project in 2016, titled 'The Great Divide: How Westerners and Muslims View Each Other' (2016), which showed that reciprocal opinions held by these two groups varied markedly amongst the surveyed societies—one which was a major driver behind the current project. The survey revealed that Muslims were more positive than the general public in their adopted country about the way things are going for them and their future, but many worried about the future of Muslims in their country of origin. Their greatest concern was unemployment. Islamic extremism emerged as the second concern. By and large however, several advocacy groups, Human Rights advocates, and others within the mainstream society do not regard most non-Muslims as hostile towards Muslims. Their commitment and advocacy are inarguably genuine. Their knowledge of what constitutes a Muslim self-identification, or for that matter the self-identification of Christian minorities in Muslims countries, is often incomplete. This in fact constitutes much of the blurred vision and misconstrued attitudes between both communities—Muslim and mainstream Australians. Little is known, for example, that being identified as a Palestinian, Lebanese, Egyptian, and the like entails that one's identity is synonymous with affiliation to a particular religion (see also, Sklare 1957). In such countries the law dictates that all—Christian and Muslim—citizens must identify 'their' religion in their passport. Whether they attend a mosque or a church is immaterial, and is instantly defaulted to adopting one's ancestral religion. In extreme, but not unusual cases, to claim irreligiosity (or secularism) is a punishable offense.

Australians and other Westerners may find this reasoning odd at best. To them Christianity and nationality are distinct, separable, and hence a private matter. To be a secular humanist posits that human beings are capable of being ethical and moral without religion or *a God*.

A pioneer Muslim writer drives this point further. As Muhyi states, 'Islam is not merely a body of religious doctrine and practice; it is also a form of social and political organization [whereby] most (minority) Christian sects are also governed by religious law. In the Middle East there is no clear distinction between religious and secular life' (1959: 51).

To an Australian, and other Westerners, who are brought up in a secular state, the complex web of religious and civil authority amongst Muslims and minority non-Anglo Christians appears incomprehensible.

There is little published research however beyond the Pew Centre's which has examined specifically the extent to which false facts relate to attitudes of Muslims towards Australia (Rabasa and Benard 2014). Much less is reported on what may constitute negative attitudes towards Australia, understandings that could be predicted from the scale of our knowledge, fashionable or well worn. It is held that many of the false beliefs play a crucial role in perpetuating negative attitudes, legitimizing social distance, and justifying blatant and subtle prejudice (Eagely 1992; Pedersen, Walker, and Wise 2005). In other words, they interlink with generalizable attributes and stereotyping, extending portrayal and the like.

Results from studies on anti-prejudice education showed that participants believed that factual information about out-groups is crucial in challenging negative feelings and improving positivity towards them (Dunn 2001, 2004, 2005; Pedersen, Walker, and Wise 2005).

Several researchers from Europe and Australia, for example, found that low- and high-prejudiced people share the same knowledge of cultural and ethnic stereotypes of minority, thus signifying that the level of knowledge and depth of prejudice are independent of one another (Augoustinos and Quinn 2003; Gordijn, Koomen, and Stapel 2001; Lepore and Brown 1997; Sidanius et al. 2001). This could, however, relate to the validity of the test itself. Gordijn, Koomen, and Stapel argue that the measuring instrument may be insensitive enough to detect finer 'differences in the knowledge of cultural stereotypes as a function of level of prejudice when the free response method' (2001: 157).

This chapter analyses the attitudes and state of knowledge of Australian Muslim students—both males and females—and their views towards the wider mainstream Australian community and culture. Extracted below are selected results of a five-year long national survey which was conducted during 2010–13. The main aim of the survey was to investigate the knowledge, values, and attitudes of 430 Muslim students in Classes 11 and 12, in 10 Muslim High schools, towards the mainstream Australian society. The current study drew its survey sample from Muslim denominational schools, it included few if any non-Muslims; it can therefore fairly be said to represent how the overwhelmingly Muslim student community views mainstream Australian society. A number of theoretical orientations supporting the study are discussed before the results are discussed.

The current study follows a previous national survey on attitudes of Australian students towards Islam and Muslims (Chapter 2) hereafter referred to as 'The Companion Study'. The two studies are largely complementary in the sense that both explore how one community perceives the other.

Survey Method and Sample Characteristics

The survey unit was the high-school student. Over 430 completed questionnaires were obtained from students at eight schools (six high schools and two community schools (that is, those which involve a partnership between the school and other resources) in Victoria, New South Wales, Queensland, and Western Australia. South Australia, Northern Territory, Australian Capital Territory, and Tasmania did not take part for logistical reasons. Two schools catered mainly for students of Turkish background.

Schools were requested to survey students of Class 11, these being considered mature enough to give informed answers, yet unencumbered by year 12 exams in each selected school. The survey was administered to eligible students present on the day of the survey. Even so four of the schools chose to administer the survey to students of classes 10 and 12.

The survey (see Table 1.1) was refined in the light of the pilot after which 431 students were administered the full survey form. The percentage of female participant students (57 per cent) was slightly higher than male students (43 per cent). Almost the entire sample (93 per cent) declared themselves to be Muslim; the remainder who were also of Muslim descendants chose not to do so in writing. We do not know the circumstances of those who gave 'Other' (that is, not Muslim) as their religion. It is possible that some were children of interreligious marriages, and others just rebellious. There were more students born in Australia (61 per cent) than overseas (39 per cent). However, the percentage of fathers (3 per cent) and mothers (9 per cent) born in Australia was significantly lower.

Over 66 per cent indicated that their friends were mostly Muslim and 3 per cent indicated that they were mostly non-Muslim and the remainder were 'half and half'.

Most students (93 per cent) spoke 'other languages' at home. This accords with the finding that most parents were born overseas. In The

TABLE 1.1   Participant characteristics (N = 431)

Sex	Male	43 per cent
	Female	57 per cent
School gender composition	Co-educational school	90 per cent
	Girls/boys only school	10 per cent
Place of birth	Australia	61 per cent
	overseas	31 per cent
Language spoken at home other than English		93 per cent
English only spoken at home		7 per cent
Religion	Muslim	93 per cent
	Not declared	7 per cent
Parental background (Parents born in Australia)	Father	3 per cent
	Mother	9 per cent
Metropolitan (Sydney, Melbourne, Perth, Brisbane, Adelaide)		100 per cent
Rural		none
Religious background of Friends of participant	Muslim	66 per cent
	Non-Muslim	3 per cent
	Half Muslim, half non-Muslim	31 per cent

Source: Ata (2009).

Companion Study only 19 per cent non-Muslim Australian students spoke 'other languages' at home.

Respondents were presented with 18 statements concerning subjective attitudes towards Islam and Muslims and asked to rate their agreement on a three-point scale of 'Agree' through 'Neutral' to 'Disagree'.

Findings and Discussion

On many questions between a third and a half of the sample was neutral, indicating that they neither agreed nor disagreed with the statement (Figure 1.1). This could signify honest ignorance of the

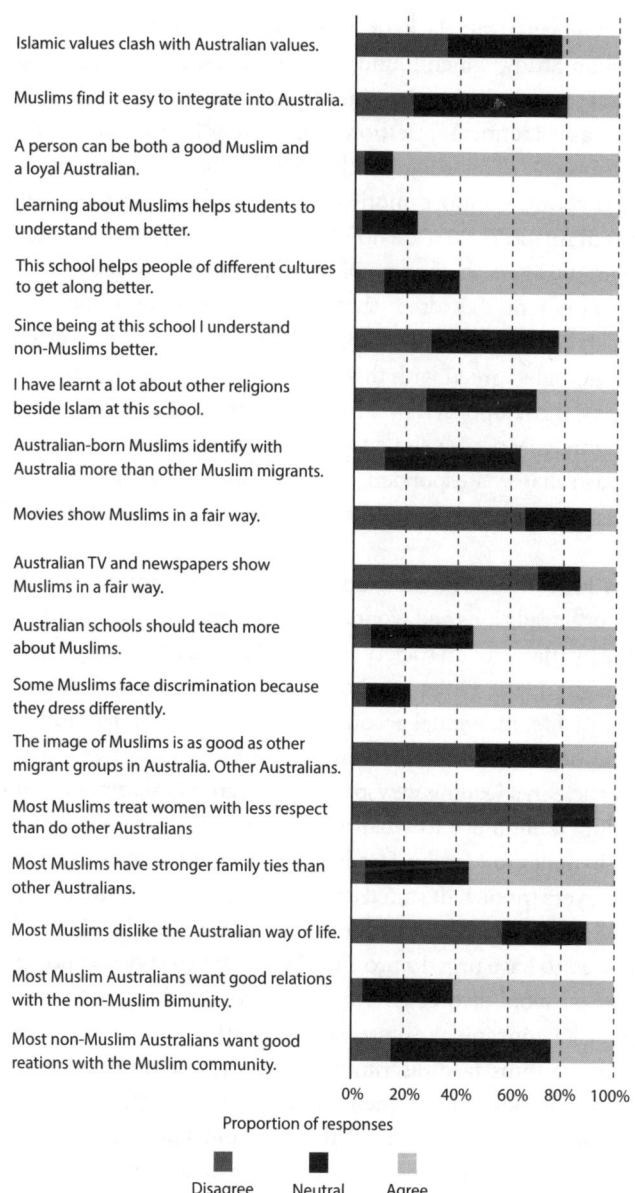

FIGURE 1.1   Responses to select statements reflecting attitudes towards Australia and Australians

Source: Ata (2016a).

issues or alternatively lack of motivation. This contrasts with The Companion Study, which found that a considerably higher proportion of neutral responses given by non-Muslim students to comparable (and in some cases identical) questions concerning Islam and Muslims (see also, Chapter 2). This suggests that Muslim students are either more informed about, or more motivated to comment on the position of Muslims in Australia than are non-Muslims—understandably so, as they are commenting on their own community, not someone else's.

The statement that drew that higher agreement response was 'A person can be both a good Muslim and a loyal Australian'. Respondents overwhelmingly agreed with this statement, with those in support outnumbering those opposed by 11 to 1. The reverse was found regarding the statement 'Most Muslims treat women with less respect than do other Australians'. Respondents overwhelmingly disagreed with this statement, with those opposed outnumbering those in support by 10 to 1.

Many Muslims in Australia find themselves caught in the middle of two cultural traditions and wonder if their growing community is being accepted by mainstream society (see also Ata and Batrouney 1989; Cahill and Gundert 1996). Differences of interpretation towards social values and way of life, individual accountability, consensual decision-making, and attitudes towards implementing moral imperatives do exist. A recent article in a leading newspaper, for example, slammed Centerlink for turning a blind eye to what was termed 'Islamic Polygamy', paying spousal benefits to Muslim families with multiple wives in an effort to save taxpayers money'. It stated the following explanation as further evidence of the practice being widespread 'Muslim leader Keyser Trad is understood to have urged a pro-marriage event to consider polygamous marriage to avoid divorce.... We are always the data [at Centerlink] is not kept ... a convenient excuse' (Maiden 2016: 4).

'Some Muslims face discrimination because they dress differently' was another important statement that, not surprisingly, drew the second largest response. At the centre of this attitudinal position is the premise that modesty and integration into the mainstream society are strongly linked. Modesty is a key value within the Muslim community and cannot be separated from its teachings of *akhlaq* or Islamic etiquette. It is built on the family unit and is prescribed by God (Qur'an, 24: 30–1). The degree to which modesty *akhlaq* (or lack of it) regulates inter-gender relations, taking part in mixed sport activities involving immodest outfits, visual effects, behaviour, or language, for example, swimming, dancing, school camps, partying, TV commercials and films, art galleries, and magazines will be examined.

Other statements however drew a variety of responses. For example, 'The image of Muslims is as good as other migrant groups in Australia', many students overwhelmingly disagreed with this statement, with those opposed outnumbering those in support by 2.3 to 1.

As regards the statement 'Australian-born Muslims identify with Australia more than other Muslim migrants', students were divided on this statement. Most were neutral, but of the minority who took sides, those in support outnumbered those opposed by 3.1 to 1.

Importantly students were divided on the statement 'Islamic values clash with Australian values'. A sizable proportion of 43 per cent were neutral, but of those who took sides, those opposed outnumbered those in support by 1.6 to 1.

The findings overwhelmingly contrast with those analysed in the following Chapter 2 in this volume. The latter revealed a considerably higher proportion of neutral responses given by non-Muslim students to comparable (and in some cases identical) questions concerning Islam and Muslims. This suggests that Muslim students are either more informed about, or more motivated to comment on the position of Muslims in Australia than are non-Muslims—understandably so, as they are commenting on their own community, not someone else's.

Words That Come to Mind 'When You Hear the Word "Australian"'

When asked for the first words that come to mind when the word 'Australian' is mentioned, just under one third (29 per cent) offered neutral or negative comments specifically relating to cultural images or symbols including the words 'Cronulla, bogan, boogan, beer, drugs, the bush, Howard, Christian, blonds, fags, pussies, gay, cricket, Freckles, BBQ, and thongs' (see Figure 1.2). About 21 per cent offered positive qualities including 'peaceful, cultured, nice, easy going, O.K. people, and freedom'. A smaller group (8 per cent) referred to multiculturalism; 12 per cent referred to patriotic qualities including 'Australia my country, I am born in Australia'; 3 per cent referred to culture-based

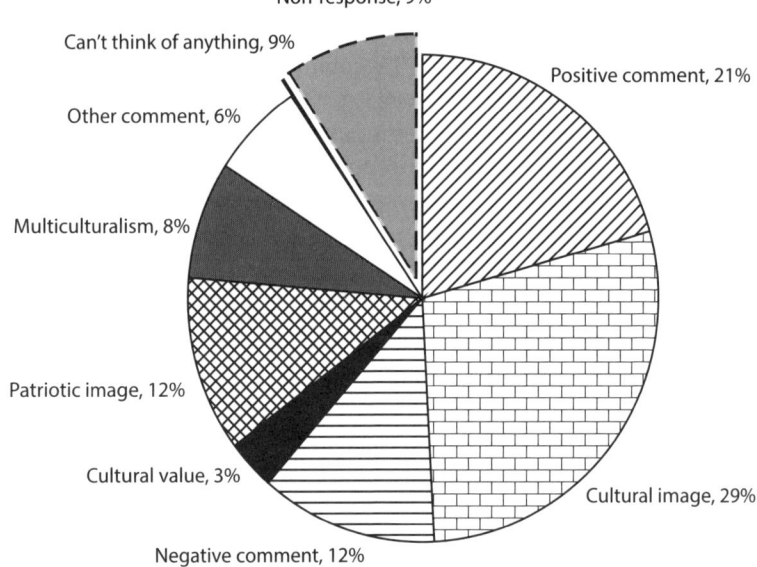

FIGURE 1.2   Response to 'What are the first words that come to your mind when you hear the word "Australian"?'
Source: Ata (2016b).
Note: Apparent errors in addition are due to rounding off. N = 431 (inc. non-response)

Box 2   Selected responses to *'What are the first words that come to your mind when you hear the word 'Australian'?*

- People that try to make a better community and people who just laze around with a VB can in their hand.
- I seriously think of alcohol ... but I also think of hard working people and kind people.
- Homeland, Australian flag?
- People with beers in their hand watching footy.
- Dirty people and drinking and drugs.
- Fear, because I have the fear of being abused for being a Muslim.
- Australians are European people who think of Jesus to be son of God which is impossible, and are fairly good people.

Source: Ata (2016a).
Note: All quotes above are verbatim.

values including 'a fair go and mateship'. One in 10 (12 per cent) offered generalized negative comments including 'being lost, confused, dick-heads, rednecks, hostile, arrogant, greedy, non-believers, and racist'. About one respondent in 11 (9 per cent) offered no response.

Words That Are Liked Most 'When You Hear the Word "Non-Muslim Australians"?'

When asked what they liked most about non-Muslim Australians roughly half (46 per cent) offered positive comments (compared with 31 per cent regarding Muslim Australians) (see Figure 1.3). These include phrases such as 'solidarity and uniqueness, smile back, relaxed life, car-ing, even handed, not judgmental, enjoy life, don't act mean, down to earth, and kind'. It is noteworthy none of these comments was given in response to Muslim Australians, possibly because of difference in the

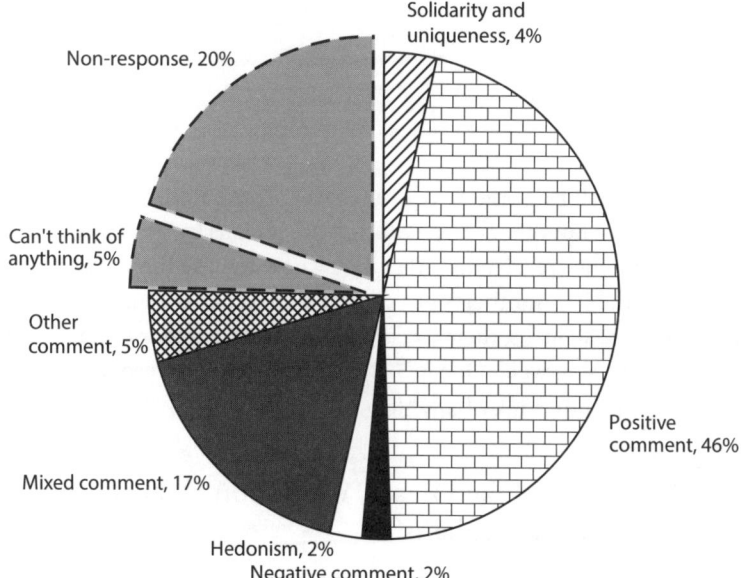

FIGURE 1.3   Response to 'What do you like most about non-Muslim Australians?'
Source: Ata (2016a).
Note: Apparent errors in addition are due to rounding N = 431 (inc. non-response)

Box 3   Selected responses to *What do you like most about non-Muslim Australians?*

- Their curiosity to always try and learn about others.
- Their struggle in asking a question to Muslims about religion.
- I like how it's not obvious what religion non-Muslims came from.
- How they seem so interested about Islam ... and how they are fascinated when they discover the truth.
- They are underestimating most of them and are good to get advice from.
- Some of them are nice but other judge Muslim Australians by what they see in the media.
- They want to live in a country that is multi-cultural and everyone is treated the same.
- The general non-Muslim Australian community is extremely gentle and understand that Muslims are not 'terrorists' and it's just a 'media story'.
- Some are friendly—they know how to have fun without getting into trouble.
- They want to know the truth but they do not have the initiative to seek the truth.

Source: Ata (2016a).
Note: All quotes have been presented verbatim.

hierarchy of values. Some 17 per cent gave mixed comments including: 'Some are nice but others judge Muslim Australians by what they see in the media; some are friendly—they know how to have fun without getting into trouble'. Another 5 per cent offered 'other comment' including 'look nice; sheilahs, their accent, world soccer, care for nature, their food, and dressing well'. One in 5 (20 per cent) gave no response, and 5 per cent could not think of anything.

Words That Are Liked Least 'When You Hear the Word "Non-Muslim Australians"'

Combined, the majority of negative categories including racism, ignorance, and other judgmental criticisms are reflected in the responses below quoted verbatim—reflecting fear and anger that the society at large is Islamophobic (see also, Brasted 2001; Briskman 2015; Hargreaves 2016; Poynting 2002; Poynting and Mason 2008).

When asked about what they like least about non-Muslim Australians roughly 1 out of 3 (27 per cent) gave a 'no response'; whilst 6 per cent could not think of anything—a significantly smaller percentage than that in the previous finding (see Figure 1.4). 'Racism' drew the next highest response (19 per cent); 'ignorance' 14 per cent; 'being judgmental of Muslims' drew 13 per cent; 'other negative comment including meaningless life, disrespectful, selfish too relaxed, overreact, denigrating our clothes, and abusive' consisted 12 per cent; and other comment including 'they don't drive good cars like us in Lebanon, freedom of women, complain a lot, because they are pigs' drew only 6 per cent.

Moderate Muslims who keep their faith on a personal level avoid bringing religion into politics, and who feel embarrassed at violent actions taken under the banner of their religion, are in particular need of such an endorsement (Asmar 2001; Muslim Community Reference Group 2006). Absence of a religious hierarchy—one that is

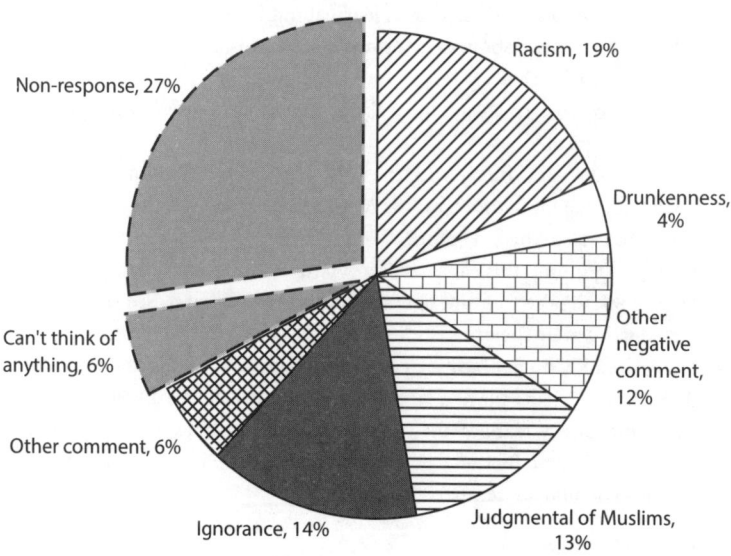

FIGURE 1.4   Response to 'What do you like least about non-Muslim Australians?'
Source: Ata (2016a).
Note: Apparent errors in addition are due to rounding. N = 431 (inc. non-response)

Box 4   Selected responses to *What do you like least about non-Muslim Australians?*

- They can underestimate us.
- They are racist and have a grudge inside them against Muslims; some of them show it while others force it inside.
- Most of them have no fathers.
- Sometimes they can be very hostile to Muslims.
- I don't like non-Muslim Australians because they think that Australia only for Aussie.
- How they are rude and do not care who is next to them and use course language.
- When non-Muslim put down Muslims because of September 11 and other activities that show Islam as a bad religion.
- It takes ages to break the ice.
- Some of them drink too much.
- Disrespect for Muslim, isolate Muslim, call Muslim girls weird names because of the scarf. Harass Muslims.
- Their treatment of women.
- They don't go out of their way to learn about Muslims.
- I like to learn more about all Muslims + non Muslim. To love each other not dislike each other.
- When John Howard always talks about 'Australian values'. Most of them are stereotypical.
- The way they eat is funny with the knife and forks. It's weird.
- Their judgmental nature towards Muslims even though they have never seen/spoke to a Muslim before.
- They are ignorant, this causes stereotyping and prejudice.
- They think they're free and liberated but are too blind to see that they're still controlled by society.
- They generally do not have a clear and valid understanding and education about Islam. Media plays a large role in brainwashing Australian public into unnecessary fears of the 'unknown'. For example, the boogy man, Osama Bin Laden. By the way Americans still proved it was him who was the mind behind September 11.

Source: Ata (2016a).
Note: All quotes presented verbatim.

similar to the Catholic one with the Pope at is pinnacle, has prompted many moderate Muslims to take matters into their own hands and become more organized. For a self-serving extremist minority of a mainstream society it may be politically convenient to demonize others on the basis of race or religion, but it never defeats their own phobias (Parliamentary Joint Committee on Intelligence and Security 2006).

Does the Religion of One's Friends Make a Difference?

In a word, the results show that they actually do.

Those with mostly Muslim friends differed significantly from those with mostly non-Muslim friends (though not significantly from those with a balance from both communities) on four out of 18 statements as shown in Figure 1.1.

Not surprisingly, those with mostly Muslim friends held more empathetic attitudes towards Muslims than did those with mostly non-Muslim friends (though we are naturally not in a position to distinguish cause and effect on this evidence alone). How Muslims are portrayed by the media is a statement that triggered the widest range of views which have been grouped into two camps: those with mostly non-Muslim friends indicted that the media portrays Muslims fairly; those with only or mostly non-Muslim friends demurred.

Those with mostly Muslim friends agreed more than others on the following statements:	Those with mostly non-Muslim friends agreed more than others on the following statements:
Some Muslims face discrimination because they dress differently.	Most Muslims treat women with less respect than do other Australians.
I have learnt a lot about other religions beside Islam at this school.	Australian TV and newspapers show Muslims in a fair way.
Since being at this school I understand non-Muslims better.	Movies show Muslims in a fair way.
A person can be both a good Muslim and a loyal Australian.	

Students' Knowledge and Attitudes to Australia

The survey of Muslim students revealed a moderate lack of knowledge of Christianity as shown in Figure 1.5. Students were presented with 10 statements concerning objectively verifiable facts about Christianity. Muslim students' knowledge of Christianity was, however, noticeably better than non-Muslims' knowledge of Islam. On two particular questions—Jesus wrote the Holy Bible and Christians believe that Jesus was the son of God—respondents were overwhelmingly correct in their responses. This may be because on these points Christianity and Islam disagree most starkly in matters of fundamental doctrine.

The results show that participants who spontaneously mentioned false beliefs and had low levels of knowledge reported significantly

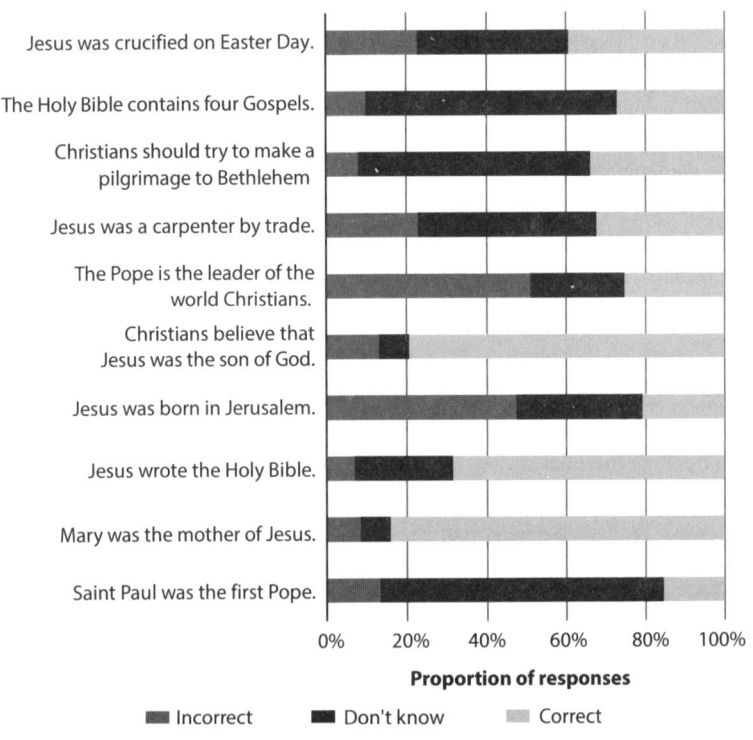

FIGURE 1.5   Proportion of correct and incorrect responses
Source: See 'Survey Method and Sample Characteristics' in this chapter.

more negative attitudes towards Christians than those who did not. This is an important result because it is possible that accepting incorrect information may be shaping negative attitudes towards Christians.

Given the high bidirectional relation between the two variables, surprisingly no group is found to fall in the middle, that is, one showing a flat lining. That is expected in that a knowledgeable person will answer in one way and others with little knowledge will answer in another. It is clear that the hypothesis is corroborated by evidence—one that suggests bigots to be ignorant but those who have a high level of knowledge are not. More to the point: if a person is knowledgeable about Christianity s/he will not be bigoted (a reasonable assumption). It is possible, though, that people can dislike Christians and be knowledgeable, because of their ethnic and religious affiliation; that one is swayed to express tendencies that they believe they share with the rest of the community.

We conclude that although ignorance of Christianity is widespread, those who are on balance correctly informed outnumber the incorrectly informed in the ratio of 6 to 1. This is considerably better than the comparable ratio for non-Muslim students, 2.5 to 1.

The assumption behind cross-tabulating the two variables was—a knowledgeable person (in this case Muslim students) will answer in one way and those with little knowledge will answer in another.

Figure 1.6 shows that people who are knowledgeable about Christianity, at a high ranking of 2.4 and above generally, disagree with the statements outlined below—negative and positive. It is shown in particular that the five statements, for example, 'Most Muslims dislike the Australian way of life' ranked highest (at 2.9) on the knowledge scale.

On the other hand the statement 'Movies show Muslims in a fair way' ranked lowest (at 2.45). As discussed above, it is clear that the hypothesis is corroborated by evidence—one that suggests bigots to be ignorant but those who have a high level of knowledge are not.

These results show that participants who spontaneously mentioned false beliefs and had low levels of knowledge reported significantly more negative attitudes to mainstream Australian Christians than those who did not. This is an important result because it is possible that accepting incorrect information may be shaping negative attitudes towards Christians.

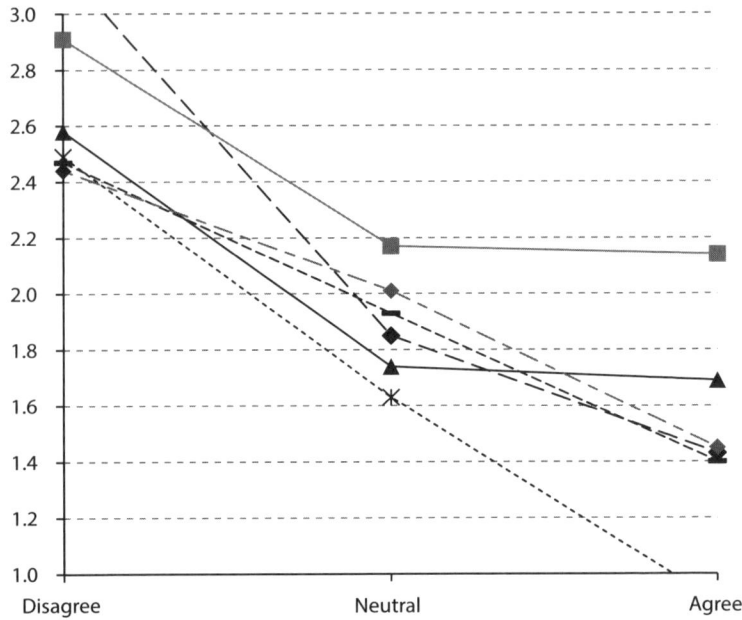

FIGURE 1.6 The relationship between knowledge and select attitudinal statements
Source: See 'Survey Method and Sample Characteristics' in this chapter.

Way Forward: Towards 'Multiculturalism'

The general picture that emerges from analysis of the data in this project is somewhat daunting and yet provides information that is relevant to ongoing debates and public concerns such as social integration, cultural harmony, religious tectonics, and fragmentation of values.

Findings in this chapter, and Chapter 2 'How Mainstream Australian Students Perceive Muslims and Islam: A National Survey', reveal unequivocally that cultural background and religious affiliation are strong indicators of the individual's attitudes towards and behaviour and knowledge of the other, in this case, Australia and mainstream Australians.

A sizable proportion of the students found themselves caught in the middle of two cultural traditions and wonder if their growing community is being accepted by mainstream society. The survey, for example, found considerable lack of knowledge of Christianity; almost half of the students recorded a 'don't know' response of all questions; and only 17 per cent correctly disagreed with the statement 'Jesus wrote the Bible'. There are profound implications for Western educators and community at large. The premise that Muslim students (and by extension students at large) who are more knowledgeable about Christianity would express more favourable opinions of Australians and that through knowledge, greater levels of awareness come from equal status interaction between the two. It is thus argued that the scale of our knowledge, fashionable or well worn, and negative attitudes are interrelated—a clear falsehood in our findings.

It is possible that incorrect information about the religion of other be it Christianity, Islam, or Judaism, can lead, without any exception, to significantly stronger negative attitudes. Similarly, being knowledgeable about Islam makes one more likely to see recent terrorist attacks as part of a conflict.

In Australia, the separation between one's religious and public identities is a cultural and political given. Many Australians may have been influenced by Christian values, but, unlike citizens of many Muslim countries, their identity is not exchangeable with their religious affiliation. That said, significant differences between the two religions, Christianity and Islam, are not to be side-stepped. This could lead to a false sense of security. Differences in interpretation of social values and way of life, individual accountability, consensual decision-making, and attitudes towards implementing moral imperatives do exist. It is feasible that we should be able to acknowledge them, respect them, and address them without necessarily aiming for compromise.

Clearly much work is needed to bring about a remedy. Providing awareness sessions to students and parents which address critical social, religious, and cultural issues including stereotyping and inclusivity, freedom of expression and the media, sexual permissiveness and conservativeness, secular and religious identity, individual and community basic rights, and social justice and foreign policy is one of several measures to take.

There are clearly grounds for this belief. Because in most Muslim countries the mass media is controlled, the question of why Australian television does not help change the negative image and dispense with some honest remains a moot one. The perception that local television is market-oriented and is not a free medium to educate the public but is dedicated to the perpetuation of social structure remains strong.

Moderate Muslims who keep their faith on a personal level, avoid bringing political issues out of it, and feel embarrassed at actions made under the banner of their religion are in particular need of such an endorsement. Absence of religious hierarchy has prompted many moderate Muslims to take matters into their own hands and become more organized. For a self-serving minority it may be politically convenient to demonize others on the basis of race or religion, but it never defeats their own phobias (Windle 2004; Wise and Ali 2008).

Another major finding was linked to their views regarding the way Muslim schools promoted intercultural understanding. Once again, the survey found that students were equally divided on statements that their school teaches them.

The degree to which Muslim students feel that their school is appropriately educating pupils about Australia and Australians was an important predictor of certain levels of tolerance (Ata 2009, 2014, 2016b, 2016c; Simkin and Gauci 1992). This suggests that it is the atmosphere created by the school that can lead to increased acceptance of mainstream Australians, rather than the level of pure factual knowledge. Therefore, it is not just a matter of knowing more facts about religious and cultural congruence, but perceiving that the school cares enough to educate students on these issues that are important as well as acknowledging worldview differences.

This was the belief of the majority of those surveyed. A case in point was their reaction to the statement 'Australian schools should teach more about Muslims'. The results show that those who agreed with it and those who did not were 5 to 1. By the same token those with mainly Muslim friends strongly agreed than those without on the following statements 'I have learnt a lot about other religions beside Islam at this school and since being at this school I understand non-Muslims better'.

One of the critical steps is to engage with educational curriculum consultants nationally and at a state level. They may propose inclusion of subjects relating to their current and eventual contribution to the building of multicultural Australia, the diversity of Muslim cultures and diverse Christian (and Jewish) minorities in their countries of origin, the emerging identities of children within Christian–Muslim marriages, their willingness and eventual participation in the cultural, artistic, literary, and political expression of the mainstream society (Asmar 2001; Ata, Bastian, and Lusher 2009).

That said, significant differences in the teaching and attitudes between the two religions are not to be side-stepped due to a false sense of security. Differences of interpretation towards social values and way of life, individual accountability, consensual decision-making, and attitudes towards implementing moral imperatives do exist. It is feasible that we should be able to acknowledge them, respect them, and address them without aiming at a fine compromise. Not because we no longer need a dialogue, but because these different approaches have concrete implications to both communities living together in a shared place. Professor Robert Manne has, on several occasions, referred to this capacity of accommodating many cultural and religious expressions—within a single language, law, and polity—'multiculturalism'.

References

Augoustinos, M. and C. Quinn. 2003. 'Social Categorization and Attitudinal Evaluations: Illegal Immigrants, Refugees, or Asylum Seekers?', *New Review of Social Psychology* 2: 29–57.

Asmar, C. 2001. 'A Community on Campus: Muslim Students in Australian Universities'. In *Muslim Communities in Australia*, S. Akbarzadeh and A. Saeed (eds), pp. 136–60. Sydney: University of New South Wales Press.

Ata, A. 2009. *Us and Them: Muslim-Christian Relations and Cultural Harmony in Australia*, Brisbane: Australian Academic Press.

———. 2014. *Education, Integration, Challenges: The Case of Australian Muslims.* Melbourne: David Lovell Publishing.

———. 2016a. 'How Muslim Students Perceive of Australia and Australians: A National Survey', *Journal of Intercultural Communication*, 41, July.

———. 2016b. 'How Muslims Are Perceived in Catholic Schools in Contemporary Australia: A National Survey', *Journal of Intercultural Communication* 41: 337–51.

————. 2016c. 'How Muslim Students' Knowledge of Christianity Is Related to Their Attitudes to Mainstream Australia and Australians: A National Survey (Project Report)', *Social Science* (Europe) 4(3): 800–5; doi:10.3390/socsci4030800.

Ata, Abe, Brock Bastian, and Dean Lusher. 2009. 'Intergroup Contact in Context: The Mediating Role of Social Norms and Group-Based Perceptions on the Contact–Prejudice', *International Journal of Intercultural Relations* 33(6): 498–506.

Ata, A. and T. Batrouney. 1989. 'Attitudes and Stereotyping in Victorian Secondary Schools', *The Eastern Anthropologist* 42(1).

Brasted, H. 2001. 'Contested Representations in Historical Perspective: Images of Islam and the Australian Press 1950–2000'. In *Muslim Communities in Australia*, S. Akbarzadeh and A. Saeed (eds.), pp. 136–60. Sydney: University of New South Wales Press.

Briskman, Linda. 2015. 'The Creeping Blight of Islamophobia in Australia', *International Journal for Crime, Justice and Social Democracy* 4(3): 112–21.

Cahill, D. and A. Gundert. 1996. *Immigration and Schooling in the 1990s*. Canberra, Australia: Bureau of Immigration Multicultural and Population Research and Department of Immigration and Multicultural Affairs.

Donohoue Clyne, I. 2000. *Seeking Education: The Struggle of Muslims to Educate their Children in Australia*. PhD thesis, University of Melbourne.

————. 2001. 'Educating Muslim Children in Australia'. In *Muslim Communities in Australia*, S. Akbarzadeh and A. Saeed (eds), pp. 219–44. Sydney: University of New South Wales Press.

Dunn, K. 2001. 'The Geography of Racisms in NSW: A Theoretical Exploration and some Preliminary Findings from the Mid 1990s', *The Australian Geographer* 32(1): 29–44.

————. 2004. 'Islam in Australia: Contesting the Discourse of Absence', *The Australian Geographer* 53(3): 333–53.

————. 2005. 'Australian Public Knowledge of Islam', *Studia Islamika: Indonesian Journal for Islamic Studies* 12(1): 1–32.

Eagely, A.H. 1992. 'Uneven Progress: Social Psychology and the Study of Attitudes', *Journal of Personality and Social Psychology* 63(5): 693–710.

Gordijn, E., W. Koomen, and Stapel, D. 2001. 'Level of Prejudice in Relation to Knowledge of Cultural Stereotypes', *Journal of Experimental Social Psychology* 37: 150–7.

Hargreaves, Julian. 2016. '*Islamophobia: Reality or Myth?*', PhD Thesis, Lancaster University..

Lepore, L. and R. Brown. 1997. 'Category and Stereotype Activation: Is Prejudice Inevitable?', *Journal of Personality and Social Psychology* 72(2): 275–87.

Muhyi, I. 1959. 'Women in the Middle East', *Journal of Social Issues* 15(3): 51.

Maiden, S. 2016. 'Welfare Wives Cash In', *The Heraldsun*, 11 December, p. 4.

Muslim Community Reference Group. 2006. *Building on Social Cohesion, Harmony and Security*. Canberra: Dept. of Immigration and Citizenship (series).

Parliamentary Joint Committee on Intelligence and Security. 2006, *Review of Security and Counter Terrorism Legislation*. Canberra: Parliament of Australia.

Pedersen, A., I. Walker, and M. Wise. 2005. 'Talk Does Not Cook Rice: Beyond Anti-Racism Rhetoric to Strategies for Social Action', *Australian Psychologist* 40: 20–31.

Pew Research Center. 2016. 'The Great Divide: How Westerners and Muslims View Each Other'. Washington, DC: Global Attitudes & Trends.

Poynting, S. 2002. '"Bin Laden in the Suburbs": Attacks on Arab and Muslim Australians before and After 11 September', *Current Issues in Criminal Justice* 14(1): 43–64.

Poynting, Scott and Victoria Mason. 2008. 'The New Integrationism, the State and Islamophobia: Retreat from Multiculturalism in Australia', *International Journal of Law, Crime and Justice* 36 (4, December): 230–46.

Rabasa, Angel and Cheryl Benard. 2014. *Eurojihad: Patterns of Islamist Radicalization and Terrorism in Europe*. London: Cambridge University Press.

Sklare, M. 1957. 'The Function of Ethnic Churches'. In *Religion, Society and the Individual*, J. Yinger (ed.), pp. 459–60. New York: McMillan.

Sidanius, J., S. Levin, C. Federico, and F. Pratto. 2001. 'Legitimizing Ideologies: The Social Dominance Approach'. In *The Psychology of Legitimacy: Emerging Perspectives on Ideology, Justice, and Intergroup Relations*, J.T. Jost and B. Major (eds), pp. 307–31. New York: Cambridge University Press.

Simkin, K. and E . Gauci. 1992. 'Ethnic Diversity and Multicultural Education'. In *Contemporary Perspectives in Comparative Education*, R.J. Burns and A.R. Welch (eds), pp. xlv, 432. New York: Garland Publications.

Skelton, R. 2005. 'Muslims Sound Alarm Over Schools', *The Age*. 31 July.

Windle, J. 2004. 'Schooling, Symbolism and Social Power: The Hijab in Republican France', *Australian Educational Researcher* 31(1): 95–112.

Wise, A. and J. Ali. 2008. *Muslim-Australians and Local Government [electronic resource]: Grassroots Strategies to Improve Relations between Muslim and Non-Muslim-Australians: Final Research Report*. Canberra: Department of Immigration and Citizenship.

2

ABE W. ATA

How Mainstream Australian Students Perceive Muslims and Islam

A National Survey

Since mass immigration to Australia began after the World War II, official policy has passed through several phases. In the 1950s the aim was 'assimilation' when migrants would become Australian as quickly as possible and to that end were dubbed 'New Australians'. By the 1960s native Australians were more accepting and 'integration' was officially the goal, but the authorities 'still sought social cohesion but more gently' (Hirst 2016: 160). And by the 1970s a more socially relaxed Australia was ready to embrace difference and 'multiculturalism' became the catchword.

Australia is now entering a new phase, but one for which there is no ready policy nostrum. Now the issue is not what 'Old Australians' demand of the New, but what New Australians (or more likely some of their descendants) demand of the Old. Australia is not alone in confronting this issue of course; it is a global phenomenon.

Like other Western multicultural societies the Australian community continues to look for ways to mount an inclusive action on behalf of the common good; it takes time to appreciate all the diversities and discover common values between groups and in this case between mainstream Australian community and the Muslim community. Clearly the cultural and historical differences between Christian and Muslim communities in our society are too wide to make a complete reconciliation, but, given the alternatives, a creative dialogue must continue (see also Benard 2015). Just like mixed marriages, certain differences between the two faiths may be identified, without being fully reconciled. A starting point towards this end is identifying misconceptions, misgivings, and the roots of grievances.

Encounters on a large scale between the Christian and other sections of mainstream Australia and Muslims have become a reality only recently. Social media are abuzz with daily articles asking the same questions: Do Muslims find it harder than other migrants to integrate, or is the bigotry of some that perpetuates it? Is Islamophobia the flipside of inherent racism that some Australians lashed in stages against Aboriginals, Greeks, Italians, Chinese, Africans, and Middle Easterners? Or perhaps it is the cultural and historical (and religious) differences between the Christian and Muslim communities worldwide that are too wide to make a complete reconciliation? Why do religious minorities in Muslim countries have fewer rights than Muslims do in Western societies? Do Muslims need reform and reflection similar to those of Catholic Priests? Are Muslim and Australian identities compatible with one another or are they mutually exclusive? And lastly, are the schools doing enough in fostering goodwill and inter-communal relationship?

A recent grievance about the way mainstream Australians are being 'taken for a ride by the growing number of Muslim and other people who exploit the benefits and goodwill of the very country they might live in but refuse to join', was pointed out in a major headline 'Community turns a blind eye to changes in our culture: Biting the hand that feeds you'. The writer, Peta Credlin remarks that 'things have got so bad in NSW that they passed a special law a year or so ago to deal with the growing numbers of Muslim men (and now women) refusing to acknowledge the jurisdiction of the court and show necessary respect to the bench.... Despite the concessions, Mrs Elzahed refused to remove her veil and also refused to stand when the judge entered the room, because, as her legal counsel explained, she stood only for "Allah"' (2016: 31).

The mainstream community at large may differ on the nature, causes, and consequences of vulnerability and volatility of such youngsters, and on their implications for policy, but there remains much common ground, particularly on why 'unease' and potential radicalism happens and who is most at risk. What are some common elements in the experiences of most people who have become disenchanted in Australia, regardless of their beliefs or motivations?

In two recent reports by the Pew Research Center (2006, 2008) the opinions held in several European countries by the two communities—Muslim and Christian—were found to vary markedly except for a fundamental variable: Muslims were decidedly found to be more positive than the general public in their adopted country about the way things are going for them and their future, but many worried about the future of Muslims in their country of origin. Their greatest concern was unemployment. Islamic extremism emerged as the number two concern. The majority do not regard most non-Muslims as hostile towards Muslims (Ata 2009, 2014).

The study of acculturation, and by implication integration, social harmony or lack of it arguably dates back to the 1930s when sociologists and anthropologists coined the term and explicitly explored acculturation at the group level. They were followed in the 1960s by psychologists investigating acculturation at the individual level. Berry (2008) famously developed his influential fourfold model. He identified these as follows: (*i*). *integration* which results in the maintenance of existing cultures and behaviours while peoples engage in day-to-day interaction within an evolving civic framework; (*ii*). *separation* which leads to avoidance of interaction with the dominant group in favour of holding on one psychological and cultural qualities; (*iii*). *assimilation* whereby minority groups, referred to as 'non dominant' lose distinctive chore cultural and behavioural features and gradually absorb those of the dominant ones, and (*iv*). *marginalization* resulting in cultural and psychological loss, particularly among non-dominant populations, along with their exclusion from full and equitable participation in the larger society.

For all its elegance, however, Berry's model has come under criticism for its static approach. The field is now characterized by lively debate, with more complex, dynamic models competing for relevance. These newer models seek to answer such questions as how acculturation happens and why biculturalism is so hard to sustain. In recent years this debate has largely focused on Muslim migrants' integration and social harmony in Western countries.

Others, however, believe that the majority of European (and arguably by implication Australian) Muslims are neither well-integrated nor radicalized (Rabasa and Benard 2014). Rabasa and Benard point out that for the minority amongst second generation who are disaffected, some find it difficult to live within either the traditional culture of their parents or the modern Western culture where they reside. Extremist ideologies offer a new identity that allows the individual to identify with an imagined worldwide community.

The grievance for the second generation are no longer shaped by the experiences of their parents in the countries of their origin, it is the marginalization in the new country.

Benard who has written widely on political Islam posits however that Islamic violence is on the rise. She points out with equivocation

> What we lumped together as moderates includes what we might better have termed aggressive traditionalists, people who believe that Muslims living in the West must struggle to remain external to Western values and lifestyles, and should owe little or no loyalty to Western institutions and persons. They might be against violence, but they are also against integration. Divided loyalties can cause individuals to stay silent when they notice suspicious activity in their neighborhood or family or social circle.
>
> (Rabasa and Benard 2014: 1–2)

Results from studies on anti-prejudice education showed that participants believed that factual information about out-groups is crucial in challenging negative feelings, and improve positivity towards them (Dunn 2005; Nelson, Dunn, and Paradies 2011; Pedersen 2005). Several researchers from Europe and Australia found that low- and high-prejudiced people share the same knowledge of cultural and ethnic stereotypes of minority, thus signifying that the level of knowledge and depth of prejudice are independent of one another (Gordijn, Koomen, Stapel 2001; Lepore and Brown 1997; Walton et al. 2015). This could, however, relate to the validity of the test itself. Gordijn, Koomen, and Stapel (2001: 157) argues that the measuring instrument may be insensitive enough to detect finer 'differences in the knowledge of cultural stereotypes as a function of level of prejudice, namely due to providing an open-ended response option'.

This chapter is concerned with understanding what may drive negative attitudes and behaviours of non-Muslim mainstream Australians towards Muslims and Islam, which posits the premise that Australians who are more knowledgeable about Muslims would express more favourable opinions of Muslims and Islam. The chapter argues that through knowledge, greater levels of awareness come from equal status interaction between the learner and individuals of Muslim background. It is thus argued that scale of our knowledge, fashionable or well worn, and negative attitudes are interrelated.

The analysis and understanding of what it means to be perceived by the mainstream community as a Muslim, and its consequences in a growing multicultural, multi-religious, and technological, contemporary Australia presents a difficult and sensitive task. And yet this chapter provides a stepping stone on that journey, and I commend it to those who wish to develop a better broader understanding of Muslims within the broader Australian cultural and religious traditions—an environment where the separation between the religious and secular identities is a cultural and political given. The mainstream community may have been influenced by Christian values, but, unlike citizens of Muslim countries, their identity is not exchangeable with a religious affiliation.

To the Australian society, composed of both Anglo and non-Anglo Australian born, expressions of opinion—acceptance, concerns, or criticism of their lifestyle—is often driven by patriotism, separation, in-group protection, lack of knowledge, cultural centricism, or a combination thereof.

The aim of this presentation is to identify, analyse and interpret the knowledge, perception and attitudes of Australian students with respect to Islam and the Muslim migrant communities in Australia. It will also explore the extent the media and political forces impact on attitude formation and the extent to which they overshadow common values, perception and select social and cultural issues. Indeed we will look behind those walls and explore the issues challenging the mainstream Australian community and their struggle against apathy, misunderstanding, and integrating the Muslim community with Western values and lifestyle mannerisms.

Survey Method and Sample Characteristics

The participants are 1,000 students at 20 secondary schools around Australia (excluding the Northern Territory and Western Australia)[1] who were administered a full-length survey[2] examining general attitudes towards Muslims and Islam. Participating students were from Classes 10–12.

The sample consisted of just under half boys (43 per cent) and over half girls (57 per cent). This may be because among single-sex schools, girls' schools were slightly more likely to agree to participate than were boys' schools. We found that the principals of boys' schools were more inclined than those of girls' schools to think that the survey might disturb school harmony. About half the sample came from Catholic schools (53 per cent) and roughly a quarter each from other Christian schools (26 per cent), and non-denominational schools (21 per cent). The predominance of Catholic students was a consequence of the relative reluctance of state schools to participate. Secondary schools of Muslim or Jewish affiliation were not approached for this survey, nor were Muslim or Jewish students. It is anticipated that differences will exist with these groups towards Muslims and Islam, and it is intended to survey these groups in subsequent surveys. But primarily, the responses of Muslim and Jewish students were likely to be unrepresentative of most Australians. The particular characteristics of our sample are presented in Table 2.1 .

Findings and Discussion

Three open-ended questions were put to respondents and the answers coded into a manageable number of categories as follows. Naturally this entailed a degree of subjective judgment.

---

[1] These locations were excluded as it would have been costly to survey them for logistical reasons and in any case it was thought they would not contribute to survey accuracy as there was no reason to suppose their responses would differ from those in other states.

[2] A Pilot Study was conducted at nine schools with 552 students in 2012, and a Short Form survey was conducted at 13 schools with 682 students.

TABLE 2.1   Participant characteristics by gender (N = 1000)

		Female (n = 655)	Male (n = 340)	TOTAL
Language	English only	518	289	807
	Other/English & Other	136	50	186
Religion	Christian	490	259	749
	Non-religious	152	74	226
Do you have Muslim friends?	Yes	171	452	216
	No	482	93	775
Do you have Muslim neighbours?	Yes	43	11	54
	No	612	329	941
Location	Metropolitan	256	46	302
	Non-metropolitan	399	294	693
School Type	Private	569	311	880
	State	86	29	115
School Type	Coeducational	385	320	705
	Girls only	270	0	270
	Boys only	0	20	20
Year Level	10	21	11	33
	11	329	219	548
	12	295	107	402
State	NSW/ACT	292	181	473
	VIC	119	82	201
	QLD	31	0	31
	SA	90	18	108
	TAS	123	59	182

Source: Author.

What are the first words that come your mind when 'Muslim' is mentioned?

When asked for 'the first words that come [to] mind when the word "Muslim" is mentioned', few respondents (7 per cent) mentioned anything unequivocally positive (Figure 2.1). About a quarter (28 per cent)

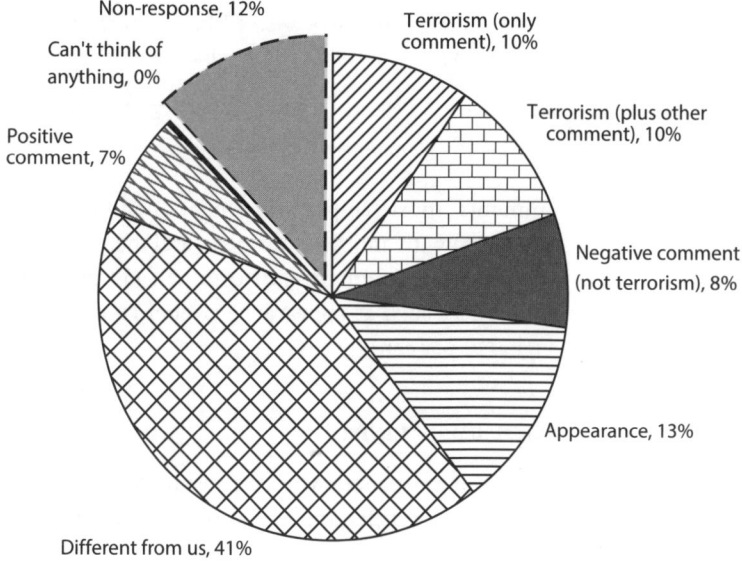

FIGURE 2.1   Response to 'What are the first words that come into your mind when "Muslim" is mentioned?'

Source: Ata (2016c).

Note: Apparent errors in addition are due to rounding.

N = 2023 (inc. non-response)

Box 1   Selected responses to *What are the first words that come into your mind when ... 'Muslim' is mentioned?*

- **Terrorism (only comment)**: ... they are all terrorists wanting to blow people.
- **Terrorism (plus other comment)**: honestly, the first word that comes to mind is f-----g terrorists. You, Bin Laden, Arabics, turban, Cronulla, Lebos, stupid heads, different looks, everything.
- **Negative comment (not terrorism)**: Iraq, Afghanistan, refugees, cover up, Mecca, Middle East ... and they don't show love or manners. Why don't they love Jesus anyway?
- **Appearance**: The towels on their head make them look like penguins.
- **Different from us**: I know they have their own values but it is shit they threatened my sisters school not to sing carols or have Christmas plays at the end of the year.

(Cont'd)

- **Positive comment:** Many things like family oriented, brave, peaceful, normal people, treated badly, bullied, beautiful people, discriminated against and traditional.

Source: Ata (2016c).

offered negative comments; most (20 per cent) mentioned terrorism, half of them in combination with another comment; and the rest (8 per cent) gave some other negative comment. Just over half (54 per cent) alluded to neutral differences such as appearance (13 per cent). About one respondent in eight (12 per cent) gave no response.

What Do You Like Most about Muslims?

When asked what they liked most about Muslims, just under two-thirds offered a comment of some kind (Figure 2.2). Some 44 per cent gave

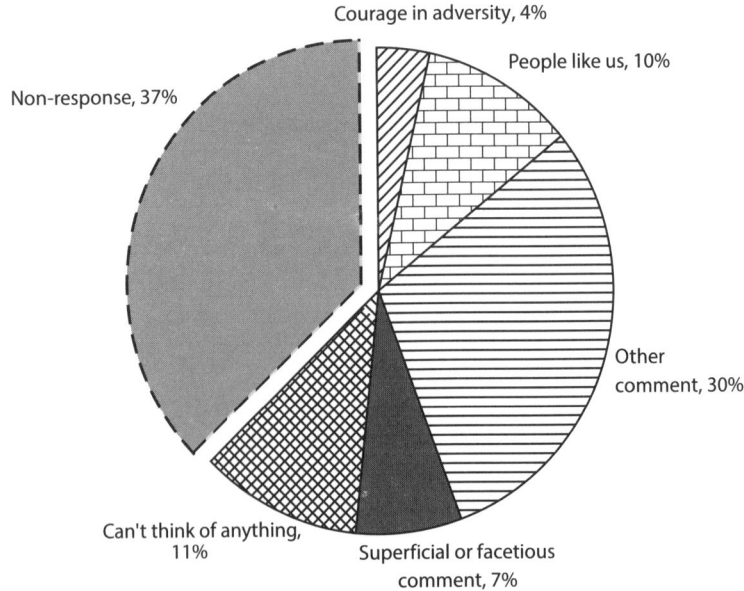

FIGURE 2.2   Response to 'What do you like most about Muslims?'
Source: Ata (2016c).
Note: Apparent errors in addition are due to rounding.
N = 2023 (inc. non-response)

Box 2   Selected responses to: *What do you like most about Muslims*

- **Courage in adversity:** Coping it both ways ... they survive prejudice / racism in Australia and they suffer solemnly at their country home.
- **People like us:** ... they are normal and we are all different. Most like Australia and respect other cultures and religions. Isn't this multiculturalism?
- **Courage in adversity:** I like their bravery, courage, being honest about peace; they are friendly and give everything for being religious.
- **Superficial or facetious comment:** I don't know anything about them so how the hell will I know.
- **Superficial or facetious comment:** I like their curry and kebabs. They have funny accent.
- **Other comment:**
  - I don't think Australians have close families who stick to each other like them. They can also be cool and very generous when you visit them ... even open the door to strangers.
  - Other comment: I am really not phased. I don't judge them by their looks or culture, that's my view.
  - Other comments: The innocent Muslims are OK. I have a Muslim friend, really generous, and cool, confident and well mannered. I like them and treat them just as I want to be treated.
  - They have nice skin.
  - Their falafel.
  - No one particular aspect.
  - They are people.
  - They don't speak to me.
  - The way they say "Peace upon Him".
  - They don't underestimate themselves.

Source: Ata (2016c).
Note: All responses above were recorded verbatim.

positive comments, 4 per cent alluded to courage, often with a mention of the difficult time Muslims have in Australia, 10 per cent saw Muslims as benign just like other Australians and 30 per cent gave other positive comments. Some 17 per cent of respondents gave superficial or facetious comments (7 per cent), or explicitly stated that they could not think of anything they 'liked most about Muslims' (not to be confused with non-response, which might signify simply lack of motivation to respond). Just over a third of respondents (37 per cent) gave no response.

What Do You Like Least about Muslims?

When asked what they liked least about Muslims, just under two-thirds offered a comment of some kind (Figure 2.3). Some 27 per cent mentioned terrorism, 8 per cent alluded to the poor media image[3] of Muslims, 5 per cent alluded to threats to the Australian way of life, and 9 per cent stressed the strangeness of Muslims. Some 7 per cent of respondents gave ambivalent comments of some kind, and 9 per cent explicitly stated that they could not think of anything they 'liked least about Muslims' (not to be confused with non-response, which might signify simply lack of motivation). Just over a third of respondents (38 per cent) gave no response.

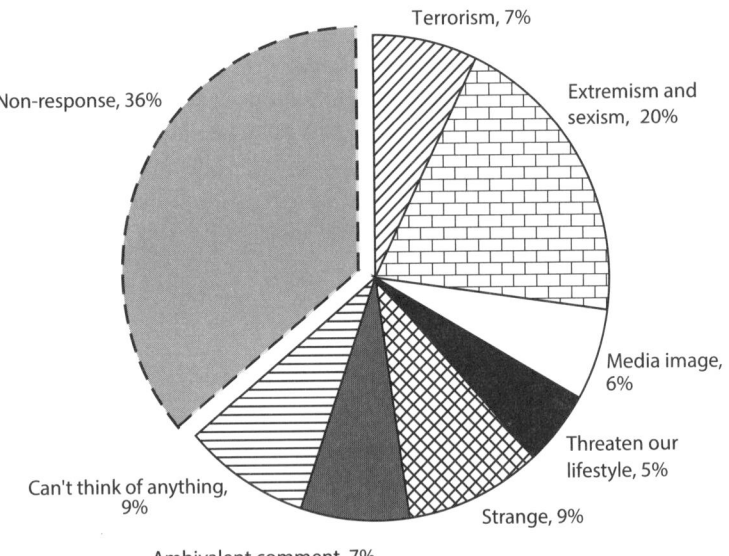

FIGURE **2.3**   Response to 'What do you like least about Muslims?'
Source: Ata (2016c).
Note: Apparent errors in addition are due to rounding
N = 2023 (inc. non-response)

---

[3] This comment might be taken in two ways depending on whether the media image is assumed to be accurate or not. If accurate, then it is a negative comment; if inaccurate, it could be taken as at least neutral, and possible as expressing solidarity—'Muslims are okay; it's the media I don't like.'

Box 1.3   Selected responses to: *What do you like least about Muslims?*

- **Terrorism:** They are all wrong. All this terrorism stuff happened because of Muslims. They just look really filthy.
- **Extremism and sexism:** The way they treat women, women's clothes, over the top, violence, ruthless, how they believe killing is a good thing.
- **Media image:** The way media portrays them, and the way all of us are sucked in bouncing off what we hear about them again and again. There is bad in every culture.
- **Threaten our lifestyle:** ... frightening our culture and not wanting to assimilate cause they don't live by the rule lifestyle, etc., riots and every-thing, they should go back home.
- **Strange:** The way they stare at you and their attitude to parties or school camps. They don't want to assimilate or be social like Italians or Greeks.
- **Ambivalent comment:**
  - Because they ... wear heavy clothes.
  - I have not met any. I don't know them well enough to know and judge them badly ... There is bad in every culture. This questionnaire is racist.
  - For one hundred years Australian schools used to play Xmas carols; this does not happen anymore. WHY!

Source: Ata (2016c).

The reference to extremism and terrorism has in recent years been at the centre of public debate. Even where consensus exists, the problem is recognized as complex. The causal factors—psychological, sociological, historical, and institutional—that give rise to violent extremism combine with and interact in ways that make it extremely hard to predict which particular individuals will succumb. According to US researchers Denoeux and Carter 'There can be no general theory about "why and how the turn to [violent extremism] occurs", because the answer to that question will vary from one set-ting to another' (2009: 84). Edmund Rice Centre (2006) listed several falsehoods held by the mainstream community about Muslims. They contend that such falsehoods have long-term implications in that they are negative and passionate reactions. For example, words like *jihad* have come to overshadow what is a religion of many perspectives. *Jihad* does not mean 'holy war', but refers to 'any action by which one makes sincere and conscious effort for a collective benefit' and wearing a *hijab* is a testimony of faith not subjugation. It is pointed out that differences of world view between the two societies and their traditions will continue to exist.

Where might have false beliefs about Muslim minorities originated? It is argued that attitudes are not only formed by the media but can also be formed by other more individual social-psychological variables. Utsey, McCarthy, Eubanks, and Adrian (2002) found that people with high self-esteem were more prejudiced. Pedersen and Walker (1994) found the same individuals often have varying prejudiced views depending on the target group whereby indigenous Australians were at the bottom of the pecking order, followed by Asian Australians (see also Habtegiorgis, Paradies, and Dunn 2014; Walton et al. 2015).

Rabasa and Benard (2015) have challenged the widely held view that violent extremism is borne of 'relative deprivation', 'religion', or any number of other causes. In Benard's words, 'If we take a closer look at "moderate Islam" we find that one slice of it—the "aggressive traditionalist" slice—incites not violence against the West, but rejection of Western values, modern life and integration. It demands of its followers that they be in the West but not of it, that they maintain emotional, social and intellectual separation' (2015: 1). And it is this sense of separation that makes violence possible.

That said, this analysis does not attempt to expand this already extensive body of knowledge, a task better tackled by national agencies with an international remit.

How Do Students Differ in Their Attitudes?

So far we have explored the attitudes of the sample as a whole. They covered a range of themes including cultural pluralism, the media, religious education, civic engagement, spiritualism and interfaith dialogue, the role of women, asylum seekers, sexual abuse, mental health, mixed marriages, identity, social services and institutions, conversion to and from Islam, tolerance and factionalism, apologists and the faithful, schools and universities, challenges and future directions.

But does this mask differences within the sample? For instance, do boys differ systematically from girls in their attitudes towards Islam and Muslims? To answer this and similar questions, we used statistical techniques to determine if there were significant differences in the mean attitudes of all the demographic groups measured in the survey. The result is outlined as follows:

Gender Differences

Significant differences were found between the responses of boys and girls (see Figure 2.4). Boys and girls differed significantly on the following statements.

Boys agreed more than girls with the following statements:	Girls agreed more than boys with the following statements:
Most Muslims treat women with less respect than do other Australians.	Most Muslims have good feelings for Australia and Australians.
Muslims threaten the Australian way of life.	This school helps people of different cultures to get along better.
Most religious fanatics these days are Muslims.	Learning about Muslims helps students to understand them better.
Most migrants are racist.	A person can be both—a good Muslim and a loyal Australian.
Most Australians are racist.	Muslims have made a major contribution to Australia.
Australian TV and newspapers show Muslims in a fair way.	Most Australians have good feelings for Muslims.
Muslims do not belong to Australia.	The image of Muslims is as good as other migrant groups in Australia.
If I saw a Muslim student being abused in a public place I wouldn't care.	Australian schools should teach more about Muslims.

These findings show that boys were less accepting of Muslims and Islam than were girls. Interestingly, boys agreed more than girls with the statement 'Most Muslims treat women with less respect than do other Australians'—clearly a view not founded in direct experience. Removed statement does not account for possibility of boys seeing women treated with disrespected—which is near enough the meaning of 'direct experience'. Note that we are not suggesting that either boys

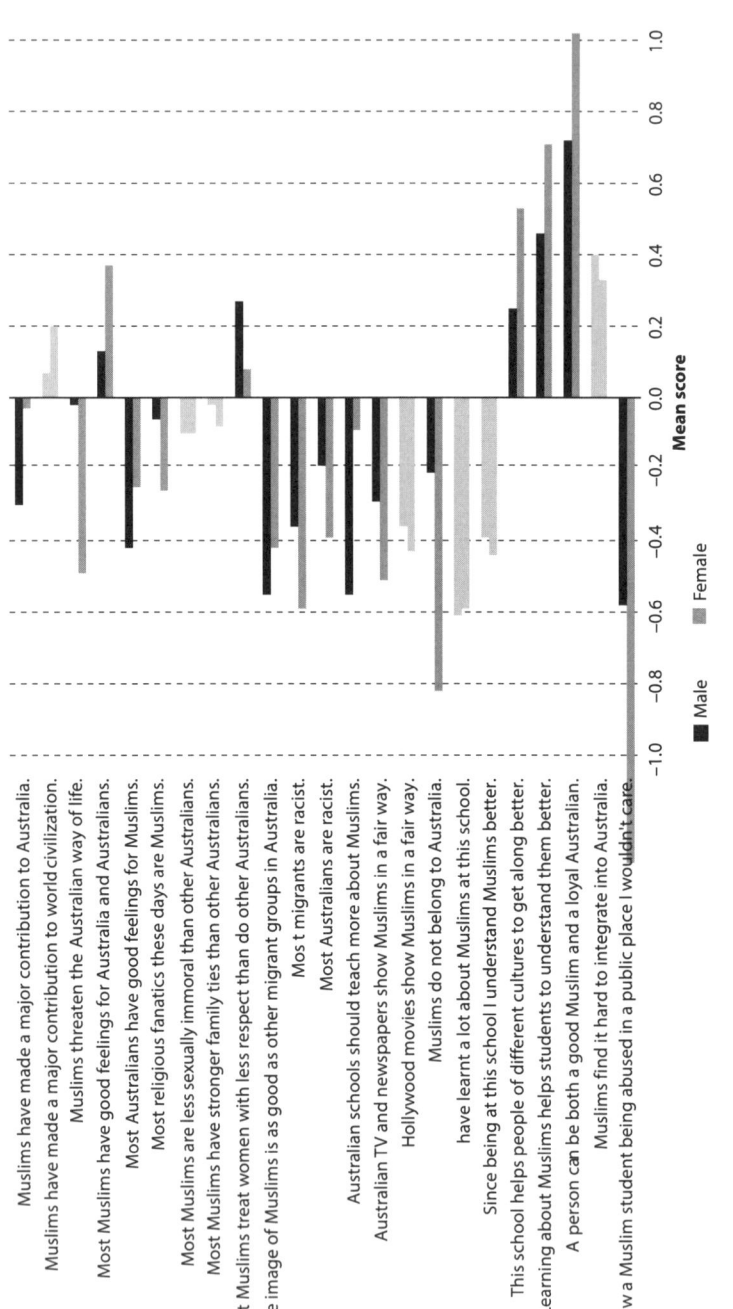

FIGURE 2.4 Mean attitude scores by gender

Source: Author.

or girls are being treated with less respect, only the possibility of this being true and our concern with the wording of the statement.

The Role of Religion

Significant differences were found between the responses of respondents according to their religious affiliation (or lack of one) (Figure 2.4).

On many statements, there was a strong tendency for the two Christian groups—Catholics and other Christians—to resemble each other and to differ from the non-religious.

Non-religious agreed more than Christians with the following statements:	Christians agreed more than non-religious with the following statements:
Muslims have made a major contribution to world civilization.	Most religious fanatics these days are Muslims.
Muslims have made a major contribution to Australia.	Most migrants are racist.
Most Muslims have good feelings for Australia and Australians.	Muslims do not belong to Australia.
Australian schools should teach more about Muslims.	

On two statements, all three religious affiliations differed significantly from each other as follows:

- On the statement 'Muslims threaten the Australian way of life', all disagreed, but to different degrees, non-religious most, Catholics next, Other Christians least.
- On the statement 'Most Muslims treat women with less respect than do other Australians', they all agreed, other Christian most, Catholics next, non-religious least.

On one statement, 'Australian TV and newspapers show Muslims in a fair way', other Christian and non-religious did not differ significantly, but did differ from Catholics: all groups disagreed, Catholics least.

These findings show that the two Christian groups were significantly less well-disposed towards Muslims and Islam than were the non-religious (see Figure 2.5).

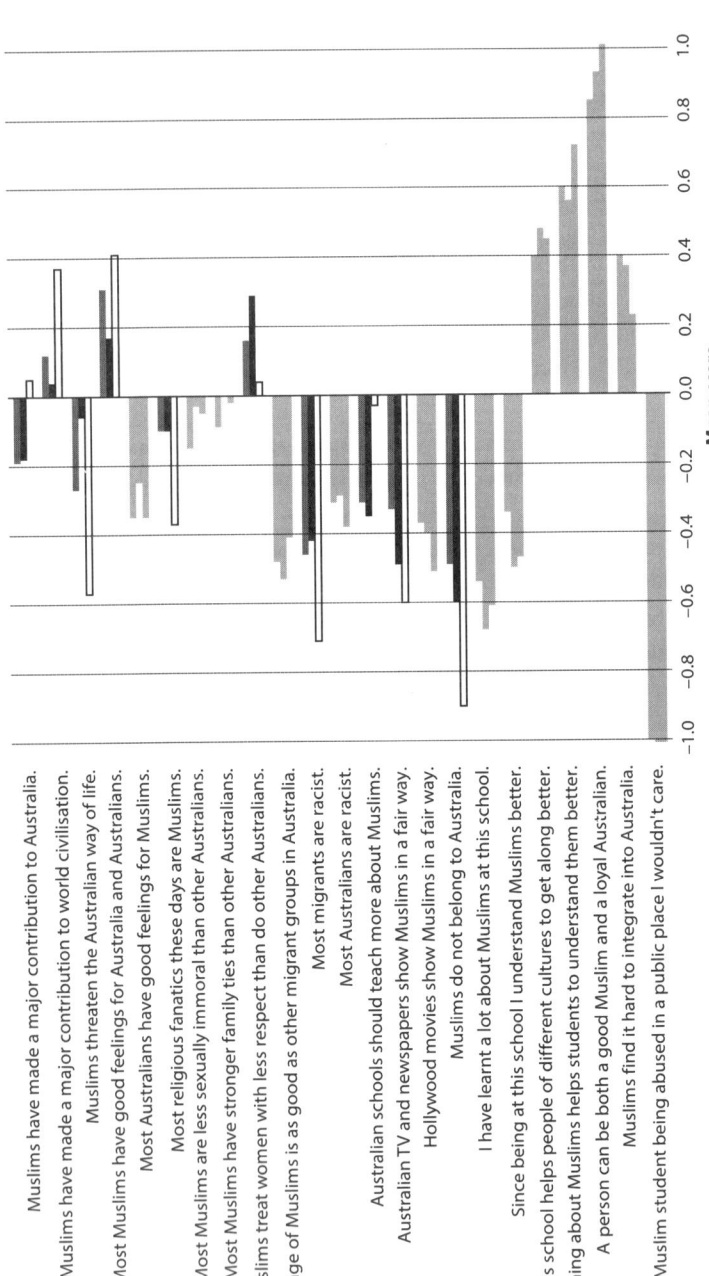

FIGURE 2.5   Mean attitude scores by religion

Source: Age (2016)

Does Having Muslim Friends Make a Difference?

In a word, yes. Significant differences were found between the responses of those with Muslim friends and those without. Those with Muslim friends differed significantly from those without on the following statements.

Those with Muslim friends agreed more than those without with the following statements:	Those without Muslim friends agreed more than those with the following statements:
Muslims have made a major contribution to Australia.	Muslims find it hard to integrate into Australia.
Muslims have made a major contribution to world civilization.	Muslims threaten the Australian way of life.
Most Muslims have good feelings for Australia and Australians.	Most migrants are racist.
Most Muslims have stronger family ties than other Australians.	Hollywood movies show Muslims in a fair way.
Australian schools should teach more about Muslims.	Muslims do not belong to Australia.
This school helps people of different cultures to get along better.	If I saw a Muslim student being abused in a public place I wouldn't care.
Learning about Muslims helps students to understand them better.	
A person can be both a good Muslim and a loyal Australian.	

These findings suggest that those with Muslim friends tend to endorse positive attitudes towards Muslims and although those who lack Muslim friends do not mostly endorse negative attitudes, they do tend to disagree less with them. In other words, positive attitudes are generally embraced by both groups, but more strongly by those with

Muslim friends and negative attitudes are generally opposed by both groups, but more strongly by those with Muslim friends.

Note that these findings say nothing about causation. Having Muslim friends might give rise to positive attitudes, or alternatively having positive attitudes might predispose one to seek or accept Muslim friends. Nevertheless the two are strongly associated in a statistical sense, meaning that if one is present, the other is likely to be also.

Knowledge of Islam and Muslims

A study by the Pew Research Center (2006) showed that those who are more knowledgeable about Muslims express favourable opinions of Muslims and Islam. It was noted that through knowledge, greater levels of awareness come from equal status interaction between the learner and individuals of Muslim background. The study showed that the ability to identify both Allah and the Qur'an correctly correlates with holding a favourable view of Islam. Being informed about Islam prompts people to think that Islam and their own religion have a lot in common. Similarly being knowledgeable about Islam makes one more likely to see recent terrorist attacks as part of a conflict.

Respondents were presented with 10 statements concerning objectively verifiable facts about Islam and Muslims, and asked to rate their agreement on a five-point scale from 'Strongly agree' through 'Neutral' to 'Strongly disagree'. Responses are tabulated for each question and aggregated into a score representing each respondent's knowledge. To avoid bias, questions were worded so that half had 'Agree' as the correct response, and half 'Disagree'.

The survey revealed a great lack of knowledge of Islam; on all questions about half the sample recorded a 'don't know' response (see Figure 2.6). The proportion of correct responses varied from a high of 49 per cent for 'Some Palestinians are Christian', to a low of 6 per cent for 'Iran is an Arab country'.

Some Palestinians Are Christian

The correct answer to this is 'Agree', since some 20 per cent of Palestinians are Christian. Formerly the proportion was considerably greater, but has declined in recent years due to emigration. The

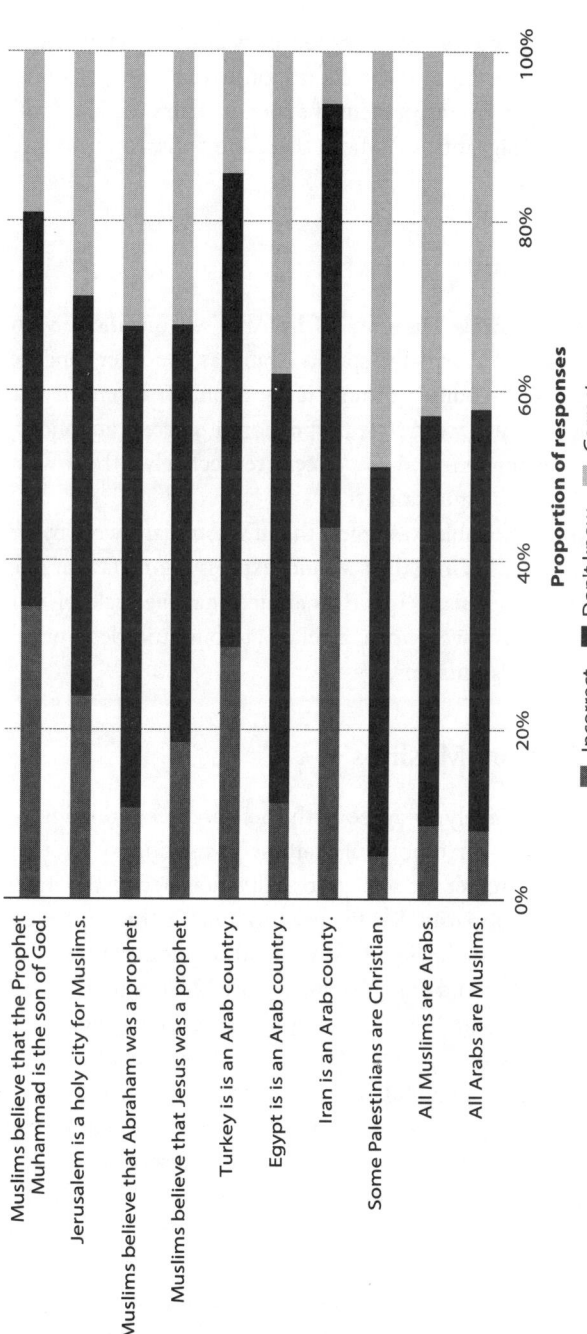

FIGURE 2.6 Proportion of correct and incorrect responses

N = 996, 997, 994, 991, 994, 989, 991, 995, 994, and 993, respectively

Source: Ata (2016c).

proportion of correct and incorrect responses was 49 per cent and 5 per cent respectively—the highest correct response of all the questions. This may be because many respondents happen to know, or know of, Christian Palestinian migrants, of whom there are a disproportionate number in Australia.

Iran Is an Arab County

The correct answer to this is 'Disagree'. If by 'Arab' we mean one who claims to be an Arab and (normally) speaks Arabic as a mother tongue, then Iran is not an Arab country, though it does contain a minority of Arabs, mainly in the south west. The proportion of correct and incorrect responses was 6 per cent and 44 per cent respectively—the lowest correct response of all the questions.

It would thus be reasonable to suggest that if Australians were more knowledgeable about Muslims they would express more favourable opinions of Muslims and Islam. It is thus argued that the scale of our knowledge, fashionable or well worn, is related to our attitudes—negative or positive—towards Muslims.

Social Distance from Muslims

Respondents were less likely to agree with the statements relating to 'Muslims' than with the corresponding statements relating to 'another race' (Figure 2.7), and greater the social proximity indicated by the statement, the greater the disparity. So, for instance, about three-quarters agreed with 'I would enjoy having a close friend of another race', but only about half with 'I would enjoy having a close Muslim friend', and while about half agreed with 'I would marry someone of another race', only a fifth did so for 'I would marry a Muslim'. At that level of proximity about 20 per cent of respondents strongly agreed with the statement 'I would marry someone of another race', but only 7 per cent did so when that 'someone' was a Muslim. This shows that respondents were more reluctant to engage socially with Muslims than those of 'another race'. Furthermore, it cannot be explained by a generalized racism but is specific to Muslims.

In order to highlight the differences between social distance towards Muslims as compared to persons of 'another race', the difference in

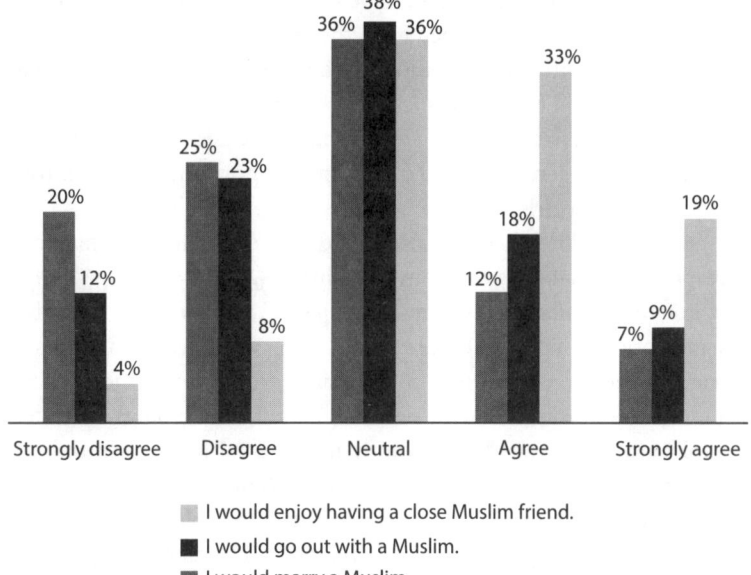

FIGURE 2.7   Proportion of respondents by social distance of self from
Muslims
Source: Author.

responses were ranked (Figure 2.6).[4] Respondents favoured persons of
'another race' over Muslims on all three measures of social distance, but
much more so when the degree of intimacy was greater.

These findings show that the social distance of respondents and that
of their parents (as perceived by the respondents themselves) were very
similar, and where the difference was significant, the parents' social
distance was generally slightly greater than that of their children—an
unsurprising finding if the older generation is perceived to be socially
more conservative than the younger. Because the parent's perceived

---

[4] For this purpose responses were scored as follows: 'Disagree strongly' =
−1, 'Disagree' = 1, 'Neutral' = 0 etc. All differences were significant at the 5 per
cent level on paired t-tests. No analogous comparison was made for parents'
perceptions as it was considered unnecessary since perceptions of non-religious
resembled perceptions of Christians.

social distance scores were found to be little different from those of the respondents, they were dropped from the analysis.

A significant difference was found between boys (mean score 9.6) and by girls (8.6) in respect of social distance from Muslims (F (1,979) = 26.9, $p <$ .001). These findings show that boys desired not only more social distance in general than did girls, but proportionately more from Muslims than did girls.

A significant difference was also found between religious affiliations in respect of social distance from Muslims (F (2,961) = 11.7, $p <$ .001). Post hoc tests (Student-Newman-Keuls, $p <$ .05) showed that Catholics (mean score 9.1) and Other Christians (9.4). While not differing significantly one from another, both desired significantly more social distance from Muslims than did non-religious. These findings show that Catholic students desired significantly more social distance from both 'another race' and Muslims than did non-religious. Other Christians were ambivalent, vis-à-vis 'another race' they resembled Catholics, but vis-à-vis Muslims they resembled non-religious. The differences, though significant, were not large, however.

For many attributes, there was little difference in the perceptions of the religious groups, but on some the Muslims stood in sharp contrast to the others (refer to Figure 2.7).

No current test can do that without producing either an unacceptable number of 'false positives' (harmless but flagged as harmful), or an unacceptable number of 'false negatives' (harmful but flagged as harmless, which is worse), or both. Pre-emptive screening of this kind has its place and will no doubt improve, but is best done by national agencies with wider powers and bigger budgets.

In order to highlight the differences between how Muslims were perceived as compared to how Christians were perceived, the difference in proportional responses were ranked (see Figure 2.8 as follows).[5] Muslims were perceived (in decreasing order of importance) as more victimized,

[5] Differences were calculated as in the following example: 69 per cent of respondents regarded Muslims as 'victimized' as compared to 23 per cent who regarded Christians as 'victimized', hence the difference was 23 per cent − 69 per cent = −46 per cent. All differences were significant at the 5 per cent level on paired t-tests. No analogous comparison was made between Muslims and non-religious as it was considered unnecessary since perceptions of non-religious resembled perceptions of Christians.

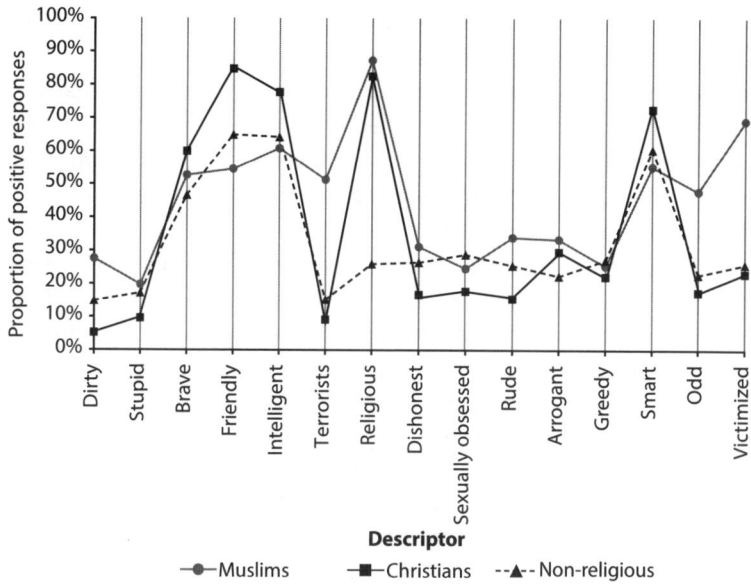

FIGURE 2.8   Proportion of positive responses to attributes of selected
religious groups
Source: Author.

terrorists, odd, dirty, rude, dishonest, stupid, sexually obsessed, religious, arrogant and greedy than Christians, while Christians were
perceived (in decreasing order of importance) as more friendly, smart,
intelligent and brave than Muslims. Differences were calculated as in
the following example: 69 per cent of respondents regarded Muslims
as 'victimized' as compared to 23 per cent who regarded Christians
as 'victimized', hence the difference was 23 per cent − 69 per cent =
−46 per cent. All differences were significant at the 5 per cent level on
paired t-tests. No analogous comparison was made between Muslims
and non-religious as it was considered unnecessary since perceptions of
non-religious resembled perceptions of Christians.

Unexpected Findings

This survey revealed a trajectory of unexpected findings of attitudes,
feelings, and knowledge towards Muslims in Australia. The themes

addressed and the cultural and historical differences between Christian and Muslim communities in our society are too wide to make a definitive statement or a complete reconciliation, but, given the alternatives, a creative dialogue must continue. Just like mixed marriages, certain differences between the two faiths may be identified, without being fully reconciled. A starting point towards this end is identifying misconceptions, misgivings, and the roots of grievances.

Three open-ended questions were put to respondents and the answers coded into a manageable number of categories as discussed below. Naturally this entailed a degree of subjective judgment. Widespread negative stereotypes and the relatively new presence of the Muslim community in Australia tend to suggest non-Muslim students may not be well informed, while the longstanding multicultural posture of educational policy suggests otherwise. Variation in response between boys and girls, religion or non-religious affiliated also revealed a high level of significance. The findings show Australian students are generally ignorant about Muslims and Islam, and few believe that schools are filling the gaps in their knowledge. While non-Muslim students agree that acceptance of Muslims does not come easily in Australia, school does not emerge as a site for change.

The survey found that students are divided in the degree and nature of prejudice and tolerance towards Muslims in Australia. One of the main findings was with regards to gender differences were boys were less accepting of Muslims and Islam than were girls. Interestingly, boys agreed more than girls with the statement 'Most Muslims treat women with less respect than do other Australians'—clearly a view not founded in direct experience. A significant difference was also found between boys (mean score 9.6) and by girls (8.6) in respect of social distance from Muslims including aspirations to friendship, neighbourhood, and intermarriage. They showed that boys significantly desired not only more social distance in general than did girls, but proportionately more from Muslims than did girls. They also show that social distance is linked to the degree to which students felt that their school was educative about Islam. Knowing more facts about other groups, Muslims or non-Muslims, is less predictive of tolerance that one's feeling of the school caring to educate students about each other.

On the question of the relationship between attitude formation and religious friendship the following was revealed: those with mostly

Muslim friends agreed more than those with mostly non-Muslim friends that 'Some Muslims face discrimination because they dress differently' and, that 'a person can be both a good Muslim and a loyal Australian'. Those with mostly non-Muslim friends agreed more than others on the following statements: 'Most Muslims treat women with less respect than do other Australians; Australian TV and newspapers show Muslims in a fair way; and Movies show Muslims in a fair way'. There was also a strong tendency for the two Christian groups—Catholics and other Christians—were significantly less well-disposed towards Muslims and Islam than were the non-religious.

On two statements, all three religious affiliations differed significantly from another. On the statement: 'Muslims threaten the Australian way of life', all disagreed, but to different degrees, non-religious most, Catholics next, other Christians least. On the statement 'Most Muslims treat women with less respect than do other Australians', they all agreed, other Christian most, Catholics next, non-religious least. Goodwill towards the Muslim community resonated with more participants than otherwise. There were twice as many respondents (35 per cent + 7 per cent contrasted with 19 per cent + 2 per cent) who believed that most Australians have good feelings for Muslims. And subsequently it is correct to conclude that they are perceived as being accepted in the wider mainstream society. Those who expressed neutrality (38 per cent) may want to seek a wider occurrence or firmer evidence of this reality.

It was found that Australian students, a clear majority (64 per cent), felt that they have learnt little or nothing about Muslims at their school, with over a fifth strongly disagreeing with the proposition. A mere 2 per cent felt they could give the most positive response. The small response (16 per cent) by those who learnt a lot about Muslims at their school is understandable. Similarly, a large percentage of respondents (49 per cent) disagreed/strongly that they understand Muslims better since being at their school—22 per cent. The absence of Muslim students from a large number of non-public schools and regional Australia may have contributed to the direction of responses, although having Muslim friends does not make a significant difference.

The results show that participants who spontaneously mentioned false beliefs and had low levels of knowledge reported significantly more negative attitudes to Christians than those who did not. This is an

important result because it is possible that accepting incorrect information may be shaping negative attitudes towards Christians. That said,
cultural background and religious affiliation continue to be strong indicators of the individual's attitudes and behaviour towards and knowledge of the other. The relationship between prejudice and the degree of
knowledge, or cultural perception, of Muslims in the Australian society,
is not conclusive.

References

Ata, Abe. 2009. *Us and Them: Muslim-Christian Relations and Cultural Harmony in
  Australia*. Brisbane: Australian Academic Press.
———. 2013. *Christian Muslim Intermarriage in Australia: Social Cohesion or
  Cultural Fragmentation*. Melbourne: David Lovell Publishing.
———. 2014. *Education, Integration, Challenges: The Case of Australian Muslims*.
  Melbourne: David Lovell Publishing.
———. 2016a. 'How Muslim Students' Knowledge of Christianity Is Related
  to Their Attitudes to Mainstream Australia and Australians: A National
  Survey (Project Report)', *Social Science* (Europe) 4(3): 800–5. doi:10.3390/
  socsci4030800
———. 2016b. 'How Muslim Students Perceive of Australia and Australians: A
  National Survey', *Journal of Intercultural Communication* 41, July.
———. 2016c. 'Research Note: How Muslims are Perceived in Catholic Schools
  in Contemporary Australia: A National Survey', *Intercultural Education* 27(4):
  337–51.
Ata, A., B. Bastian, and D. Lusher. 2009. 'Intergroup Contact in Context: The
  Mediating Role of Social Norms and Group-Based Perceptions on the
  Contact–Prejudice', *International Journal of Intercultural Relations* 33(6):
  498–506.
Ata, A. and T. Batrouney. 1989. 'Attitudes and Stereotyping in Victorian
  Secondary Schools', *The Eastern Anthropologist*, 42(1): 35–49.
Bastian, B., D. Lusher, and A. Ata. 2012. 'Contact, Evaluation and Social
  Distance: Differentiating Majority and Minority Effects', *International
  Journal of Intercultural Relations* 36: 100–7.
Benard, C. 2015. 'Moderate Islam' Isn't Working', *The National Interest*, 20
  December, pp. 1–2.
Benard, C. and A. Angel. 2015. *Eurojihad: Patterns of Islamist Radicalization and
  Terrorism in Europe*. New York: Cambridge University Press.
Berry, J.W. 2008. 'Globalisation and Acculturation', *International Journal of
  Intercultural Relations* 32(4): 328–36.

Brasted, H. 2001. 'Contested Representations in Historical Perspective: Images of Islam and the Australian Press 1950–2000'. In *Muslim Communities in Australia*, S. Akbarzadeh and A. Saeed (eds), pp. 136–60. Sydney: University of New South Wales Press.

Briskman, Linda. 2015. 'The Creeping Blight of Islamophobia in Australia', *International Journal for Crime, Justice and Social Democracy* 4(3): 112–21.

Cahill, D. and A. Gundert. 1996. *Immigration and Schooling in the 1990s*. Canberra, Australia: Bureau of Immigration Multicultural and Population Research and Department of Immigration and Multicultural Affairs.

Credlin, P. 2016. 'Community Turns a Blind Eye to Changes in Our Culture: Biting the Hand that Feeds You', *The Heraldsun*, 11 December, p. 31.

Denoeux, G. and L. Carter. 2009. *Guide to the Drivers of Violent Extremism*. Washington: USAID.

Donohoue Clyne, I. 2000. *Seeking Education: The Struggle of Muslims to Educate their Children in Australia*, PhD thesis, Melbourne: University of Melbourne.

———. 2001. 'Educating Muslim Children in Australia'. In *Muslim communities in Australia*, S. Akbarzadeh and A. Saeed (eds), pp. 219–44. Sydney: University of New South Wales Press.

Dunn, K. 2001. 'The Geography of Racisms in NSW: A Theoretical Exploration and Some Preliminary Findings from the Mid 1990s', *The Australian Geographer* 32(1): 29–44.

———. 2004. 'Islam in Australia: Contesting the Discourse of Absence', *The Australian Geographer* 53(3): 333–53.

———. 2005. 'Australian Public Knowledge of Islam', *Studia Islamika: Indonesian Journal for Islamic Studies* 12(1): 1–32.

Edmund Rice Centre. 2005. *Debunking Myths about Muslims in Australia*. ERC, Strathfield: NSW.

Gordijn, E., W. Koomen, and D.A. Stapel. 2001. 'Level of Prejudice in Relation to Knowledge of Cultural Stereotypes', *Journal of Experimental Social Psychology* 37: 150–7.

Habtegiorgis, A., Y. Paradies, K. Dunn. 2014. 'Are Racist Attitudes Related to Experiences of Racial Discrimination? Within Sample Testing Utilising Nationally Representative Survey Data', *Social Science Research* 47: 178–91, Amsterdam: The Netherlands.

Hargreaves, Julian. 2016. *Islamophobia: Reality or Myth?* PhD Thesis, Lancaster University.

Hirst, John. 2016. *Australian History in 7 Questions*. Melbourne: Black Inc.

Human Rights and Equal Opportunity Commission. 2004. *Ismau Listen: National Consultations on Eliminating Prejudice against Arab and Muslim Australians*. Sydney: Human Rights and Equal Opportunity Commission.

Kabir, N. 2007. 'What Does It Mean to Be Un-Australian? Views of Australian Muslim Students in 2006', *People and Place* 15: 62–79.

Lepore, L. and R. Brown. 1997. 'Category and Stereotype Activation: Is Prejudice Inevitable?', *Journal of Personality and Social Psychology* 72(2): 275–87.

Muslim Community Reference Group. 2006. *Building on Social Cohesion, Harmony and Security*. Canberra: Dept. of Immigration and Citizenship (series).

Nelson, N., K. Dunn, and Y. Paradies. 2011. 'Australian Racism and Anti-racism: Links to Morbidity and Belonging'. In *Migration, Citizenship and Intercultural Relations: Looking through the Lens of Social Inclusion*, F. Mansouti and M. Lobo (eds), pp. 159–75. Surrey, England.

Parliamentary Joint Committee on Intelligence and Security. 2006. *Review of Security and Counter Terrorism Legislation*. Canberra: Parliament of Australia

Pedersen, A., A. Aly, L. Hartley, and C. McGarty. 2009. 'An Intervention to Increase Positive Attitudes and Address Misconceptions about Australian Muslims: A Call for Education and Open Mindedness', *The Australian Community Psychologist* 21(2): 81–93.

Pedersen, A. and F. Barlow. 2008. 'Theory to Social Action: A University Based Strategy Targeting Prejudice against Aboriginal Australians', *Australian Psychologist* 43: 148–59.

Pedersen, A. and I. Walker. 1997. 'Prejudice against Australian Aborigines: Old Fashioned and Modern Forms', *The European Journal of Social Psychology* 27: 561–87.

Pedersen, A., I. Walker, and M. Wise. 2005. '"Talk Does Not Cook Rice": Beyond Anti-Racism Rhetoric to Strategies for Social Action', *Australian Psychologist* 40: 20–31.

Pettigrew, T.F. and L.R. Tropp. 2008. 'How Does Intergroup Contact Reduce Prejudice? Meta-Analytic Tests of Three Mediators', *European Journal of Social Psychology* 38: 922–34.

Pew Research Center. 2006. *Conflicting Views in a Divided World*. Washington DC: The Pew Global Attitudes Project.

———. 2008. 'Unfavorable Views of Jews and Muslims on the Increase in Europe: Ethnocentric Attitudes Are on the Rise in Europe', 17 September. Washington D.C.

Poynting, S. 2002. '"Bin Laden in the Suburbs": Attacks on Arab and Muslim Australians before and after 11 September', *Current Issues in Criminal Justice* 14(1): 43–64.

Poynting, Scott and Victoria Mason. 2008. 'The New Integrationism, the State and Islamophobia: Retreat from Multiculturalism in Australia', *International Journal of Law, Crime and Justice* 36(4): 230–46.

Rabasa, A. and C. Benard. 2014. *Eurojihad: Patterns of Islamist Radicalization and Terrorism in Europe*. London: Cambridge University Press.

Shahram, Akbarzadeh and Abdulla Saeed (eds). 2001. *Muslim Communities in Australia*. Sydney: University of New South Wales Press.

Sherman, J.W., C. Groom, K. Ehrenberg, and K.C. Klauer. 2003. 'Bearing False Witness under Pressure: Implicit and Explicit Components of Stereotype-Driven Memory Distortions', *Social Cognition* 21: 213–46.

Sidanius, J., S. Levin, C. Federico, and F. Pratto. 2001. 'Legitimizing Ideologies: The Social Dominance Approach'. In *The Psychology of Legitimacy: Emerging Perspectives on Ideology, Justice, and Intergroup Relations*, J.T. Jost and B. Major (eds), pp. 307–31. New York: Cambridge University Press.

Simkin, K. and E. Gauci. 1992. 'Ethnic Diversity and Multicultural Education'. In *Contemporary Perspectives in Comparative* Education, R.J. Burns and A.R. Welch (eds), pp. xlv, 432. New York: Garland Pub.

Utsey, S.O., E. McCarthy, R. Eubanks, and G. Adrian. 2002. 'White Racism and Suboptimal Psychological Functioning Among White Americans: Implications For Counseling and Prejudice Prevention', *Journal of Multicultural Counseling and Development* 30(2): 81–95.

Walton, J., Y. Paradies, N. Priest, E. Wertheim, and E. Freeman. 2015. 'Fostering Intercultural Understanding through Secondary School Experiences of Cultural Immersion', *International Journal of Qualitative Studies in Education* 28: 216–37.

Windle, J. 2004. 'Schooling, Symbolism and Social Power: The Hijab in Republican France', *Australian Educational Researcher* 31(1): 95–112.

Wise, A. and J. Ali. 2008. *Muslim-Australians and Local Government [electronic resource]: Grassroots Strategies to Improve Relations between Muslim and Non-Muslim-Australians: Final Research Report*. Canberra: Department of Immigration and Citizenship.

3

ALI GHANBARPOUR-DIZBONI
CHRISTIAN LEUPRECHT

Framing, Branding, and Explaining

A Survey of Perceptions of Islam and Muslims in the Canadian Polls, Government, and Academia

Over the years, prominent commentators have praised Canadian multiculturalism as a model of successful integration and recommended its lessons for emulation to other Western countries. A number of them in fact pointed to Canada's record of positive interethnic and interfaith relations as exceptional within the Western world. In what follows, we will explore if Canada is as exceptional as portrayed and will review some of the key findings from public opinion polls, government discourse, and academic research on the perceived and conceived linkages between Islam/Muslims and terrorism/radicalization. This chapter is an attempt, possibly the first, to examine the securitization of Islam and Muslims in Canada at these three levels and offers a somewhat different perspective on the issue. In fact, the thrust of public polls, academic research, and government discourse does associate the presence of Muslims with security issues. Nevertheless, what may make Canada somewhat exceptional is the fact that the current government's discourse categorically dissociates a correlation between Islam and security threats. Put simply, the ways in which Canada's new government articulates its statements on the securitization of Islam and Muslims clearly diverges from its predecessor as well as from the mainstream public polls and academia.

The presence of Muslims[1] in Canada came to be viewed through different lenses post 9/11 and is described as Muslim exceptionalism[2] and at times even in alarming terms as in the book *The Muslim Question in Canada*. Accordingly—and notwithstanding some impressive achievements—Canadian exceptionalism in immigration should be weighed against the *problematization* of this presence in Canada. Although compared to other Western countries, this presence is viewed as less *problematic* it has not escaped securitization discourses, processes and practices, especially in French Canada (Quebec).[3] Like France, Germany, and the UK, the post 9/11 period in Canada has been marked by the tensions of terror incidents, wedge politics, and vehement controversies over public policy issues such as sharia court, *niqab*, funding of religious schools

---

[1] Faith-based statistics in Canada are long overdue. As Kazemipur (2014: 26–7) says, 2001 census in Canada was the last one in which demographic count on the basis of religious groups was conducted. From 579, 640 Muslims (forming 20 per cent of total immigrants arriving to Canada in 2000–01), the number is estimated to be 940,000 in 2011 and the rough forecasts for 2021 and 2031 respectively are 2 and 3 million.

[2] First, unlike Algerians in France, Canadian immigrants from a Muslim background lack resentments towards their host society based on memories of a charged colonial history. Second, unlike French Speaking North-Africans in Hexagon, or Pakistanis and Bengalis in UK, Canadian Muslims originate from very diverse ethnic, linguistic, cultural, sectarian and regional backgrounds. And unlike Turkish migrant workers in Germany, immigrants are selected on the basis of merit points system under the Canadian Immigration Act (expertise, market employability, language ...)

[3] The mosque shooting in Quebec City by a right-wing extremist on January 29, 2017 was a first of the kind in Canada. Comparing Quebec with the rest of Canada, Muslims in Quebec express higher levels of concern over racial, cultural and religious experiences and their future in terms of discrimination, unemployment and negative attitude towards Islam (Environics Institute 2006 quoted in Kazemipur 2014: 113).

and reasonable accommodation.[4] In view of this, Muslim exceptionalism within the Canadian immigrant population gives pause for a deeper consideration of the securitization of the Muslim presence in Canada.

Two methodological notes are in order here. First, while associationist hypothesis refers to the perceived or conceptualized linkages between Islam, Muslims, and security concerns, the non-associationist (or dis-associationist) thesis refutes such linkages. The latter sees the linkage as superficial or accidental and calls for the consideration deeper causes of radicalization and terrorism. Second, given the vast scope of this topic and the implied complexities of human and social research, findings emanating from such work should be treated with care. Poll results are generally fraught with methodological challenges and pitfalls including sampling, scaling, and timeline setting. Meanwhile, government (Conservative or Liberal) discourses and practices are shrouded in secrecy and bound by political expediency. Academic writings, as will be explored later, bear their own limitations, especially when the subject pertains to the current security issues.[5]

---

[4] Islam could be a multiplier factor in the Canadian general malaise with the process of immigration. Compared to 29 per cent before 9/11, Canadian support for reduced immigration rose to 45 per cent after the September 11 and more importantly, 80 per cent of surveyed Canadians called for stricter controls over immigration (Adelman 2002: 15). Again, according to Angus Reid public opinion poll on 14 September 2010, 46 per cent vs. 34 per cent of surveyed sample attribute negative effect to Immigration in Canada. Overall and generally comparable to levels in US, in Canada since 1997, there is an increased framing of immigration within the prism of Terrorism (Frederking 2012: 291).

[5] Since 9/11, there have been five known foiled terrorist attacks by Islamist extremists in Canada. The Toronto 18 in 2006, sometimes referred to as the Canadian 9/11, Project Samossa in 2010, two plots in 2013 namely the planned attack on Via Rail and the planned bombing of the British Columbia Legislature on Canada Day (Gorski 2016: 98–99), and an attack in Strathroy Ontario in August 2016, when Aaron Driver, an ISIS inspired homegrown jihadist, was killed in a confrontation with police. Based on later Governmental releases, the Toronto 18 terrorist plans included truck bombs and the beheading of the federal prime minister. Sadly, two successful terrorist acts occurred in Saint-Jean-Sur-Richelieu and Ottawa on 20 and 22 October 2014. Two Canadian ISIS inspired homegrown jihadists, a Muslim, Michael Zehaf-Bibeau and a convert, Martin Couture-Rouleau, killed a Canadian soldier and a reservist corporal

Canadian Public Opinion on Muslims, Islam, Security, and Counterterrorism

Why do public opinion polls matter? There is an increasing body of theory on radicalization in Canada that calls for *micro relational, situational* analysis in social research and argues that the study of the linkages between radicalization and religion should move beyond structural, institutional, legal, case studies or event-based perspectives and focus greater attention on daily micro social interactive levels. Amiraux and Araya-Moreno (2014: 93) thus describe this methodological shift as a move towards

> [...] a much larger set of processes encompassing the daily interactions of individuals living in pluralistic societies. Radicalization from this perspective stems from the way people feel about sharing common space in a pluralist neighborhood (whether a courtyard, a sidewalk, a mall, a playground, or a line at the bank or post office) and the way they react to the constant exposure to otherness and differences. This broader framing brings us to the unspoken and silent social routine in which hate, love, rejection or isolation emerge, influence social life, and eventually degenerate into stronger hostility towards those who gradually come to embody difference.

These micro interactions operate at a social nucleus level—affecting citizens' sense of national connectivity, solidarity, and identity within societal groups (see Kazemipur 2014: 63). Such a focus can be significant—as gaps between public policy on Muslim immigration on one hand and the social interactivity and receptivity of such groups on the other could render the former less effective.

Any comprehensive account of public opinion in its attitudinal, longitudinal, and demographic complexity and diversity is beyond the focus of this chapter. Most available polls generally look at the immigrant population as a whole through the prism of social indicators such as employment and poverty and less at its Muslim component and at views of security and counterterrorism. Polls conducted on safety and

---

in separate attacks. Zehaf-Bibeau was later shot dead when he attempted an unsuccessful attack on the Parliament building in Ottawa.

security perceptions, few as they are, can nevertheless yield interesting insights.

An overview of available polls including the most recent trans-Canadian opinion poll (Jedwab 2015), sponsored by the Association of Canadian Studies (ACS) and supported by the *Kanishka* project of the Ministry of Public Safety Canada is revealing. Leger marketing, one of the leading polling agencies in North America was commissioned by ACS to conduct this multi-year opinion survey.

With regard to the definition of terrorism, surveyed Canadians across different age groups perceive terrorism as the use of violence to advance political and religious values and beliefs. On a second question concerning the two most important causes of terrorism, 40 per cent of respondents pointed to religious fundamentalism as one of the root causes. And a clear 75 per cent of respondents divided by religious and non-religious affiliation identified religious fundamentalism as one of the essential factors of terrorism. Notably those ranking religious fundamentalism highly as root cause were found to support tougher security and safety measures, stricter immigration laws and policies (Jedwab 2015: 70–1).[6]

Much like other Western countries, intra-Canadian debates on security often become intertwined with immigration and multiculturalism. Multiculturalism is a federal state law and policy introduced by the Liberal Prime Minister Pierre-Elliott Trudeau in 1971 to manage Canada's demographic diversity (aboriginal peoples, French Canadians, and the English Canadian majority) and to ultimately forge a Canadian identity based on shared civic democratic values. With the exception of Muslims and Jewish groups (who both support religious pluralism) polls reveal that most Canadians believe that religious diversity is less an asset than a risk to unity (Jedwab 2015: 35). This majority also holds a strong unfavourable perception of Muslims in Canada and a negative view of relations between Muslims and non-Muslims. Similarly, based on multiple surveys between 2012 and 2015, 55 per cent to 60 per cent of Canadians believe that there is an irreconcilable clash between the West and Muslims. Two-thirds of biblical religious denominations (that is, Jews, Catholics, and Protestants) express the same view (Jedwab

---

[6] Kelly Leitch one of the Conservative candidates in the party leadership race has campaigned for introducing new citizenship (that is cultural) exam.

2015: 98–9). The result holds when Canadians of French, English, or other origin are asked about the trust towards Muslims in Canada. Here those who hold very negative views of Muslims rank highest (70 per cent) in their lack of trust and are equally concerned about the prospect of terrorist activity in Canada (Jedwab 2015: 111). The data is reinforced by the fact that a strong majority of Canadians are worried about the rise of anti-Muslim and to slightly lesser extent anti-Semite feelings in Canada.[7] This finding is corroborated by 2011 Ipsos Reid survey which finds that the majority of the Canadian population (60 per cent) sees increased discrimination against Muslims compared to 10 years ago (Jamil 2014: 148). Earlier polls pointed to such feelings among Muslims themselves. A 2006 poll conducted by Environics finds that 55 per cent of Muslims said they were somewhat or very concerned about the future of Muslims in the country and 50 per cent of Muslim Canadians expressed anxieties about the occurrence of discrimination, unemployment, and extremism among Muslims (Kazemipur 2014: 109).

Understandably, the terrorist incidents in Ottawa and Saint-Jean-sur-Richelieu by homegrown jihadists in 2014 reinforced the perception of insecurity. In a 2014 poll (Jedwab 2015: 38), on threat perceptions, Islamic fundamentalism outranked other security concerns such as a nuclear Iran, Russia, China, or North Korea. This finding is in sync with the view expressed by most Canadians 80 per cent plus that imported conflicts create internal racial and intercommunity strains and tensions within Canada. A greater level of Canadian anxiety is linked to terrorist incidents internationally rather than domestically across all age and linguistic categories (Jedwab 2015: 48–9). This level of anxiety is commensurate with a perception among the majority of Canadians that terrorist abilities to deliver another major attack have not decreased (Jedwab 2015: 51). And a minority of Canadians agree that public safety measures nationally or internally have decreased the likelihood of terrorist attacks in the West or in Canada (Jedwab 2015: 61–2).

---

[7] In a 2003 poll conducted by Statistics Canada, Muslims draw the second lowest trust (after Jehovah's Witnesses) from their fellow Canadian citizens. In a 2005 survey, Canadian Muslims rank low (this time fourth lowest out of 16 faith groups) in the question on Trust in neighbours. In a 2003 poll by Environics Institute, native-born Canadians have low level of contact with Muslims with 55 per cent having rarely or never contact with Muslims (Kazemipur 2014: 103–5).

Another group of polls examined possible associations between anti-Muslim sentiments and anti-Islam feelings (Jedwab 2010). In other words, the polls were conducted to determine whether Canadians distinguished between anti-Islam (as faith) attitudes and their anti-Muslim feelings. The results are both comforting and worrisome! About 60 per cent of those polled expressed a negative view of Muslims while only 20 per cent registered a negative assessment of Islam. It could be interpreted that Islam as faith does not condone terrorism but, in reality, individual Muslims' behaviour matters the most. This interpretation is compatible with the fact that a great number of Canadians acknowledge knowing very little about non-Christian religions such as Islam,[8] a condition possibly reinforced by the character of coverage provided by mass media (for example, relatively little conceptual and theoretical examination of terrorism).

Mass media is a key force in shaping public opinion.[9] Mass media preys on public fears and anxieties and often spins Muslim-related news in a manner which feeds such emotions. The famous Bouchard-Taylor Report refers to the populist treatment of facts by mass media (Bouchard-Taylor Report 2008). For instance, the appetite of major Canadian news media (both French and English) for extensive coverage of the sharia court story in Ontario in 2005–6 and their previous total lack of interest in the Arbitration Act (enjoyed by Christians and Jews for 15 years) is telling. So, too, is the framing of Muslims and Islam in coverage of current affairs. In a recent study of the coverage which three major Canadian newspapers (English and French) devoted to terrorism from 2006 to 2013, these media-branded incidents as Islamic or Muslim in 87 per cent of international terror events and 95 per cent of terror events occurring domestically, using phrases such as: 'inspired by Al-Qaeda', 'Islamic fundamentalism', 'Islamist jihadists', or, for that

---

[8] In a 2006 poll by Environics Institute, the native–born Canadians having negative view of Islam was 40 per cent *v.* 45 per cent for positive view (Kazemipur 2014: 100).

[9] A Canadian-based national survey in 2006, show the influence of mass media framing of terrorism on their interpretation of reality. The national phone interview survey of terrorism-related risk perceptions (based on a sample of 1,502 adult Canadians) reveal that Canadian mass media are the most often referred news source when seeking credible information about terrorism (Lemyre et al., [2006: 756] quoted in Malo, Ouellette, and Vucetic [2014]).

matter, 'moderate Muslims' in their coverage. Branding such events as Islamic or Muslim associates the threat with a faith, essentializes Islam and threat, and implicitly characterizes Muslims as a unified entity and a menace to public safety (Malo, Ouellette, and Vucetic 2014).[10]

In sum, regardless of the causes/reasons and for the purpose of this chapter, we can confidently establish that in view of available poll results, the *Muslim question* hypothesis is not far-fetched and the thrust of the Canadian public holds a associationist perception on the linkages between Muslim presence and security/safety concerns. Other expert observations on the public mood often echo such conclusion. The following observation from a known scholar of the field is striking.

> Discussion of counterterrorism in conjunction with identities can be particularly toxic for persons identifying as Muslim. When the threat of terrorism is evoked in a conversation about religion, Islam often comes to mind. These days, the expression of concern about religious minorities, religious diversity or religious pluralism is almost always a euphemism for anxieties about Muslims. [...] the expression of concern about non-Christian immigrants also tend to be a cover for anxieties about Muslims.
>
> (Jedwab 2015: 96)

Ian Reader describes the *response mode* reaction in Canada as the '[...] immediate knee-jerk assumption when acts of horrific public violence occur, (that) they must somehow be connected with Islam [...] the focus on religious violence after September 11 reflects an ethnocentric perspective' (Reader 2014: 55–6).

Canadian Academia and Linkages between Muslim Presence and Safety/Security

Secular academic literature in Canada, in social science and mainly political science, has resisted the consideration of religion in their research (foci) methodologies. The concepts of Islam and Muslims have

[10] The debate over Islamist extremism, terrorism and homegrown-jihadist occupied a central place in Canada's 2015 federal election. Throughout, candidates' views and positions on Islam, terrorism and national security were constantly and extensively broadcasted by a media, which played on the sensitivities of the electorate. Meanwhile, party candidates accused each other of unpatriotic views, fear mongering and divisive politics.

gradually made headway through current Canadian research on terrorism, radicalization, and counterterrorism. The available data is not as abundant as in other major Western countries and even less so with regard to Islam as an analytical factor. Most Canadian writings focus on religion and the public sphere and involve typical Canadian debates on multiculturalism (or *interculturalisme*), integration, *accommodement raisonnable* rather than security matters per se.

The debate on the clash of civilizations echoed in Canada in terms of the future of Islam in open societies, its *violent aspects* and its reconcilability with democracy. Others such as the political critics of Canadian multiculturalism and proponents of assimilationist theory have embraced variants of the 'clash' vision. Before getting into empirical research on radicalization in Canada, it would be useful to mention two Canadian associationist writings on Islam and Jihad. Irshad Manji, a Canadian Muslim scholar from lesbian, gay, bisexual, and transgender (LGBT) community and author of the non-apologist book *The Trouble with Islam: A Muslim's Call for Reform in Her Faith* (2003), was one of the first to break the taboo. Manji argues that the orthodox understanding of Islam is in fact incompatible with modernity and democracy and proposes a re-interpretation of the Quran to liberate Islam from the preachers of violence. Similarly the book *Islam and War* (a pre-9/11 study by one of the authors of the present chapter), suggests that classical Islam including its largest component the sharia, is in paradigm crisis and that its epistemological and methodological characteristics impede its internal dynamism for reform and for inter-subjective, inter-horizon dialogue with broader aspects of human philosophy and science. The work focuses on the case of war (jihad) to demonstrate the a-empirical and ahistorical thinking of later generations of Muslims on jihad. Relying on the insights of the hermeneutic school, the book suggests paradigmatic changes in Muslim thinking in the modern age in terms of a methodological shift towards the historical and empirical interpretation of foundational texts and events.

As mentioned earlier, the post 9/11 empirical research on Islam, terrorism, and radicalization in Canada is plagued by methodological limitations but most specifically in three areas: explanatory gaps, primary data, and heterogeneity problems (Dawson 2014). The explanation problem refers to establishing a specific type of explanatory correlation to account for why and how some, out of many *n*, walk the path of violent radicalization. The second problem refers not only to the fact that occurrences of radicalization are limited but more importantly, given legal and security measures, to gaining access to sources. As Dawson says, interviews, provided they can be conducted, have dubious credibility. Finally, the heterogeneity issue refers to the variety and the diversity of types of discourses, actors, and processes of jihadism and radicalization. For example, determining how to distinguish between non-religious and religious motivations and reasons of violence or between processes of home-grown radicalization and foreign-origi-nated terrorism are given visibly different experiences and paths.

Mindful of these limitations, the few available Canadian social sci-ence research works on Islam/Muslims and Canadian security and radi-calization can be categorized as associationist and non-associationist. Empirical research on Islam and terrorism in Canada tends to focus on the weight of the Muslim faith in the process of radicalization. Peer-reviewed literature is cautious and nuanced in establishing a causal relation between Islam and home-grown jihadist incidents. The reason is either related to the three methodological pitfalls mentioned above or—as noted earlier—to general resistance of a paradigm on the part of social scientists.[11]

A small amount of surveyed literature can be categorized as non-associationist, that is, rejecting a correlation between Islam and terror-ism for lack of consistent proof. Here Islam is not viewed as a primary factor nor a secondary one of violence. The work of Peter Beyers is illustrative. Using different samples and methodology, Beyers (2014), *à la Cavanaugh*, does not find enough evidence to establish causality or a significant correlation between Islamic faith and practice on one hand and a potential for violent radicalization on the other. In fact, he even suggests that Islam could be an immunizing factor against radicalization.

Yet the vast majority of current researchers on Islam and terrorism in Canada are associationist in varying degrees. Ian Reader (2014), for example, acknowledges the significance of the correlation. Although admitting that violence is not the monopoly of a religion, ideology, or a state, Reader rejects Cavanaugh's thesis on *the Myth of Religious*

---

[11] This resistance brushes aside the faith as an ontologically independent variable or explanatory factor reducing it to its social effects and functions in a broader context and nexus of human and group motivations and interests.

Violence, and believes that removing the religious component from violence would be very misleading from both academic and practitioners' perspectives.

> Those who seek either to separate religion from violence on the grounds that religion is peaceful and 'good' or to deny that there can be a category of religious violence are evading the reality of religion as part of the human world and as potential factor in and qualifying agent of violence. Certainly 'religion' is not some fixed identifiable entity with a timeless nature; rather it is a conceptual category created by humans as a means of explaining or analysing the world.
>
> (Reader 2014: 57)

Reader's chapter is representative of that part of the academic tradition that views religion as a significant explanatory factor in understanding violent groups such as Al-Qaeda, ISIS, Aum Shriynko, Zen monks, Christian medievalists, bible-reading British racists, and so on (2014: 58).

This finding echoes in Dawson's research on the explanatory weight of Islam in inspiring or motivating the so called Toronto 18 terrorist plot—although he is more cautious in establishing any explanatory linkage between Islamic faith and the plot itself. Indeed, Dawson proposes that religion per se was less a factor of violence but that its linkages with other factors such as identity and age created a more explosive cocktail. On the Toronto 18 case, he concurs with the current research on religion and radicalization, 'Given the age-old functional linkages between religion and identity [....] and the role of the transcendent in sacralising causes, it should come as no surprise that religious ideologies-no matter how unsavory-can continue to play a role in the contention over ultimate ends in our cultures and lives' (Dawson 2014: 86).

Unlike previous researchers who focused on actual terrorist events and actors, another set of quantitative and high-impact research (Skillicorn, Leuprecht, and Winn 2012) in Canada examines the radicalization process among *at-risk* communities. In general, radicalization is defined very broadly in such work and can range from sympathizing to actual support and engagement. Indeed, one such article notes that 'Radicalization per se ... is not necessarily problematic ...' and adopts as its focus '... a particular subset of radicals: people who sympathize with, justify or feel a personal obligation towards politically motivated violent extremism or associated illegal acts' (Skillicorn, Leuprecht, and Winn 2012: 929).

Surveying an at-risk Muslim community in the nation's capital (Ottawa), the research focuses on attitude variation towards issues (such US politics in Middle East, views on states such as Israel and Iran, and/or groups such Hamas and Hezbollah) relevant to three following radicalization factors:

> [First,] general social, financial and political satisfaction or dissatisfaction; a second related to moral and religious satisfaction or dissatisfaction, including dissatisfaction associated with political support for groups such as al Qaeda, Hamas and Hezbollah; and a third [dependent variable] (among Muslims only) related to high levels of religious activity, small religious group participation and support for groups that break the law.
>
> (Skillicorn, Leuprecht, and Winn 2012: 930)

The article concludes that these dissatisfactions will create likely conditions for radicalization in at-risk communities:

> As dissatisfaction with life increases across the social, financial and political dimensions, respondents become more active and involved with political groups. As dissatisfaction with the religious and moral world increase, respondents become more overtly religious and more positive towards terrorist groups. As dissatisfaction with both life and the religious and moral world increases, respondents become more overtly religious in ways that involve high-frequency and small-group religious activity, and they show a willingness to admit to supporting organizations that fight oppression even if they break the law."
>
> (Skillicorn, Leuprecht, and Winn 2012: 951)

Simply put, a coexistence of frustrations with life and with the religious world significantly increases the possibility of at-risk Muslim individuals engaging in violent radicalization.

Another more qualitative example of the associationist thesis can be found in recent research focusing on new ways of conceiving home-grown terrorists in Canada. Typical is the work of Zekulin (2015) who suggests using the 'Islamist inspired' epithet for home-grown jihadism. By doing this, he argues, the current literature gains in clarity and the response to home-grown terrorism would be more focused and mindful of its transformations. Thinking on *Islamist inspired home-grown terrorism* will shift our focus from the 'endgame' to its original inceptions and drivers, that is, from prevention of actual violent acts to the detection of radicalization symptoms. It will also help to distinguish between home-grown extremists based on domestic issues (such as right wing violence) from domestic terrorism that is directly inspired by an age-old international Islamist ideology. This ideology survives and transcends lone wolves, cells, and groups and inspires Islamists in different shapes and forms. Here, Zekulin calls for recognizing, '[...] that the primary driver behind this type of terrorism is the global jihadist narrative [...] those traveling from Western countries to Syria and Iraq are predominantly doing so of their own volition. They are not necessarily in contact with leadership or recruiters from specific groups who assist them or facilitate their travel and assimilation' (Zekulin: 2015). The latest peer-reviewed research in Canada on Canadian Jihadi Fighters goes in the same direction establishing a stronger correlation between faith and the decision to join the jihadism in Syria (Dawson and Amarasingam 2017)

In sum, the securitization of Islam is not exclusive to the general public opinion. The data from the academic research, too, nuanced as it is, show that associationist thesis seems to dominate the surveyed research in French or English Canada establishing varying linkages between Islam, terrorism, and radicalization.[12] The securitization of Muslims as perception becomes now a conception.

Government and the Break Away (Rupture) from the Dominant Associationist Views and Theses

The previous Conservative government (2006–15) persistently and increasingly branded, portrayed, and presented terrorism as linked to Islam. Indeed, Prime Minister Stephen Harper labelled *Islamic terrorism* the biggest threat to Canada on many occasions, a stance interpreted by many as populist but also one seemingly ideologically inspired and in line with the Conservative platform and value system. Titles and contents of reports by CSIS provide telling explicit and implicit examples: From Radicalization to Jihadization: The radicalizers: the Islamist extremism threat to Canada from within (2006); Radicalization in Canada: Current State of Knowledge Counter Radicalization in the West (2007); Radicalization: State of Knowledge, Scope of the Problem, and Effectiveness of Counter Measures (2008); A Study of

---

[12] Limitations on chapter length preclude a discussion of literature on Muslim integration in Canada.

Radicalization: The Making of Islamic Extremists in Canada Today (2011). As Monaghan (2014) says,

> ... CSIS integrated an Islamic-component with their definition of radicalization. Indeed, they define radicalization as 'the process of moving from moderate beliefs to extremist belief—whereby Muslim radicalization is the process of moving from moderate, mainstream Islamic beliefs to a belief that violence can legitimately be used to defend Islam against its enemies, support and promote a fundamental view of Islam and an intolerance of both non-believers and those deemed to be impure Muslims.

Although the current government, like the previous one, continues to abide by the toughest antiterror laws ever devised in Canada and voted for them while in opposition, it's tone and discourse changed significantly. The *letter of Mandate* for the current Minister of Public Safety issued by the PMO (Prime Minister Office) does not question C51, but requires the minister to work towards proposing amendments in order to strengthen its accountability and the judiciary oversight clauses. Furthermore, the brand awareness and implicit references matter when it comes to discourses and official declaratory framing of antiterrorism. Under the Liberal Government (elected since October 2015), official framing of Muslims and Islam in securitization discourses[13] has undergone significant shifts. In a recent internal administrative order by the government, all public institutions were directed to refrain from making reference to ISIS as the *Islamic State* and instead to use its Arabic abbreviation DAESH in all communications (Public Safety 2016). In his foreword to the Annual Report, Canada's Minister of Public Safety Ralph Goodale explained the decision to dissociate Islam and Terrorism by noting, '

> It is a serious and unfortunate reality that terrorist groups, most notably the so-called Islamic State of Iraq and the Levant (ISIL), use violent extremist propaganda to encourage individuals to support their cause. This group is neither Islamic nor a state, and so will be referred to as Daesh (its Arabic acronym) in this Report.

The government in fact branded its public safety programme as Countering Violent Extremism (CVE) a title which by definition covers

---

[13] Another important indication for this shift was that unlike most other Western countries, the new government, as promised, admitted 6,064 Syrian refugees by January First 2016 only few months after its election.

violent extremism across the political and religious spectrum (that is, from left to right, from secular to religious), a significant shift from Conservatives' framing of terrorism. This religion-neutral discourse unfolds in greater detail in statements of the Ministry of Public Safety outlining new CVE thinking (Public Safety 2015),

> Building Resilience against Terrorism is the Government of Canada's Counter-terrorism Strategy. It provides a framework for addressing domestic and international terrorist threats. The Strategy has four elements: Prevent, Detect, Deny and Respond. Prevention is a major aspect of countering violent extremism. The Prevent element of the Counter-terrorism Strategy aims to get at the root causes and factors that contribute to terrorism by actively engaging with individuals, communities and international partners. Research is also critical to better understanding these factors and how to counter them. Success in this work requires the support and participation of all levels of government, civil society and, most of all, local communities and individual Canadians. Raising awareness among youth and adults within our local communities is an important step in preventing and countering violent extremism. That is why the Government reaches out to active and interested community representatives in order to build trust and partnerships. Families and community groups are the foundation of a safe and resilient Canada. Everyone plays a part in keeping our communities safe.

This new CVE vision bears two important contrasts with previous Conservative government narrative. The first involves the general approach taken to addressing the terrorist challenge. The second concerns the controversial issue of root cause of terrorism.

As to general approaches, the present government stresses more vigorously and actively an inclusive collaboration with communities, creating a federal office of Community Outreach and Counter-Radicalization Coordinator. This comprehensive approach is highlighted in the PSE report. As Minister Goodale (Public Safety 2016) states in his foreword,

> [W]e are launching a new national office for community outreach and engagement to pursue research, mobilize resources, and help coordinate work at all levels to detect and prevent tragedies before they occur. In addition, for the first time ever, we are beginning focused consultations with Canadians about our country's national security framework—all in pursuit of two essential goals which must be achieved simultaneously.

In contrast, the Tory government relied on co-optation of supportive electoral bases, marginalizing less significant voting blocks and emphasized a stricter—and decidedly more limited—version of a comprehensive approach focusing on the whole-of-government, (that is, intragovernmental streamlining in antiterrorism) at the expense of inclusive community outreach.

The Conservatives also categorically rejected the concept of the *root cause* (that is poverty, regional conflicts, foreign intervention, and weak states)approach in counterterrorism, arguing that this offered legitimacy or justification to the terrorism and hid the real evil that is, radical Islamism and its fanatic will to destroy the free world. This Conservative rhetoric, much like its American counterpart, recurrently pointed to cultural barbarian practices—a narrative which played well with a large number of Canadians—especially in Quebec.[14] On the contrary, the liberal narrative re-engineers its political discourse by shifting the threat from its most common visible association to a general concept, that is, extremism broadly defined and caused by real or perceived factors (Public Safety 2015),

> Violent extremism, broadly speaking, refers to the process of taking radical views and putting them into violent action. While radical thinking is by no means a problem in itself, it becomes a threat to national security when Canadian citizens, residents or groups promote or engage in violence as a means of furthering their radical political, ideological or religious views. The motivations and drivers that inspire them towards violent action may be due to real or perceived grievances, for example,

---

[14] In reaction to *Reasonable* Accommodations, viewed as threat to French Quebec Identity (Language, laïcité and gender equality, six municipalities 2010 issue a *code de vie* (norms of life). The following passage explicitly addresses immigrants: 'We would especially like to inform the new arrivals that the lifestyle that they left behind in their birth country cannot be brought here with them and they would have to adapt to their new social identity.' Article 6 of the Act 94 in Quebec to establish guidelines governing accommodations denies accommodation for wearing Niqab on the basis of security reasons. In 2013, Parti Quebecois proposed Bill 60 called *Charte affirmant les valeurs de laïcité et de neutralité religieuse de l'État ainsi que d'égalité entre les femmes et les hommes et encadrant les demandes d'accommodement.* The political objective was to mobilize the support of Quebec electors and to address the issues related to *accomodements raisonnables.*

animal rights, white supremacy, Al Qaida-inspired, environmentalism and anti-capitalism. Homegrown and imported violent extremism has been on the Canadian scene for many decades. It is not limited to any specific race, ethnicity, religion or culture. There is no single profile or pathway for individuals who come to embrace violent extremism. It is important to note that the threat of violent extremism in Canada evolves constantly. Today's threat is not necessarily the threat of tomorrow.

In sum, under the current government, the CVE discourse has dropped references such as the Islamic State or caliphate, Islamist terrorism, and Jihadi ideology. The primary objective is to disentangle the war on terror from a war against Islam (a new Crusade), and to avoid antagonizing Muslim communities in order to strengthen Canadian resilience to prevent, detect, and disrupt radicalization processes and cases. Rather than engaging in populist and wedge politics, it appears that the new government's strategy is to stay at the centre left of the continuum— closing the gap between the extremes. One may add that in its anti-radicalization approach, the liberal government prefers a return to Canadian multiculturalism as opposed to the policy of assimilation. This recognizes Islamic identity as part of the Canadian mosaic—dissociating Islam as faith from violent extremism and acknowledges the latter as a more complex political phenomenon.[15]

The Muslim Question: Securitization in Canada

The question of how host societies and Muslim communities in the West perceive each other is multifaceted and can be addressed from a range of angles and approaches. Grosso modo in toto, Islam and Muslims are heavily securitized in Canada. If we take a cursory look at the definitions of securitization, it is possible to draw at least one key conclusion from this chapter. Canada's exceptional success in immigration is mitigated by the fact that Muslims and Islam are perceived and conceived as objects of securitization by the public and in academic research. On the bright side, the current government discourse in Ottawa breaks away from these positions and rejects *essentialist* or sweeping statements towards securitizing Islam and Muslims.

---

[15] Again the Bouchard-Taylor Report (2008) stressed that that multiculturalism must first be reflected at the public policy and discourse levels (see for example the Bouchard-Taylor 2008).

Securitization represents a major component of the debate on Muslim communities. In general, the term 'securitization' refers 'to the ways specific ethnic and religious groups become the targets of broad social stigmas and suspicion, surveillance and often harassment [...] the ways state and society frame the individuals and groups to radical religious subcultures' (Bramadat 2014: 3,8). This definition is broadened by another researcher (Jamil 2014: 146) by giving it a deeper and more encompassing social content, '[...] securitization affects more than the individuals and groups drawn to radicalization. Securitization is part of the contemporary sociopolitical context which shapes the way Muslim communities are perceived in society, particularly the way in which they are collectively identified as "guilty by association" and viewed as potential threats, terrorists, fifth columnists, or a danger to national security'.

In both cases, it is clear that there is a *Muslim question* (or a Muslim exceptionalism) when it comes to issues of security and terrorism in Canada. Repeatedly, it has been emphasized that 'placing Islam at the forefront of the current security environment profoundly affects Muslims in their day-to-day lives' (Keeble 2014: 279). Clearly, 9/11 changed the world and the lives of Muslims and non-Muslims alike. Perceptions of securitization are not only confirmed by accounts of Muslims themselves but also by their fellow Canadian citizens as well as in the academic literature in general.[1]

The Liberal government's commitment to multiculturalism, its Islam-neutral public declarations on terrorism, radicalization and public safety and its declared support for national outreach to communities to counter violent extremism should be welcomed. This policy is both a reflection of Canada's cautious attitudes towards unconditional acceptance of the religious drivers of political violence and more importantly, a re-direction of the society towards peace, order and good governance.

References

Amiraux, V. and J. Arya-Moreno. 2014. 'Pluralism and Radicalization: Mind the Gap!'. In *Religious Radicalization and Securitization in Canada and Beyond*, P. Bramadat and L. Dawson (eds), pp. 92–120. Toronto: University of Toronto Press.

Adelman, Howard. 2002. 'Canadian Borders and Immigration post 9/11', *International Migration Review* 36(1): 15–28.

Beyer, P. 2014. 'Securitization and Young Muslim Males: Is None too Many'. In *Religious Radicalization and Securitization in Canada and Beyond*, P. Bramadat and L. Dawson (eds), pp. 121–44. Toronto: University of Toronto Press.

Bouchard, G. and C. Taylor. 2008. 'Fonder l'avenir: Le temps de la conciliation' (Build the future : Time for Reconciliation). Available at: https://www.mce.gouv.qc.ca/publications/CCPARDC/rapport-final-integral-fr.pdf. Accessed on 13 February 2017.

Bramadat, Paul. 2014. 'The public, the Political and the Possible: Religion and Radicalization in Canada and Beyond'. In *Religious Radicalization and Securitization in Canada and Beyond*, P. Bramadat and L. Dawson (eds), pp. 1–34. Toronto: University of Toronto Press

Dawson, L. 2014. 'Trying to Make Sense of Home-Grown Terrorist Radicalization: The Case of Toronto 18'. In *Religious Radicalization and Securitization in Canada and Beyond*, P. Bramadat and L. Dawson (eds), pp. 64–91. Toronto: University of Toronto Press.

Dawson, Lorne L. and Amarnath Amarasingam. 2017. 'Talking to Foreign Fighters: Insights into the Motivations for *Hijrah* to Syria and Iraq', *Studies in Conflict & Terrorism* 40(3): 191–210.

Frederking, Lauretta Conklin. 2012. 'A Comparative Study of Framing Immigration Policy after11 September 2001', *Policy Studies* 33(4 July): 283–96.

Gorski, P. 2016. *The Threat from Within: Recognizing AL-Qaeda-Inspired Radicalization and Terrorism in the West*. Maryland: Rowman & Littlefield Publishing.

Jamil, U. 2014. 'The Impact of Securitization on South Asian Muslims in Montreal'. In *Religious Radicalization and Securitization in Canada and Beyond*, P. Bramadat and L. Dawson (eds), pp. 145–63. Toronto: University of Toronto Press.

Jedwab, J. 2015. *Counterterrorism and Identities: Canadian Viewpoints*. Westmount (Quebec), Linda Leith Publishing Group Inc.

Kazemipur, A. 2014. *The Muslim Question in Canada*. Vancouver: UBC Press.

Keeble, E. 2014. 'The Cross-Cultural Roundtable on Security as a Response to Radicalization: Personal Experiences and Academic Reflections'. In *Religious Radicalization and Securitization in Canada and Beyond*, P. Bramadat and L. Dawson (eds). Toronto: University of Toronto Press.

Malo, J., V. Ouellette, and S. Vucetic. 2014. 'Simplifying Terrorism: An Analysis of Three Canadian Newspapers, 2006-2013', *Canadian Political Science Review* 8(2): 59–73.

Monaghan, J. 2014. 'Security Traps and Discourses of Radicalization: Examining Surveillance Practices Targeting Muslims in Canada', *Surveillance & Society* 12(4): 485–501.

Public Safety Annual Report on the Terrorist Threats in Canada. 2016. Available at: https://www.publicsafety.gc.ca/cnt/rsrcs/pblctns/2016-pblc-rpr-trrrst-thrt/index-en.aspx. Accessed on 13 February 2017.

Public Safety Countering Violent Extremism. 2015. Available at: https://www.publicsafety.gc.ca/cnt/ntnl-scrt/cntr-trrrsm/cntrng-vlnt-xtrmsm/index-en.aspx. Accessed on 13 February 2017.

Reader, I. 2014. 'Beating a Path to Salvation: Themes in the Reality of Religious Violence'. In *Religious Radicalization and Securitization in Canada and Beyond*, P. Bramadat and L. Dawson (eds), pp. 34–63. Toronto: University of Toronto Press.

Skillicorn, David B., C. Leuprecht, and C. Winn. 2012. 'Homegrown Islamist Radicalization in Canada: Process Insights from an Attitudinal Survey'. Available at: http://post.queensu.ca/~leuprech/docs/articles/Skillicorn_Leuprecht_%20Winn_2012_Homegrown%20Islamist%20Radicalization%20in%20Canada_Process%20Insights%20from%20an%20Attitudinal%20Survey_Canadian%20Journal%20of%20Political%20Science.pdf. Accessed on 13 February 2017.

Zekulin, M. 2015. 'Endgames: Improving Our Understanding of Homegrown Terrorism', *Studies in Conflict & Terrorism* 39: 46–66.

PART TWO

INCLUSION AND EXCLUSION

4

HISHAM M. ABU-RAYYA

Integrated Acculturation and Contact Strategies to Improve Anglo-Muslim Relations in Australia

Muslims are a cultural minority group in Australia. According to the 2016 Australian Census, 604, 240 Muslims live in Australia and comprise 2.6 per cent of the total population. Of the total Australian Muslim population, 63.61 per cent were born overseas and almost 50 per cent are aged below 25 years (Australian Bureau of Statistics 2017). Australian-Muslims[1] are citizens in a country that explicitly adopts a multicultural policy. On 16 February 2011, the Australian government launched 'The People of Australia: Australia's Multicultural Policy' and reaffirmed the importance of a culturally diverse and socially cohesive nation (Department of Immigration and Citizenship 2011). The policy emphasizes, among other things,

---

[1] Muslims in Australia come from multiple and heterogeneous cultures. Despite their cultural heterogeneity, Islam provides a common identity and has a strong cultural influence in the lives and worldview of Muslims in Australia (Akbarzadeh and Saeed 2001). To escape reference to each specific Muslim cultural group, the term 'Australian-Muslims' is used throughout the chapter.

(i) the expression of cultural values and benefits for all Australians, within the broader aims of national unity, community harmony, and maintenance of Australia's democratic values; (ii) a commitment to a just, inclusive, and socially cohesive society where everyone can participate in the opportunities that Australia offers and where government services are responsive to the needs of Australians from culturally and linguistically diverse backgrounds; and (iii) a commitment to promote understanding and acceptance while responding to expressions of intolerance and discrimination with strength and law enforcement.

In principle, the Australian multicultural context provides a space for cultural minority individuals to practice their own cultural identity while being expected that they develop identification with Australian mainstream culture, as well as to freely practice their religion and flourish personally. This in turn may promote cultural minority youth's psychological and sociocultural adaptation and contribute to the fostering of good intergroup relationships. However, the space provisioned by the Australian context may not be equally welcoming of all cultural minority groups. Islam is perceived in Australia as a threat to the Australian way of life, and as a consequence, prejudice towards Muslims is deep-rooted (Abu-Rayya and White 2010; Pedersen et al. 2009). Australian-Muslims are perceived as culturally inferior, devalued, or the 'dangerous other', and incompatible with or radically different from the non-Muslim Australian culture (Dunn, Klocker, and Salabay 2007), with over 50 per cent of non-Muslim Australians reporting never having contact with Muslims (Ryan and McKinney 2007). Likewise, the Scanlon Foundation Surveys found a large measure of consistent negative attitudes towards Australian-Muslims (25 per cent) across the years 2010–14 compared to Australians' negative attitudes towards Christians (less than 5 per cent) or Buddhists (less than 5 per cent) (Markus 2014).

These negative perceptions did not develop out of the blue. Islam, in fact, has been propagandized to be an inherently violent religion following post-11 September 2001 terrorist attack, strengthened by the Cronulla riots of 2005, where a clash between Anglo-Australian and Australian-Muslim youths resulted in injuries to 25 people, and followed by the Sydney Siege in 2014, ending after 16 hours of terror for captives. This has fuelled a climate of animosity, suspicion, insecurity, fear, and discrimination in Australia, resulting in vandalism, threats against Mosques, Muslim schools, and Muslim centres, assaults of hijab-wearing women, telephone and mail threats to Muslim community leaders, and verbal abuse of Muslims (Browning, Jakubowicz, and Gold 2003). Relatedly, the Australian Human Rights Commission launched the 'IsmaU', which means 'listen' in Arabic, project in 2003 to find out whether Muslim (and Arab) Australians had become targets of increased hostility since 11 September 2001. The Commission 'listened' to the experiences of over 1,400 adult Muslim (and Arab) Australians from around the country. The research found that participants identifiable as Muslim (or Arab) by their dress, language, name, or appearance told of having been abused, threatened, and spat on. 'Terrorist', 'dirty Arab', 'murderer', 'raghead', 'bloody Muslim', 'Bin-Laden', and 'illegal immigrant', are just some of the labels and profanities that participants said have been used against Muslims (and Arabs) in public places.

The aforementioned 'politics of fear' may ultimately create, at the societal level, social segregation and undermine social inclusion in a culturally diverse society like Australia. Thus, effective intergroup bias reduction strategies need to be developed to promote cooperative intergroup contact as a first step to resolving these tensions. School classrooms have long been shown to be an effective context for implementing cooperative contact programmes and improving intergroup relations (Aboud and Fenwick 1999; Houlette et al. 2004). Early interventions within school settings in Australia are urgently sought to foster the required skills in Australian-Muslims and Anglo-Australians to be cooperative youths and adults. With this in mind, the aim of this chapter is to review and discuss research-based and theory-driven strategies that would help in promoting relationships between Australian-Muslims and Anglo-Australians, as emerged in recent acculturation and social psychological research. Specifically, the *Interactive Acculturation Model* (IAM; Bourhis et al. 1997), and *Direct* and *Indirect* (distal) contact strategies (for example, Allport 1954; Brown and Paterson 2016; Crisp and Husnu 2011; Gómez and Huici 2008; Pettigrew and Tropp 2005; White and Abu-Rayya 2012) are integrated and applied to school settings in this review.

The Interactive Acculturation Model

Model Features

The Interactive Acculturation Model (IAM; Bourhis et al. 1997) investigates the extent to which the acculturation orientations of cultural minority members and mainstream majority members play a role in differentiating the levels of positive and negative attitudes they hold towards each other. As such, applied to the Australian context, the IAM does not treat Anglo-Australians or Australian-Muslims as homogenous groups. Instead, the IAM assumes that a wide variation of intergroup attitudes exist between Anglo-Australians and Australian-Muslims that can be understood by examining the acculturation orientations of each group. In addition, the IAM points to the acculturation orientations that their endorsement by majority and minority members would lead to harmonious and consensual minority–majority relations.

According to the IAM, cultural minority members can endorse one of five acculturation orientations, depending on their desire to maintain their culture of origin, on the one hand, and their willingness to adopt important features of the mainstream / dominant society, on the other hand. Specifically, (*i*) *Integrationist* denotes the orientation of those minority members who show a desire to maintain their own cultural identity while adopting important aspects of the mainstream / dominant culture; (*ii*) *Separationist* characterizes those who have a desire to maintain their minority cultural identity while rejecting relationships with members of the mainstream / dominant culture; (*iii*) *Assimilationist* describes minority members who relinquish their own culture for the sake of adopting the culture of the mainstream / dominant society; (*iv*) *Anomie* refers to those minority individuals who reject both their own culture and that of the mainstream / dominant society, that is, are in the state of cultural marginality; and lastly, (*v*) *Individualist* describes those minority individuals who dissociate themselves from both their own culture and the mainstream / dominant culture because they prefer to identify themselves as individuals rather than members of specific cultures.

Similarly, the acculturation orientations that mainstream majority members can endorse towards minority members may be outlined as follows:

(1) Integrationist is defined as majority respondents' acceptance of cultural minority members maintaining their heritage culture as well as adapting to important features of the mainstream majority culture.

(2) Individualist refers to majority respondents' tendency to accept cultural minority individuals as individuals rather than as representative members of given group-identity categories.

(3) Assimilationist refers to the expectation on the part of majority respondents that cultural minority members relinquish their cultural identity in order to adopt the mainstream majority culture.

(4) Segregationist is defined as majority respondents' expectation that cultural minority members would hold themselves separate from the mainstream majority culture.

(5) Exclusionist refers to majority respondents' intolerance for cultural minority members maintaining their heritage culture and refusal to accept their adoption of any features of the mainstream majority culture.

Bourhis et al. (1997) assume that the acculturation orientations endorsed by mainstream minority and majority members tend to be affected by the ideology of their context. Within a society (like Australia) which explicitly adopts a multicultural ideology towards cultural diversity, the IAM predicts that this ideology would help facilitate minority and mainstream majority members' endorsement of the Integrationist and Individualist acculturation orientations. This is presumed to be particularly correct when the minority group is a valued, that is, preferred cultural minority within the society. Additionally, the IAM predicts that the endorsement of Integrationist or Individualist acculturation orientations by minority and majority members leads to minority–majority intergroup harmony and tolerance.

Empirical Findings within the Australian Context

Empirical findings concerning the predictions of Bourhis et al.'s (1997) IAM have generally been supportive, as emerged in Australian and international research (for example, Abu-Rayya 2016; Abu-Rayya and White

2010; Bourhis and Dayan 2004; Montreuil and Bourhis 2004; Safdar et al. 2008). For instance, Abu-Rayya and White (2010) examined Anglo-Australian University students' acculturation orientations and attitudes towards Muslims, and found that despite the culturally perceived devalued status of Australian-Muslims, Anglo-Australian students still endorsed the Integrationist and Individualist acculturation orientations the most, particularly in the area of social activities.

Findings of this study also revealed that, as predicted by the IAM, Anglo-Australians' acculturation orientations played a significant role in differentiating the levels of positive and negative attitudes that Anglo-Australians hold towards Australian-Muslims. Specifically, the Integrationist and Individualist acculturation orientations of Anglo-Australians, in contrast to the adoption of the other acculturation orientations, correlated positively with their positive attitudes towards Australian-Muslims and negatively with negative attitudes.

Unfortunately, Abu-Rayya and White's (2010) study relied exclusively on a university student sample and it also did not examine the acculturation preferences and out-group attitudes of Australian-Muslims, so that important features of the IAM remain obscured when applied to the Australian context. A subsequent study (Abu-Rayya 2018) was carried on a relatively large sample ($n = 536$) involving Australian-Muslims (44 per cent) and Anglo-Australians (56 per cent) who were recruited from universities, community organizations ($n = 233$), and high schools ($n = 303$) in Sydney and Melbourne metropolitan areas. In support of Abu-Rayya and White's (2010) findings, the study revealed that high school and adult Anglo-Australians endorsed the Integrationist and Individualist acculturation orientations the most towards Australian-Muslims. The other orientations were present among Anglo-Australians to a lesser degree. The study also revealed that high school and adult Australian Muslims preferred the Integrationist and Individualist orientations, and less so the other orientations. Refer to Table 4.1 for means and standard deviations of all acculturation orientations' scores.

In addition, Anglo-Australians' Integrationist and Individualist acculturation orientations, were positively correlated with positive attitudes towards Australian-Muslims and negatively correlated with negative attitudes, subtle prejudice, and perceived threat with absolute correlations ranging from 0.34 to 0.50, as shown in Table 4.2. Australian-Muslims'

TABLE 4.1 Differences between the acculturation orientations within the Anglo-Australian and Australian-Muslim samples

M [range = 1-7]		SD
Anglo-Australian Overall Sample		
Integrationist	5.46[a]	1.19
Individualist	5.23[b]	1.12
Assimilationist	2.91[c]	1.47
Segregationist	3.79[d]	1.21
Exclusionist	1.78[e]	1.11
Australian-Muslim Overall Sample		
Integrationist	5.16[a]	1.30
Individualist	4.99[a]	1.42
Assimilationist	2.50[b]	1.70
Separationist	3.98[c]	2.02
Anomie	1.63[d]	1.78

Source: Abu-Rayya (2018).

Note: Means with different subscript letters for the Anglo-Australian and Australian-Muslim samples differed significantly, $p < .05$ and $p < .001$, respectively.

TABLE 4.2 Bivariate correlations (r's) between acculturation orientations and intergroup measures within the Anglo-Australian and Australian-Muslim samples

	Positive Attitudes	Negative Attitudes	Subtle Prejudice^	Perceived Threat
Anglo-Australian Overall Sample				
Integrationist	.42***	−.34**	−.47***	−.34***
Individualist	.43***	−.46***	−.50***	−.39***
Assimilationist	−.37***	.39***	.54***	.25*
Segregationist	−.45***	.44***	.49***	.30**
Exclusionist	−.47***	.43***	.57***	.47***
Australian-Muslim Overall Sample				
Integrationist	.52***	−.41**		−.24*
Individualist	.40***	−.35***		−.21*
Assimilationist	.57***	−.48***		−.09
Separationist	−.54***	.59***		.41***
Anomie	−.23*	.18*		.06

Source: Abu-Rayya (2018).

Note: ^ the subtle prejudice measure used in this study was designed for majority members only, ***$p < .001$, **$p < .01$, * $p < .05$.

Integrationist and Individualist acculturation orientations were also positively correlated with positive attitudes towards Anglo-Australians and negatively correlated with negative attitudes and perceived threat with absolute correlations ranging from 0.21 to 0.52. A reverse pattern of relationships was evident between most other acculturation orientations and intergroup measures.

Importantly, Abu-Rayya's (2018) findings held true even when social desirability, that is, the tendency of participants to report the socially desirable acculturation orientations, was taken into account in the analyses. It is very interesting that despite the negative stereotypes and attitudes that Australian-Muslims suffer (for example, Markus 2014; Pedersen et al. 2009), which would potentially encourage them to psychosocially adopt a 'separationist' style of acculturation and undermine their sense of Australian belonging, adult and high school Australian-Muslims showed a preference towards the Integrationist and Individualist orientations. This finding converges with recent research (Abu-Rayya et al. 2018) on Australian-Muslim students studying in public or Muslim high schools showing that the majority (59.5 per cent) of them preferred an Integrationist acculturation orientation, regardless of the school type—public versus Muslim—they attend. Australian-Muslim schools and community/organizations' leaders should be encouraged by Abu-Rayya's (2018) findings and may want to put further efforts into the current practices/initiatives they have and develop new ones to strengthen students' preference of the Integrationist orientation. This is particularly important because the endorsement of the Integrationist orientation among Australian-Muslims does not only promote intergroup harmony, as evident in Abu-Rayya's (2018) findings, but also seems beneficial to students' psychological and sociocultural adaptation, compared to the other orientations, as shown in Abu-Rayya et al.'s (2018) study.

Contact Strategies to Promote Endorsement of the Integrationist and Individualist Orientations

Abu-Rayya's (2018) and Abu-Rayya and White's (2010) research findings accord with Pettigrew and Tropp's (2006) meta-analysis showing that intergroup contact, in the form of attitudinal acculturation preferences here, reduces intergroup prejudice within the context of cultural minority and majority groups. Anglo-Australians' and Australian-Muslims' Integrationist and Individualist acculturation orientations, most specifically, contain positive attitudes to social activities and contact involving outgroup members, and these orientations were shown here to be better for intergroup relationships. From a multicultural educational perspective, then, it might be effective to encourage joint sociocultural activities between Anglo-Australians and Australian-Muslims in school settings when it comes to promoting endorsement of the Integrationist and Individualist acculturation orientations. Certain evidence-based strategies may be applied to foster endorsement of the Integrationist and Individualist acculturation orientations among Anglo-Australians and Australian-Muslims including direct contact (for example, Cooperative Contact), and indirect contact (for example, Extended Contact, Vicarious Contact, Imagined Contact, and Electronic Contact), discussed in what follows. These strategies need yet to be empirically studied by acculturation researchers working within the IAM tradition.

Direct Contact

Within the tradition of Allport's (1954) *Contact Hypothesis*, a plethora of research suggests that intercultural understanding and greater intergroup harmony can be fostered through *direct* (that is, face-to-face) contact between minority and majority members in the presence of the following conditions: (*i*) a perception of equal status amongst both groups within the contact situation (for example, school/education setting); (*ii*) institutional support (for example, school policies); and (*iii*) working cooperatively in order to (*iv*) achieve a common goal (Pettigrew and Tropp 2005). Furthermore, Pettigrew (1998) has pointed to the potential for friendship to develop beyond the social interaction itself, as additional facilitating factor. I propose that cooperative contact between Australian-Muslim and Anglo-Australian school students (such as working together on planning a joy trip that will include members from both groups or working collaboratively on a school cultural task) has the potential to shape their preference towards the Integrationist and Individualist acculturation orientations, which will in turn have a positive effect on their intergroup relations, a hypothesis that future acculturation work will need to test (see Figure 4.1).

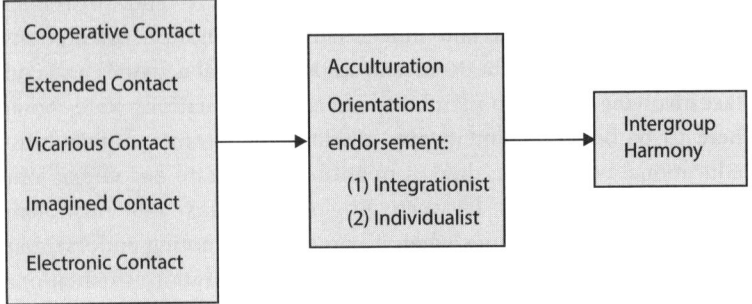

FIGURE 4.1   Effects of social contact strategies on intergroup measures via acculturation strategies
Source: Author.

Indirect Contact

Due to various settlement considerations in the immigration of Muslims to the country, they ended up concentrating in certain suburbs in Australian major cities, a matter that practically limits, to a degree, their opportunities for significant *direct* contact with Anglo-Australians in school and other settings. When *direct* contact between minority and majority members may be limited or difficult due to geographic dispersion or high intergroup tension, research indicates that still the deployment of *indirect* (that is, *distal*) forms of contact such as extended, vicarious, imagined, and electronic in school settings can be useful for the promotion of intergroup harmony. These strategies, clarified as follows, do not require individuals to physically meet face-to-face in the same location. Again, I propose that positive effects of extended, vicarious, imagined, and electronic contact on relationships between Anglo-Australians and Australian-Muslims may be mediated by their endorsement of the Integrationist and Individualist acculturation orientations (see Figure 4.1).

Extended contact refers to the process by which the individual becomes merely aware that an ingroup member (minority or majority) has an outgroup friend (Wright et al. 1997). *Vicarious Contact*, in contrast, simply refers to the process of observing a positive interaction between an ingroup (minority or majority) and an outgroup member (Gómez and

Huici 2008). Minority and majority members in an extended or vicarious situation may act here as positive exemplars to their respective groups, reduce their anxiety feelings associated with hypothetical interaction with outgroup members, breakdown stereotypes, and increase the perceived variability of the outgroup. Research evidence has demonstrated the efficacy of extended contact (Brown and Paterson 2016; Cameron et al. 2011; Dovidio, Eller, and Hewstone 2011; Turner et al. 2013) and vicarious contact (Brown and Paterson 2016; Gómez and Huici 2008; Mazziotta, Mummendey, and Wright 2011) in prejudice reduction.

For instance, Cameron et al. (2011) found that UK English children who read stories (that is, extended contact) that portrayed friendships between the cultural majority and minority (Indian) children reported more positive attitudes towards minority children compared to the control condition. Likewise, Mazziotta, Mummendey, and Wright (2011) found that amongst Caucasians in Germany, video-based vicarious intergroup contact led to significantly lower levels of anxiety, higher levels of self-efficacy, greater willingness to engage in contact and more positive affect towards Chinese international students compared with either ingroup contact or presentation of the outgroup member acting alone.

Another form of indirect contact is *Imagined contact* (Crisp and Husnu 2011), a mental exercise by which an individual is asked to engage in a positive imagined interaction with an outgroup member. It is argued that imagining a positive interaction with the outgroup would activate concepts normally associated with successful intergroup interactions such as feeling less apprehensive about intergroup contact and self-attributing a positive attitudinal orientation towards interaction with the outrgoup (Crisp and Husnu 2011). Research has demonstrated that imagined contact improves intergroup relations with outgroup members and enhances future intentions regarding intergroup contact (Brown and Paterson 2016; Crisp and Husnu 2011; Miles and Crisp 2014).

In other words, merely telling Anglo-Australian and Australian-Muslim school students stories about positive contact between individuals from both groups (that is, *extended contact*), or exposing them to positive contact examples (that is, *vicarious contact*), or simply ask them to engage in imaginary positive interaction (that is, *imagined contact*) would improve their intergroup relations. Examples of positive extended/vicarious/imagined contact may take the form of reading/ hearing about/watching/imagining Anglo-Australian and Australian-Muslim students winning an educational competition, playing as partners in a soccer team, organizing a multicultural festival, working on a humanitarian cause, or working on a school interfaith dialogue project, to name a few. Since the Integrationist and Individualist acculturation orientations contain positive attitudes towards shared intergroup social activities, it becomes sensible to argue that positive effects of extended/ vicarious/imagined contact on intergroup relations occur through the Integrationist and Individualist acculturation orientations that minority and majority members would develop in the process, as illustrated in Figure 4.1.

Despite the potential efficacy of the extended, vicarious, and imagined contact strategies in shaping minority and majority Integrationist and Individualist orientations, improving intergroup relations in turn, it should be acknowledged that these strategies ignore the active role of self-engagement in the intergroup contact situation (White, Harvey, and Abu-Rayya 2015). Hearing/reading about, observing, or imagining a positive contact between minority and majority members limits the extent to which one experiences actual, real-time involvement in the contact situation. This may not be strong enough to elicit or strengthen minority and majority members' endorsement of the Integrationist and Individualist acculturation orientations.

White and Abu-Rayya (2012) have developed the *Dual Identity Electronic Contact* (DIEC) strategy which requires both minority and majority individuals to be self-engaged in real time over the electronic medium, thus overcoming shortcomings of the other indirect contact strategies. Here, ingroup and outgroup members never physically meet but engage in a synchronous text-based interaction which is mediated by online technology.

In the DIEC programme, Australian Muslim and Christian high-school students exchanged, in a guided cooperative way, information about how their respective religious beliefs and practices could work together to develop water saving, energy saving, and recycling solutions to actively contribute to an 'environmentally sustainable future for Australia', their shared community or common identity. In each of the DIEC programme's eight weekly sessions, about 200 Muslim and Christian high school students from religiously segregated schools formed 50 four-person groups, where one pair from each faith made text-based electronic contact with a pair from the other faith synchronously via eight internet chat sessions each lasting 50 minutes. Allport's (1954) and Pettigrew's (1988) optimal conditions for successful contact were incorporated in the DIEC programme, including assigning equal numbers of Christian and Muslim students to the chat groups, defining a common goal, providing the opportunity for friendliness and familiarity between participants, providing support for the programme by the school authorities, and using multiple contact sessions to allow time for friendship formation to occur.

Significant short-term and long-lasting positive attitude change was witnessed among the participants (White and Abu-Rayya 2012; White et al. 2015; White, Abu-Rayya, and Weitzel 2014). Specifically, the DIEC programme successfully produced short-term (two-weeks post-test) intergroup anxiety reduction and increased outgroup knowledge for DIEC participants. The programme also produced short-term and long-term (6 and 12 months post-test) bias reduction for the DIEC cohort. Further to these findings, the DIEC chat groups tended to progressively use more affect and positive emotion words, and less anger and sadness words than the control chat groups. Besides, analyses revealed that the DIEC intervention was most effective in decreasing intergroup bias for individuals with higher levels of ingroup (religious) identification. Outgroup friendship was also shown to moderate the relationship between electronic contact and intergroup bias reduction in the short-term and long-term for DIEC participants, such that students with greater outgroup friendships (outside their religiously segregated school) tended to benefit more from the electronic contact as evidenced by the extent of their intergroup bias reduction.

These significant research findings imply that electronic contact may offer an efficacious route to acculturation researchers interested in promoting individuals' endorsement of the Integrationist and Individualist orientations using indirect contact strategies. While White and Abu-Rayya (2012) have implemented text-based electronic contact between Australian Muslim and Christian students, this can also be expanded to include other structured collaborative forms of electronic interaction such as audio or video-based or a mixture of text and audio/video-based communication.

Summing Up

Research findings employing the Interactive Acculturation Model propose that Anglo-Australian and Australian-Muslim high school and university students are more inclined towards the endorsement of the Integrationist and Individualist acculturation orientations, and that these orientations are critical for achieving harmonious and consensual intergroup relations. Carefully structured direct and indirect contact strategies can shape Anglo-Australians' and Australian-Muslims' endorsement of the Integrationist and Individualist acculturation orientations. This proposition opens the way for applied acculturation researchers to integrate direct and indirect intergroup contact paradigms with the Interactive Acculturation Model to improve relationships between Anglo-Australians and Australian-Muslims. Given the effective context of school settings for early interventions, implementation of these ideas within school classrooms is strongly advised to foster mutually positive Anglo-Australian and Australian-Muslim generations.

References

Aboud, Frances E. and Virginia Fenwick. 1999. 'Exploring and Evaluating School-Based Interventions to Reduce Prejudice', *Journal of Social Issues* 55: 767–85.

Abu-Rayya, Hisham M. 2018. 'Mutual Acculturation Orientations of Anglo-Australians and Australian Muslims.' Manuscript under Review.

Abu-Rayya, Hisham M. and A. Fiona White. 2010. 'Acculturation Orientations and Religious Identity as Predictors of Anglo-Australians' Attitudes towards Australian Muslims', *International Journal of Intercultural Relations* 34: 592–9.

Abu-Rayya, Hisham M., Maram H. Abu-Rayya, A. Fiona White, and Richard Walker. 2018. 'Comparative Associations Between Acculturation, Ego Identity Achievement, and Religiosity and Adaptation among Australian Adolescent Muslims', *Psychological Reports* 121: 324–43.

Akbarzadeh, Shahram and Abdullah Saeed. 2001. *Muslim Communities in Australia*. Sydney: University of New South Wales Press.

Allport, W. Gordon. 1954. *The Nature of Prejudice.* Cambridge, MA: Perseus Books.

Australian Bureau of Statistics. 2017. *Census of Population and Housing.* Canberra, ACT, Australia.

Bourhis, Y. Richard and Joelle Dayan. 2004. 'Acculturation Orientations towards Israeli Arabs and Jewish Immigrants in Israel', *International Journal of Psychology* 39:118–31.

Bourhis, Y. Richard, Moïse C. Lena, Perreault Stephane, and Senécal Sacha. 1997. 'Towards an Interactive Acculturation Model: A Social Psychological Approach', *International Journal of Psychology* 32: 369–86.

Brown, Rupert, and Paterson, Jenny. 2016. 'Indirect contact and prejudice reduction: limits and possibilities', *Current Opinion in Psychology* 11: 20–4.

Browning, Julie, Jakubowicz Andrew, and A. Gold. 2003. 'What Can We Say About Racism in Australia? Discussion Paper Number 1', *Racism Monitor,* July.

Cameron, Lindsey, Rutland Adam, Hossain Rosa, and Petley Rebecca. 2011. 'When and Why Does Extended Contact Work? The Role of High Quality Direct Contact and Group Norms in the Development of Positive Ethnic Intergroup Attitudes Amongst Children', *Group Processes & Intergroup Relations* 14: 193–206.

Crisp, J. Richard, and Husnu Shenel. 2011. 'Attributional Processes Underlying Imagined Contact Effects', *Group Processes & Intergroup Relations* 14: 275–87.

Department of Immigration and Citizenship. 2011. *The People of Australia: Australia's Multicultural Policy.* Canberra, ACT, Australia.

Dovidio, F. John, Eller Anja, and Hewstone Miles. 2011. 'Improving Intergroup Relations Through Direct, Extended and other Forms of Indirect Contact', *Group Processes & Intergroup Relations* 14: 147–60.

Dunn, M. Kevin, Klocker Natascha, and Salabay Tanya. 2007. 'Contemporary Racism and Islamaphobia in Australia: Racialising Religion', *Ethnicities* 7: 564–89.

Gómez, Angel, and Huici Carmen. 2008. 'Vicarious Intergroup Contact and Role of Authorities in Prejudice Reduction', *The Spanish Journal of Psychology* 11: 103–14.

Houlette, A. Melissa, Gaertner L. Samuel, Johnson M. Kelly, Banker S. Banker, Riek M. Blake, and Dovidio F. John. 2004. 'Developing a

More Inclusive Social Identity: An Elementary School Intervention', *Journal of Social Issues* 60: 35–56.

Markus, A. 2014. *Mapping Social Cohesion*. The Scanlon Foundation Surveys. Available at: http://scanlonfoundation.org.au/wp-content/uploads/2014/10/2014-Mapping-Social-Cohesion-Report.pdf. Accessed on 15 March 2016.

Mazziotta, Agostino, Mummendey Amélie., and Wright C. Stephen. 2011. 'Vicarious Intergroup Contact Effects: Applying Social-Cognitive Theory to Intergroup Contact Research', *Group Processes & Intergroup Relations* 14: 255–74.

Miles, Eleanor and Crisp J. Richard. 2014. 'A Meta-Analytic Test of the Imagined Contact Hypothesis', *Group Processes & Intergroup Relations* 17: 3–26.

Montreuil, Annie, and Bourhis Y. Richard. 2004. 'Acculturation Orientations of Competing Host Communities toward Valued and Devalued Immigrants', *International Journal of Intercultural Relations* 28: 507–32.

Pedersen, Anne, Aly Anne, Hartley Lisa, and McGarty Craig. 2009. 'An Intervention to Increase Positive Attitudes and Address Misconceptions about Australian Muslims: A call for Education and Open Mindedness', *The Australian Community Psychologist* 21: 81–93.

Pettigrew, F. Thomas. 1998. 'Intergroup Contact Theory', *Annual Review of Psychology* 49: 65–85.

Pettigrew, F. Thomas, and Tropp R. Linda. 2005. 'Allport's Intergroup Contact Hypothesis: Its History and Influence', In *On the Nature of Prejudice: Fifty Years after Allport*, edited by Dovidio F. John, Glick Peter, and Rudman Laurie, 262–77. Malden: Blackwell Publishing.

Pettigrew, F. Thomas, and Tropp R. Linda. 2006. 'A Meta-Analytic Test of Intergroup Contact Theory', *Journal of Personality and Social Psychology* 90: 751–83.

Ryan, Pamela and McKinney Claire. 2007. *Australia Deliberates: Muslims and Non-Muslims in Australia*. SA: Issues Deliberation Australia.

Safdar, Saba, Dupuis R. Darcy, Lewis J. Rees, El-Geledi Shaha, and Bourhis,Y. Richard. 2008. 'Social Axioms and Acculturation Orientations of English Canadians toward British and Arab Muslim Immigrants', *International Journal of Intercultural Relations* 32: 415–26.

Turner, N. Rhainnon, Tam Tanya, Hewstone Miles, Kenworthy Jared, and Cairns Ed. 2013. 'Contact between Catholic and Protestant

School Children in Northern Ireland', *Journal of Applied Social Psychology* 43:E216–28.

White, A. Fiona, Abu-Rayya M. Hisham, Bliuc Ana-Maria, and Faulkner Nicholas. 2015. 'Emotion Expression and Intergroup Bias Reduction Between Muslims and Christians: Long-Term Internet Contact', *Computers in Human Behaviour* 53: 435–42.

White, A. Fiona, Harvey J. Lauren, and Abu-Rayya M. Hisham. 2015. 'Improving Intergroup Relations in the Internet Age: A Critical Review', *Review of General Psychology* 19: 129–39.

White. A. Fiona, and Abu-Rayya M. Hisham. 2012. 'A Dual Identity-Electronic Contact (DIEC) Experiment Promoting Short- and Long-Term Intergroup Harmony', *Journal of Experimental Social Psychology* 48: 597–608.

White.A. Fiona, Abu-Rayya M. Hisham, and Weitzal Chela. 2014. 'Achieving Twelve-Months of Intergroup Bias Reduction: The Dual Identity-Electronic Contact (DIEC) Experiment', *International Journal of Intercultural Relations* 38: 158–63.

Wright, C. Stephen, Aron Arthur, McLaughlin-Volpe Tracy, and Ropp A. Stacy. 1997. 'The Extended Contact Effect: Knowledge of Cross-Group Friendships and Prejudice', *Journal of Personality and Social Psychology* 73: 73–90.

5

JAN A. ALI

Australian Muslims as Radicalized 'Other' and Their Experiences of Social Exclusion

With the end of the Cold War, Muslim radicalism has emerged both as national and international security concern. This concern has risen to new heights with the events of 11 September 2001 in America and subsequent, but not the only, bombings in Bali (2002 and 2005), Madrid (2004), and London (2005) (Hillyard 2005; Mythen, Walklate, and Khan 2009). Among policymakers, politicians, journalists, security experts, some academics, and certain sections of the community, Muslim radicalism is considered to be a menacing phenomenon that threatens global security with real possibility of undermining political stability, social harmony, and civil and state wellbeing of nation states. Muslim radicalism is characterized as a global phenomenon pervading, with the exception of Antarctica, all continents of the world and causing worldwide disturbances through violent destabilization of almost all nation states on the planet. Recent terror-related activities and the successful prosecution of numerous terrorists in various countries in the world including in Australia are testimonies to such a claim.

This chapter does not contest the existence or the security threat Muslim radicalism poses in Australia and by extension globally. However, it questions the alleged scale and severity of Muslim radicalism and homogenization of Muslim radicals as active actors in the theatre of violence and terrorism. Furthermore, it queries the success of state-administered risk management plan and preventative and protective policies embodied in counterterrorist legislation under the rubric of state[1] securitization. Muslim radicalism and concomitant terrorism is a reaction to a crisis of society. This crisis manifests itself in a combination of local and international Muslim socioeconomic and political malaise including poor governance, ideological challenge, and economic failure in many Muslim countries and alienation, discrimination, and institutional and structural barriers to upward mobility in a variety of Muslim and Western societies. There are Muslims who have experienced the negative effects of the socioeconomic and political order leading to their sense of perceived or real dislocation and alienation which then impacts on their consciousness and evokes a reaction (Hassan 2015). It encourages some to attempt to resolve Muslim struggles and this resolve is radicalism.

Since around 2012 the government strategies in Australia to address Muslim radicalism have increased with a reciprocal increase of the level of experience of Muslim exclusion. This chapter argues that the introduction of various forms of counterterrorism regulation or what social scientists called state securitization has made Muslim net experience worse particularly in relation to their participation in social processes producing unsurmountable socio-spatial challenge and an experience of social exclusion and 'othering'. Australian Muslims have been depicted and have been made to feel as the radicalized 'other' and consequently this has enhanced their collective experiences of social exclusion as a 'risk community' and dangerous enemy 'other'.

Understanding Muslim Radicalization

Emerging from the degenerated social and political environment of the Middle East in the early 1970s, Muslim militancy[2] quickly spread across the Muslim world making inroads into Muslim organizations,

---

[1] By state, I mean a political organization with a centralized government which has institutions such as administrative bureaucracies, legal systems, and military.

[2] I use Muslim militancy, political Islam, Islamism, and radical Islam interchangeably as I see significant overlap between them.

movements, and communities and paved the way for Muslim radicalization. '... the failure of Arab ruling elites to modernize their countries created an institutional vacuum and enabled the radicals to present themselves as serious contenders for political authority' (Khashan 1997: 5). Since then Muslim radicalization has been growing and continues to attain a greater measure of power and influence (Kepel 2000). 'Facing serious socioeconomic problems, crises of cultural identity, government ineptitude, and rapid and disruptive change, the Middle East has turned increasingly to Islam for solace and solutions' (Marr 1994: 224).

Targeting Muslim youths (Akbarzadeh 2013: 452) and those who have a very superficial understanding of their religion and who are susceptible to extreme views and ideas, Muslim militants or Islamists have been quite successful in achieving the aims and objectives of their radicalization project. This has been made possible by them using Islam as a tool to mobilize and galvanize Muslims in a powerful manner. Islam is also being used to dominate politics, education, and ideology rendering Muslim radicalism a 'transcendentally religiously motivated' (Korteweg et al. 2010: 29). Dislocated, alienated, and 'ignorant' Muslims are constantly politically subjugated by radical interest occasionally resulting in them carrying out horrendous acts of violence.

In popular discourse, religious radicalism denotes extreme violence in the name of religion (Akbarzadeh 2013: 452). Radicals are understood to be ready to engage in violent acts in the service of God and show no mercy towards their victims because the victims are seen as the enemies of God and, therefore, their enemies too. Also, religious radicalism inculcates the will to sacrifice oneself as a 'martyr' in the perceived service of God and as means to eschew the horror of the Day of Judgment and earn the rewards in the afterlife.

However, radicalism whether religious or non-religious in nature is not always and does not necessarily have to be about extreme act of violence or terrorism. Religious radicalism is multifaceted and multidimensional and is often and in majority of the cases non-violent. This is true for Muslim radicalism. 'Far from being monolithic, the movement is composed of divergent groups ranging from the rejectionist and extremist minority to a mainstream committed to working peacefully within the existing order' (Kutty 1996: 34). Religious radicalism is initially driven by the need to expand the religious law of a particular radical group or faith community. For example, Jewish religious radicals aspire for the supremacy of the Halacha while Muslim radicals work towards the dominance of the Shari'ah (Islamic law) (Kutty 1996: 34). Since radicals are critical of existing status quo and the role of key civil institutions, they strive towards the imposition of their own pro-grammes and rebuilding of society. Another driving force is the attitude of radicals towards other members of the society who do not share their views and laws. Radicals, depending on the circumstance, either apply great efforts to convert other members of the society or steer away from them. The final driving force is the removal, by radicals, of foreign values and norms from the religion and infusing it with what radicals refer to as pure tenets, principles, and ideals of the religion. Thus, radicals protect their devotees by keeping them away from the common pattern of living of mainstream society and engage members and supporters in what they consider to be religiously sanctioned way of life.

Religious radicalism existed for hundreds of years and contrary to popular belief is neither a new phenomenon nor is it unique to Muslims (Alao 2013). Religious radicals find their society in crisis and seek rem-edy. They strive to introduce change and bring about development in society based on their understanding of religious teachings and ideals. The aim is to transition society preferably non-violently for universal benefit. Their attempts are to restructure educational and communica-tion systems, to recover interpersonal relations, to restore traditional family structures, and to reform social and political order. Korteweg notes '... radicalization is the quest to drastically alter society, possibly through the use of unorthodox *but not necessarily violent* means ...' [emphasis added] (Korteweg et al. 2010: 31).

This is exactly the goal of Muslim radicals. Muslim radicals intend to make Islamic lifestyle pervasive throughout the modern world and Islam to be a dominant global system. The strategy they adopted is by setting up boundaries of difference, identify the enemy, seek out con-verts, create and maintaining institutions, and finally work towards the establishment of the caliphate (Islamic State) with Shari'ah as its constitution in an attempt to comprehensively recreate the society. Driven by anti-materialist ideology, Muslim radicals seek to recon-struct an indigenous global Islamic culture in a modern caliphate that would itself be Islamic, in which Muslims would emancipate themselves (Abbas 2007). Muslim radicalism is intended as a solution to the 'crisis of modernity' (increasing gap between rich and poor; constant growth in urban slums; unmanageable urban growth; urban transportation, housing, and infrastructure crisis; homelessness; unemployment; poverty; under education; limited social mobility; discrimination and prejudices; injustice; disenfranchisement; intensification of class division; unfair spread of and failure to generate prosperity; political discontent; debt-driven 'growth'; and weakening of faith in reason's ability to validate its supreme aims) or as an answer to the dilemmas posed by modernity and as a positive reaction to the challenges of modernity.

Muslim radicalism, therefore, neither is anti-modernity nor pursues its destruction but '... seek peaceful and democratic change' (Kutty 1996: 34). It strives to eliminate secularism and Westernism from modernity and harmoniously blend modernity's impartial sensibilities and corpus of knowledge with traditional religious attachments and norms. Joffé posits that,

> 'The challenge embodied in radicalisation is a process of contention designed to alter order and discourse but does not necessarily seek to destroy or replace the structures through which they are articulated ... [And] ... for the radical, the state can, initially at least, be challenged in order to modify its hegemonic discourse....' (Joffé 2013: 2–3)

However, in the wake of 9/11 terrorist bombings in the United States and the subsequent bombings elsewhere, Western political discourse of Muslim radicalism has become extraordinarily compelling and is the only legitimate framework for the explanation of violent extremism and terrorism in the era of 'War on Terror'. Muslim radicalism in this framework is understood to pose a great threat to national security and, gives the authorities, therefore, the legitimacy to deal punitively with the perpetrators. Can it be then said with certainty that Muslim radicalism necessarily leads to or results in acts of violence and terrorism? The ideology and inspirations of Muslim militants or Islamists do not on their own radicalize individual Muslims but there operate a complex of pathways and series of catalysts that lead to radicalization and sometimes this radicalization may pave way to acts of violence and terrorism. Tahir Abbas notes, '... it is also palpably clear that questions in relation to what drives radicalisation and how to engage with radicalised young people remain difficult to answer'(Abbas 2007: 4). It is almost a common knowledge that Muslim radicalism has a range of explanations and in political discourse and policy formulation there are a variety of responses. This confusion in policy formulation and political discourse regarding Muslim radicalism exhibits the problematic nature of the term. Muslim radicalism is taken to refer to a phenomenon in which the process of socialization enables individuals to engage in acts of terrorism. This idea forms the core in the explanation of terrorist activities through ideology. However, it is worth noting that rendering socialization in this manner is misleading because it promotes the assumption that the process of socialization results in violent behaviour or involvement in acts of terrorism when, in fact, this does not always happen or necessarily have to be the case. The fact of the matter is that there are individuals who may adopt beliefs and show support that may be construed as 'radical' but this does not necessarily mean that the individuals concerned are 'violent' or are engaged in violence and seeking violent outcomes.

Alao in his work on Islamic radicalisation in Nigeria notes that:

> There seem to be categories in radicalisation ... those who are genuinely committed to the religion and feel concerned about whatever they see as a desecration of the religion; those who may be described as ad hoc radicals who only follow instructions to go on the rampage once there is an instruction to that effect from "spiritual" leaders and revert back to their "ordinary" ways of life afterwards; and those who may be described as "opportunistic radicals", who only seize the opportunity of the moment to loot and vandalise, after which they wait anxiously for another opportunity ... in the process of militant activities, it is difficult to identify who belongs to what among these individuals. (Alao 2013: 138)

Thus, to distinguish between non-violent radicalists and those actually involved in acts of political agitation and violence is not a simple task and this must be clearly recognized. Importantly, those within the camp of Muslim radicalism who opt to engage in acts of violence and terrorism are minute in number yet this is not particularly acknowledged in either the Western political discourse or public policy and Muslim radicalism is essentialized, communitarianized, homogeneously demonized, and its threat expediently inflated.

Social Exclusion: Muslims as the 'Other'

In the age of 'War on Terror', homogeneous notion of a Muslim in the West[3] puts all Muslims as a single family of people and labels them as the 'other' and potential risk to society who then end up being viewed as terrorists. Due to the actions of a few, the entire Muslim population gets the blame. The homogenized concept of 'the Muslim' is situated in the worldwide resurgence of Islam and exhibits the return of the supressed. Muslims are not the first to be constructed as the terrorist 'other' as this kind of functional 'othering'[4] has affected groups in the past such as the Irish Republican Army (IRA) and, therefore, has a long history (Kenny 2007). Notions of 'otherness' play a critical role in the construction of the narrative of 'Us' and 'Them' and are central to ways in which 'danger', 'threat', or 'risk' are conceptualized (Lupton 1999). The 'other' is unlike and the opposite of the 'self', of 'us', of the 'same', and collective 'self'. The 'other' is the state of being dissimilar and alien to the social identity of a person and to the identity of the 'self' and, therefore, being peculiar.

The 'othering'categorizes and refers to the characteristics of the 'other' (Who and what is the 'other'?), which are different and detached from the representational order of things; from the genuine (the authentic and fixed); from social rules and social identity; and from the Self. Cultural geographer Crang explains that 'othering' is '… a process … through which identities are set up in an unequal relationship' (Crang 1998: 61). The word 'othering' depicts the reductive action of identifying an individual as someone who is a part of a subordinate social category described as the 'other'.

> Othering is the simultaneous construction of the self or in-group and the other or out-group in mutual and unequal opposition through identification of some desirable characteristic that the self/in-group has and the

---

[3] I acknowledge that the West is not a homogeneous entity and many Western countries differ from one another particularly culturally and in terms of the political system. When I refer to the West my focus is particularly on their common secular democratic capitalist framework.

[4] By functional 'Othering' I mean that the process of Othering assumes a function in the society which works at the coalface. See 'Otherness', *The New Fontana Dictionary of Modern Thought*, Third Edition (1999: 620).

other/out-group lacks and/or some undesirable characteristic that the other/out-group has and the self/in-group lacks. Othering thus sets up a superior self/in-group in contrast to an inferior other/out-group, but this superiority/inferiority is nearly always left implicit. (Brons 2015: 70)

The operational function of 'othering' is to exclude people who do not fit in and adhere to the norms of the social group, which is a reflection of the Self. The 'other' is conceptualized as fundamentally dissimilar to the Self and, therefore a source of apprehension, concern, and danger who threatens to obscure boundaries and surpass the Self. The 'other' becomes dangerous 'risky' for the society and deserves being blamed for any dangerous conduct or activity.

In the discussion of boundaries of the self/society, the distinction between in-group and out-group, and the disenfranchised or excluded, we very much depend on metaphors of spatial orientation (which Deborah Lupton [1999] refers as 'spatial metaphors') and binary oppositions. Space is a social construction created through socio-historical, cultural, and political processes (Lupton 1999). However, when it comes to the question of riskiness the space and place are seen to have not only symbolic value but real value. The 'Risky Other' is regarded by the dominant group as contaminating public spaces and, therefore, steer away from them. In the minds of the members of the dominant group developing strategies of exclusion to keep 'Risky Others' away from public spaces is legitimate and justifiably warranted which turns the public spaces into private places.

In the countries of the West, a variety of strategies exist to regulate public spaces in an attempt to keep out or remove members of 'Risky Other' from areas considered to be appropriate only for the privileged dominant group. The body of the 'Muslim Other', for instance, is frequently delineated as dangerous and risky and necessitates exclusion from the world of 'the self'. The 'other' is unknown and a stranger and the fear of him or her violating the norms and security of the world of 'the self' is amply evident in the discourse of privileged dominant group of the 'otherness' and 'alienness' of minority cultures (Bharucha 2004; Jensen 2011). Among the minority cultures Muslims as a group, in the age of 'War on Terror', produce profound anxiety in the privileged dominant group regarding the possibility of terrorist attacks in public spaces. The possibility of the 'other' penetrating the world of 'the self' is graphically exemplified in a series of four coordinated terrorist attacks on the United States on 11 September 2001 and in the presence of Western military in the countries of the Middle East in the case of the belief of Muslim militants.

By and large, the community handles the risk of dealing in a conditioned way. For example, they develop a certain image of places considering some to be potentially 'safe' and others insecure and 'risky'. This image is not just developed based on geographical aspects or aesthetics of a public space but it draws on assumptions and narratives about social exchanges and who inhabits the public space when. Fear of terrorism tends to be located within public rather than private space because terrorists are understood to be unpredictable and unknown strangers targeting and inhabiting public space rather than being found in the confinement of a private sphere (Bharucha 2004; Jensen 2011).

In Australia, and other Western countries, the community favours an increased powers of the state to combat Muslim terrorism notwithstanding that 'Australia has not experienced Islamic terrorism on its soil' Akbarzadeh (2013: 452)[5] is bolstered by an anti-terror discourse that takes into consideration the threat posed by the stranger, that is, the 'home-grown terrorist', breaching the norms and security of the world of 'the self' who is ironically both 'of us' and 'not of us'. Contemporary fear of breaching the norms and security of the world of 'the self' by the dangerous 'Risky Other' who lives 'among us and with us' helps strengthen religious and racial intolerance promoted in the popular media in the dominant social group. The fear of the 'other' produces anxiety in people and they start to coalesce together. When they do amalgamate there emerges 'anti-other' movements who often explicitly exhibit xenophobic tendencies.

---

[5] The Battle of Broken Hill (1915) in New South Wales is sometimes referred to as the first Muslim terrorist attack on Australian soil. Two Muslim men shot dead four Australians and wounded seven others on 1 January 1915, before the police and military officers killed them. It has been noted that the shooting was politically and religiously motivated but the men were not members of any recognized religious or political movement and their acts were considered as criminal rather than terrorism. Shakira Hussein asserts that 'Investigations into these incidents are ongoing, as are heated debates as to whether they were motivated by religion, the fallout of distant wars, psychiatric illness, or the experience of racism'.

Since the terrorist attacks on the New York Twin Towers in the United States on 11 September 2001, according George Williams, Professor of Law at the University of New South Wales, Australia has passed 61 new anti-terror statutes (Williams 2017). He notes that between 2001 and 2007, under the Howard government, 48 anti-terror statutes were enacted in Australia. It was an extraordinary period of law-making that no other country in the world witnessed, even those countries facing a greater level of terrorism threat. Roach describes this as Australia suffering from 'hyper-legislation … caught up in the 9/11 effect' (Roach 2011: 309). Australia's enactment of anti-terror laws was astonishing not only in terms of number but scope. In addition to defining terrorism, Australian law also deals with a range of new offences, for instance, a person can be jailed for financing terrorism or even possessing something that is perceived by the authorities to be linked to terrorism. Also, under new laws police have been given new powers to conduct searches where they can enter properties, premises, and even people's houses without having to secure a warrant from the judge or an appropriate authority. Australia has control orders whereby an individual or a group can be detained under 'House Arrest' for up to one year and be prohibited from using the internet and other communication devices imposing restrictions on their liberty (Williams 2011). There are preventative detention orders also which enables the authorities to detain people without charge or trial for up to fourteen days (Williams 2011). Furthermore, there are other provisions that deals with matters connected with censorship and speech. For example, it is possible a person can be jailed for what he or she says restricting their freedom of speech. However, the most extraordinary anti-terror law of all, in Australia, is those powers granted to Australian Security Intelligence Organisation (ASIO). With the powers vested in ASIO, it can have any person including Australian citizens not suspected of any crime to be detained for up to a week (7 days) and compelled to answer questions. In case of a detainee who refuses to answer the questions, he or she can then be jailed for up to five years. This can apply to family members or to anyone who may not necessarily be involved in terrorism directly but might be privy to information about potential terrorist activity that ASIO can force them to reveal (Williams 2011).

Thus, the bombings of the New York Twin Towers in the United States on 11 September 2001 which were undertaken by Muslims had a global consequence. It gave impetus to the proliferation of anti-terror laws in many Western countries including Australia. In Australia, there is no doubt that anti-terror laws were enacted to be aggressively enforced in order to keep Muslims under constant surveillance and to manage them as strictly as possible. Since these new anti-terror laws came into being only Muslims have been charged and prosecuted under them. 'Thirty-eight men, all but one of them Muslim, have been charged with terrorism offences in Australia to date' (McGarrity 2013: 18). This, in itself is telling and lends support to the claim that the laws indiscriminately targets Australian Muslims. All Muslims are perceived to collectively constitute the source of the threat of terrorism. In this imagination Muslims are the target of antiterror laws because they are seen as 'strangers', the 'other', who don't respect and value Australian way of life and are bent on its destruction. Muslims are the terrorists 'other'. The popular support for the state to development of new anti-terror laws through which to secure new powers to 'fight terrorism' is a reflection of a strong anti-terror discourse that draws on the threat of the 'other' breaching the norms and security of the world of 'the self' which is whole of Australia.

Muslim Enemy 'Other' and Securitization

Some very specific local issues such as the high proportion of Muslims amongst asylum seekers and the allegations of 'illegality' and 'queue jumping' that have been levelled against them (Mares 2001), the continuous increase in drug use and trafficking and violent crime among Lebanese Muslim criminal gangs, the Sydney gang rapes committed by a group of Lebanese Australian youths in 2000 led by Bilal Skaf against Anglo-Celtic Australian women and teenage girls, the Tampa Affair in 2001, Cronulla Riots in 2005, and the Haneef Case in 2007 coupled with the international events of the bombings on London transport in July 2005 that followed bombings in Bali of 2002 and the World Trade Centre in New York and Washington attacks of 2001 among other incidents, have intensified the debates in Australia about the place of Islam in modern Australian society and how to manage Muslim minority population. These have aided in questioning Muslim national identity and their citizenship rights as well as in amplifying suspicions about Muslims in Australia and made them the target of intensified material implementation of remarkable 'counterterrorism' and 'countering violent extremism' strategies. In an attempt to combat this, departments such as Attorney-General, Australian Federal Police, Australian Security Intelligence Organization, and Australian Border Force have been given increased preventative powers by the Australian government to bolster the surveillance and manage latent invisible threats brought into open by specific local issues and international events connected to Muslims (Humphrey 2009). Key to these counterterrorism and countering violent extremism strategies has been new strict anti-terror laws, as discussed earlier in the chapter, purportedly designed and targeted at iconoclastic threats posed by terrorists but in fact are cryptogrammic instruments for the management of the risky, dangerous Muslim enemy 'other'.

> They *Muslims* (emphasis added) have become a shared 'security' concern for Western governments and been made the object of suspicion and the focus of state intervention and political management. Their citizenship has become increasingly conditional on their 'performance' as citizens measured by active efforts to integrate on the one hand and their rejection of radical Islam on the other. (Humphrey 2009: 136)

Muslim immigrants and their descendants in the West have come to be problematized inhabiting the site of the desperate, the racialized group of 'folk devils' (Cohen 2002; Poynting et al. 2004; Welch 2006), 'extremists' and 'fanatics' (Gilmore 2012), the 'suspect other' (Silverstein 2005), and 'Risky Others' (Kenny 2007). Muslims have been rendered the 'enemy within' and as a homogenous bunch of 'Arab terrorists' who are '... backward, unshaven, fanatic, robe-covered, oil-rich, lecherous, desert dwellers ...' (Wakim 1992: 58), and who make unreasonable religious, cultural, and citizenship demands and who refuse to integrate into mainstream society. Unlike the pre-9/11 caricature of Muslim immigrants as merely 'culturally incompatible' they are now considered as 'politically unfaithful', and even to be outright dangerous. The wider community in Australia as well as elsewhere in the West has been made to feel increasing levels of alarm and fear. The conceptualization of Muslims as 'Risky Others' involves xenophobia or racial hatred and the mainstream society ostensibly under threat is ethically and religiously constructed, with the racialized 'other' as the corresponding dangerous enemy 'other'. Muslims are equated with terrorism, religious and cultural difference, extremism, and 'high risk' resulting in them, in the West, being pushed to the social margins and the limits of citizenship, where constant demands are being placed on them to prove their political loyalty, demonstrate integration into the mainstream society, and justify the claims over their citizenship through 'attitude test', language competency, and knowledge of national civic values (Kaya 2009). With some exceptions where some Muslims may not feel excluded the general outcome of this is the demonization of Islam and Muslims, which weakens the sense of belonging and citizenship of Australian Muslims.

Behind the backdrop of these prejudiced perceptions and descriptions of Muslims, the political and public calls for more stringent management of Muslims is being engineered. Thus, diaspora Muslim communities and Islam have been made objects of 'securitization' as a preventative measure to secure the 'home' through policies that seek to closely scrutinize and police Muslims and place demand on them for their swift social and cultural integration. In the discourse of securitization, ethnic and religious identity claims of Muslims and the difficulties associated with integration into mainstream society, as outcomes of existing structural problems of poverty, unemployment, discrimination, disenfranchisement, inequality, upward social mobility, xenophobia, and racism, are masked by focusing on the reason of these problems.

> ... [The] states tend to employ the discourse of securitization as a political technique with a capacity to integrate a society politically by staging a credible existential threat in the form of an internal, or even an external enemy that is fabricated by security agencies (like the police and the army) through categorising migration together with drug trafficking, human trafficking, criminality and terrorism. (Kaya 2011)

The principal logic of the discourse of securitization appears to have shifted from protecting the state to protecting society or in the language of James Ferguson and Akhil Gupta from 'verticality' to 'encompassment' where verticality refers to state as an institution above society and encompassment denoting state conceptually merged with the nation encompassing its locality covering family, the local community, and the system of nation state (Ferguson and Gupta 2002). Thus, the protection of society against danger and any form of attack whether from within or without has become the heart of the discourse of securitization in such a manner that the term 'security' has been propelled into all provinces of life. In the discourse of securitization there is a framing of the 'enemy other' where the enemy 'other' is constituted as not only being violent, uncivilized, and anti-modernity but pose a global and interconnected threat that covers the entire planet. These shifts are employed to justify the new defensive responses and attacks of preventive military action on the enemy overseas and the securitization of state borders.

In the end securitization directly or indirectly impacts on many Australian Muslims with far-reaching consequences manifesting in their political alienation, socioeconomic marginalization, and Islamophobia with a cumulative effect of social exclusion. In terms of political alienation, for instance, a study commissioned by the Department of Immigration and Citizenship, exploring attitudes of young Muslims in Sydney and Melbourne, found young Muslims to have a profound sense of alienation from the Australian political system and the media (Akbarzadeh and Bouma 2009). This sense of alienation was further reinforced particularly through the securitization undertakings by the Howard Government (Leach and Mansouri 2004: 124). Furthermore, 'Legal citizenship status grants individuals full civic, social and political rights and responsibilities, including the right and duty to vote and the entitlement to run for public office. Muslims remain, however, severely under-represented in political decision-making processes' (Peucker, Roose, and Akbarzadeh 2014: 288).

Another direct or indirect consequence of securitization on many Muslims is their socioeconomic marginalization. The Australian Census data reveal a disturbing discrepancy regarding living standards and access to wealth between Muslims and non-Muslims. Using the Census data, Riaz Hassan established that in 2006 Muslim households were grouped in the low-income band, with 2 per cent recording no income. This was double the figure compared to non-Muslim Australians (Hassan 2015). Regarding home ownership, a measurement of financial security, only 14 per centof Muslims owned their homes compared to 32 per cent of non-Muslim Australians (Australian Bureau of Statistics 2011).

The figures for employment rate for Muslims are worrying too and reinforces what we have discussed above. According to 2006 and 2011 Census data, Australia's unemployment rates were marginally over 5 per cent but Muslim unemployment rates were two-and-a-half times more—13.4 per cent and 12.6 per cent, respectively (Hassan 2015). From these figures it can be deduced that financial insecurity and poverty are a major concern for Muslims.

Securitization of Muslims have also resulted in increased Islamophobia in Australia. For all Muslims, but particularly for young Australian Muslims, Islamophobia exposes them to socioeconomic marginalization and consequently problematizes their integration in Australian multiculturalism. Riaz Hassan argues that Muslim men were more likely than non-Muslim men to possess university qualification (21 percent and 15 percent respectively), however their rates of unemployment were two to four times higher (depending on age) (Hassan 2015). As a result, Muslims had considerably lower labour force participation rates than other Australians.

While the experience of Islamophobia generates feelings of harm and disrespect, there are more practical consequences for Australian Muslims, particularly young Muslims who are locally born and who expect their citizenship rights to be honoured. Patterns of discomfort and fear, distrust, and exclusion amongst Australian Muslims emphasize in a general sense that their whole way of life is not only devalued, but not to be accommodated. The pervasive sense of Islamophobia creates for Australian Muslims generally, and young Muslim Australians in particular, discomfort and fear (Dreher 2005: 1) that affects their sense of belonging both to the nation (Noble 2005: 117) and to their neighbourhoods and spaces of everyday life (Noble 2005: 117).

Securitization is a regulatory tool or strategy premised on the rationale that the power vested in some of the core institutions of government such as the security intelligence organization and the police either can restrict a person or allow him/her access to a 'space'—a place to be in. In other words, securitization regulates spatial exclusion and inclusion by concentrating on the individual—person's identity and socio-religious background—to establish his or her spatial appropriateness. Spatially anchored national sovereignty and territoriality is not a new phenomenon, what is new, however, in present securitization is the national and transnational dimensions of state-based exercise of power, control, and governance over the populace (Ferguson and Gupta 2002) and the effect transnational securitization has on citizenship where citizenship itself is contingent upon the 'citizen's' performability and loyalty. Securitization is both a state-regulated policy and a manifestation of what James Ferguson and Akhil Gupta call *transnational governmentality* (Ferguson and Gupta 2002) borrowing governmentality from Michel Foucault (1991) to develop their concept.

Securitization is 'a political technique of framing policy questions in logics of survival with a capacity to mobilize politics of fear in which social relations are structured on the basis of distrust' (Huysmans 2006: xi). The impact of securitization on migrant Muslims is the transportation of them as a social category within a distinct ethnic and racial structure and national mosaic to a wider transnational context of the West. Securitization renders migrant Muslims as a transnational social category for the purpose of scrutiny, surveillance, and policing resulting in them being conceptually separated from their particular social, political, and national settings but at the same time produces a discourse in which diverse Muslim communities are collectively considered as dangerous and a social and political threat (Risley 2006). As with the past conceptualization of migrant Muslims as a category for global monitoring and surveillance in the West so is the contemporary conceptualization in which all Muslims including locally born Muslims have been turned into a transnational category denoting risky and dangerous 'other' (Kaya 2011). Securitization means presenting Muslims as a minority group and as existentially threatening and thereby forming the basis for extraordinary political measures. Securitization is a strategy of social protection characterizing political community at the national level and a project of transnational governmentality.

The project of securitization of Islam and Muslims in Western societies seeks to remould Islam as a moderate religion in a serious attempt to weakening or even eliminating the appeal of radical Islam. Thus, Islam has become a focus of governmentality, a project of governance whereby the state moving into civil society in an attempt to regulate Muslims by restructuring and legitimating local religious institutions and generating a discussion on moderate Islam (Bowen 2003). Securitization denotes political control and regulation of Islam and Muslims because they are seen to represent global threat through international migration and the formation of a Muslim diaspora. Securitization cancels out of the democratic process the voices of securitized Muslim minority communities and represents the dual strategies of exclusion or inclusion.

Like in other Western nation-states, Muslims in Australia are conceptualized by Australian host state as a transnational category which acts as a code for differentiating the 'good' and 'civilized' from the 'bad' and 'barbaric'. This means that in the age of 'global war on terror' they are no longer considered as minority migrant community through cultural essentialization of Islam and the political construction of radical Islam as a localized phenomenon embedded in the local minority Muslim communities and non-threatening to the state but as universal enemy 'other'. Securitization of Muslims and Islam are a manifestation of transnational governmentality involving monitoring, regulating, and controlling a social category not only within state borders but beyond. They have been progressively conceptualized as a transnational homogenized entity through the fusion of public policy and law.

All Muslim immigrants and their descendants in Australia are subjected to restructuring in the 'social exclusion' discourse in an attempt to make Australia secure. This is determined through politico-cultural categorization of 'enemy Muslims' (radicals and terrorists) and 'extremist Islam' (radical Islam). Social exclusion, according to Avramov is,

> '… a condition of deprivation, that is manifested through the generalized disadvantages facing individuals of social groups due to accumulated social handicaps…. Exclusion is as a rule associated with social stigmatization, blame and isolation, which translated to low self-esteem, a feeling of not belonging and not having been given a chance to be included in society.' (Avramov 2002: 26-7)

Social exclusion then denotes a policy designed to keep Australia protected and directed at social and cultural removal. Social exclusion relating to Muslims addresses social incorporation and cultural harmonization. It seeks to introduce cultural change through the de-domestication and de-nationalization of radical Islam and domestication and nationalization of 'moderate Islam' by aligning it with Australian values and the 'way of life'. The approach to domestication in the context of Australian multiculturalism recognizes Muslims as a distinct ethnocultural category premised on the idea that 'religion is embedded in a culture, so if one is a Muslim one belongs to a different culture' Roy (2007: 56) and if Australian Muslims are not an embodiment of moderate Islam then they have to be a part of 'bad' and 'extremist Islam' and therefore they are radicalized enemy 'other' subject to securitization.

Muslims As a Distinct Social Category

Muslim radicalism is a multifaceted and multidimensional ubiquitous phenomenon driven by anti-materialist ideology to reconstruct a scriptural global Islamic culture in a modern caliphate. It is a reaction to the crisis of society and negative consequences of modernity but is not anti-modernity. In an era characterized by modernity neither all Muslims are radicals nor are all radical Muslims violent.

The construction of Australian Muslims as the radicalized 'other' is an outcome of the state's attempt to manage 'globalized Islam' and Muslim diaspora. In doing so Muslims are rendered a distinct social category and their experiences of social exclusion enhanced.

The global rise of Muslim terrorism has produced a state response in the West to counter the supposedly invisible threat allegedly embodied in Muslim radicalism and promise national security through securitization. Securitization of Islam and Muslims is a strategy to minimize risk nationally and internationally. However, the way public safety wars are being fought against Islam and Muslims have neither tamed the invisible enemy nor removed the risk they pose but only aggravated it proving state's inability to desecuritize societal security.

References

Abbas, T. 2007. 'Introduction: Islamic Political Radicalism in Western Europe'. In *Islamic Political Radicalism: A European Perspective*, Tahir Abbas (ed.), pp. 3–14. Edinburgh: Edinburgh.

Akbarzadeh, S. 2013. 'Investing in Mentoring and Educational Initiatives: The Limits of De-Radicalisation Programmes in Australia', *Journal of Muslim Minority Affairs* 33(4): 451–63.

Akbarzadeh, S. and Bouma, G. 2009. *Muslim Voices: Hope and Aspirations of Muslim Australians*. Melbourne: Centre for Muslim Minorities and Islam Policy Studies, TheMonash University.

Alao, A. 2013. 'Islamic Radicalisation and Violent Extremism in Nigeria', *Conflict, Security & Development* 13(2): 127–47.

Australian Bureau of Statistics. 2011. *2011 Census of Housing and Population*. Canberra: Australian Bureau of Statistic.

Avramov, D. 2002. 'People, Democracy, and Social Exclusion', *Population Studies Series* 37: 26–7. Strasbourg: Council of European Publishing.

Bowen, J. 2003. 'Two Approaches to Rights and Religion in Contemporary France'. In *Human Rights in Global Perspective: Anthropological Studies of Rights, Claims and Entitlements*, R. Wilson and J. Mitchell (eds), pp. 33–53. London: Routledge.

Bharucha, R. 2004. 'Muslims and Others: Anecdotes, Fragments, and Uncertainties of Evidence', *Inter-Asia Cultural Studies*, 5(3): 472–85.

Brons, L. 2015. 'Othering, an Analysis', *Transcience*, 6(1): 69–90.

Cohen, S. 2002. *Folk Devils and Moral Panics*, Third Edition. Abingdon: Routledge.

Crang, M. 1998. *Cultural Geography*. London: Routledge.

Dreher, T. 2005. 'Targeted: Experiences of Racism in NSW after September 11, 2001', *UTS Shopfront Monograph Series No. 2*. Broadway: UTS Shopfront.

Ferguson, J. and Gupta, A. 2002. 'Spatializing States: Toward an Ethnography of Neoliberal Governmentality', *American Ethnologist* 29(4): 981–1002.

Foucault, M. 1991. 'Governmentality'. In *The Foucault Effect: Studies in Governmentality*, G. Burchell, C. Gordon, and P. Miller (eds), pp. 87–104. Chicago: University of Chicago Press.

Gilmore, J. 2012. 'Criminalizing Dissent in the "War on Terror": The Bristish State's Reaction to Gaza War protests of 2008 – 2009'. In *Global Islamophobia: Muslims and Moral Panic in the West*, G. Morgan and S. Poynting (eds), pp. 197–213. Surrey: Ashgate.

Hassan, R. 2015. *Australian Muslims: A Demographic, Social and Economic Profile of Muslims in Australia 2015*. Adelaide: International Centre for Muslim and Non-Muslim Understanding, University of South Australia.

Hillyard, P. 2005. 'The "War on Terror": Lessons from Ireland', *Essay*. Brussels: European Civil Liberties Network, ECLN.org.

Humphrey, M. 2009. 'Securitisation and Domestication of Diaspora Muslims and Islam: Turkish Immigrants in Germany and Australia', *International Journal on Multicultural Societies* 11(2): 136–54.

Hussein S. 2015. 'Battle of Broken Hill Finds a Resonance in Terrorist Incidents', *The Australian*. Available at: http://www.theaustralian.com.au/arts/review/battle-of-broken-hill-finds-a-resonance-in-terrorist-incidents/news-story/7a5da1b61d59032795cb37cb273dd037. Accessed on 2 August 2017.

Huysmans, Jef. 2006. *The Politics of Insecurity: Fear, Migration and Asylum in the EU*. London: Routledge.

Jensen, S. 2011. 'Othering, Identity Formation and Agency', *Qualitative Studies* 2(2): 63–78.

Joffé, G. 2013. 'Introduction: Radicalisation and the Arab Spring'. In *Islamist Radicalisation in Europe and the Middle East: Reassessing the Causes of Terrorism*, George Joffé (ed.), pp. 1–16. London: I.B.Tauris.

Kaya, A. 2009. *Islam, Migration and Integration: The Age of Securitization*. London: Palgrave.

———. 2011. '*Age of Securitization: Challenging Multiculturalist and Republicanist Policies of Integration*', *Netzwerk Migration in Europa*. Available at: http://www.migrationeducation.org/fileadmin/uploads/Age_of_Securitization_Ayhan_Kaya_pdf_version_02.pdf. Accessed on 7 January 2016.

Kenny, S. 2007. 'Risk Society and the Islamic Other'. In *Islam and Political Violence: Muslim Diaspora and Radicalism in the West*, S. Akbarzadeh and F. Mansouri (eds), pp. 87–106. London: I.B Tauris.

Kepel, G. 2000. 'Islamism Reconsidered', *Harvard International Review* 22 (2): 22–8.

Khashan, H. 1997. 'The New World Order and the Tempo of Militant Islam', *British Journal of Middle Eastern Studies* 24(1): 5–24.

———. 2000. *Arabs at the Crossroads: Political Identity and Nationalism*. Gainesville: University of Florida, pp. 117–18.

Korteweg, R., S. Gohel, F. Heisbourg, M. Ranstorp, and R. de Wijk. 2010. 'Background Contributing Factors to Terrorism: Radicalisation and Recruitment'. In *Understanding Violent Radicalisation: Terrorist and Jihadist Movements in Europe*, Magnus Ranstorp (ed.), pp. 21–49. London: Routledge.

Kutty, F. 1996. 'Issues in Islam: Islamists and the West; Co-existence or Confrontation?', *The Washington Report on Middle East Affairs* 14(6): 34–6.

Leach, M. and F. Mansouri. 2004. *Lives in Limbo*. Sydney: University of New South Wales Press.

Lupton, D. 1999. 'Dangerous Places and the Unpredictable Stranger: Constructions of Fear of Crime', *Australian and New Zealand Journal of Criminology* 32(1): 1–15.

Mares, P. 2001. *Borderline: Australia's Treatment of Refugees and Asylum Seekers*. Sydney: UNSW Press.

Marr, P. 1994. 'The United States, Europe, and the Middle East: An Uneasy Triangle', *Middle East Journal* 48(2): 211–25.

McGarrity, N. 2013. '"Let the Punishment Match the Offence": Determining Sentences for Australian', *International Journal for Crime and Justice Terrorists* 2(1): 18–34.

Mythen, G., S. Walklate, and F. Khan. 2009. '"I'm a Muslim, But Not a Terrorist": Victimization, Risky Identities and the Performance of Safety', *The British Journal of Criminology* 49(6): 736–54.

Noble, G. 2005. 'The Discomfort of Strangers: Racism, Incivility and Ontological Security in a Comfortable and Relaxed Nation', *Journal of Intercultural Studies* 26(1): 107–20.

Peucker, M., J. Roose, and S. Akbarzadeh. 2014. 'Muslim Active Citizenship in Australia: Socioeconomic Challenges and the Emergence of a Muslim Elite', *Australian Journal of Political Science* 49(2): 282–99.

Poynting, Scott, Greg Noble, Paul Tabar, and Jock Collins. 2004. *Bin Laden in the Suburbs:Criminalising the Arab Other*. Sydney: Institute of Criminology;

Risley, S. 2006. 'The Sociology of Security: Sociological Approaches to Contemporary and Historical Securitization'. Paper Presented at the Annual Meeting of the American Sociological Association. Montreal Convention Center, Montreal, Quebec, Canada. Online PDF 2009-03-05 available at:

http://www.allacademic.com/meta/p105192 _index.html. Accessed on 7 January 2016.

Roach, K. 2011. *The 9/11 Effect: Comparative Counter-Terrorism*. Cambridge: Cambridge University Press, p. 309.

Roy, O. 2007. 'Islamic Terrorist Radicalisation in Europe'. In *European Islam: Challenges for Public Policy and Society*, S. Amghar, A. Boubekeur, and M. Emerson (eds), pp. 52–60. Brussels: Centre for European Policy Studies.

Silverstein, P. 2005. 'Immigrant Racialization and the New Savage Slot: Race, Migration and Immigration in the New Europe', *Annual Review of Anthropology* 34: 363–84.

Wakim, J. 1992. 'The Gulf War Within the Australian Community and Arab Australians: Villains, Victims or Victors'. In *Racial Harassment*, G. Bird (ed.), pp. 41–61. National Centre for Constitutional Studies in Law, Centre for Migrant and Intercultural Studies, Clayton: Monash University.

Welch, Michael. 2006. *Scapegoats of September 11th: Hate Crimes and State Crimes in the War on Terror*. New Brunswick: Rutgers University Press.

Williams, G. 2011. 'A Decade of Australian Anti-Terror Laws', *Melbourne University Law Review* 35(3): 1136–76.

———. 2017. *Anti-Terror Laws and Australia*. Available at: https://youtu.be/k8RKVUWiZag. Accessed on 4 January 2017.

6

NAHID A. KABIR

Young Muslims' Identity in Australia and the US

The Focus on the 'Muslim Question'

Muslims have been present in Australia and the United States for several centuries but since the 1970s Muslims have migrated to both countries in large numbers. In 2016, in Australia Muslims comprised 2.6 per cent, and in 2015, in the US Muslims constituted 1.0 per cent of the total population in their respective countries (Australian Bureau of Statistics 2016; Mohamed 2016).

But the 'Muslim question' in both countries gradually began to surface with the Iranian Revolution in 1978–9, the Salman Rushdie affair in 1989 and the 1990–1 Gulf war. After the Twin Towers attacks on 11 September 2001, and now with the emergence of the Islamic State of Iraq and the Levant (ISIL), the 'Muslim question' has intensified.

Whenever there is a national or international crisis, some Muslims living in non-Muslim majority countries find their faith being questioned, and are verbally or physically vilified by some members of the wider society (Haddad 2011; Kabir 2014a, 2017).

Sometimes, the 'Muslim question' takes the form of Islamophobia or hate crime against the Muslims, while other times, the 'Muslim question' raises doubt in the minds of some non-Muslims about whether

Muslims will integrate and become loyal citizens, and whether they can ever coexist with non-Muslims. In the USA, the Council of American-Islamic Relations (CAIR) reported that since August 2014, when ISIL released a video showing the horrendous beheading of two Americans, the anti-Islamic sentiments have been rising. The horrific killings created an environment of 'toxic hate', in which some Americans turned out against their Muslim neighbours. The Islamophobic incidents in America included anti-Muslim backlash, threats and intimidation to Muslims, and mosque vandalism (Burke 2015). In Australia, a comprehensive report on Islamophobia from 2014 to 2016, highlighted that visible Muslim women wearing the *hijab* (head scraf) were mostly victims of Islamophobia (Ahmed 2017). In this chapter, I first discuss the concept of identity followed by contemporary events and issues (Australia 2005–07; America 2009) that generated the 'Muslim question'. Thereafter, I discuss my research methodology. Following which I examine the participants' identity and their views on the contemporary events and issues. Finally, I conclude that, to enhance social cohesion, appropriate measures should be taken to enhance young Muslims' self-esteem and confidence.

The Concept of Identity

Identity is the condition of being oneself (and not another). Arguably its formation is a fluid process that is shaped according to circumstances and opportunities. Identity may depend, for instance, on the family one is born into, the culture and religion one belongs to, one's membership to a community, and one's life experiences. When Muslims identify themselves with their Muslim identity, their religion can become an important element of their culture. Identity is both individual and group oriented. Jenkins stated that similarity and difference are the dynamic principles of identification. Jenkins also suggested that external factors play a significant role in group or collective identity leading to the 'us' and 'them' debate (2008: 18, 41).

Burke and Stets believe that social identity is based on membership in a group or category that gives one a shared feeling with others in the group (2009: 127). Burke and Stets have also observed that emotion can play an important role in the formation of one's identity (2009: 160–1). Emotions have an influence on the formation of social networks; people with 'shared affective meanings' are more likely to enter into and maintain social relationships. And people with intense positive emotions towards a network/group are likely to identify with it. Hall observed that identity is a fluid process, 'It always remains incomplete, is always "in process", always "being formed"' (1994: 122). Kabir found that when a person receives recognition, approval, and acceptance from a group then s/he is more likely to feel a part of that group (2012: 89–91).

Contemporary Events and Issues

With every national (or international) event concerning Muslims in Australia or the United States, the 'Muslim question' tends to appear in the mainstream society either through political rhetoric or media discourse. The 'Muslim question' such as whether Muslims will ever integrate into the mainstream society, and if they pose a national security threat, will resurface.

Certain contemporary incidents (discussed below) concerning the Muslims in Australia in 2005–07, and Muslims in the United States in 2009, raised the 'Muslim question' once again. In this chapter, as I interviewed my participants (in Australia 2006–07 and America 2009–11), I wanted to find out if the contemporary events and issues that raised the 'Muslim question' impacted on their identity. As discussed earlier, identity involves membership to a broader group or feeling a part of a broader group—be it ethnic, religious, or national and this is explored in detail below.

Australia

On 4 December 2005 a fight between three surf lifesavers and a group of four young men of Lebanese background occurred on a beach in a beachside suburb of Cronulla, south of Sydney. The Australian lifesavers had reportedly insulted their assailants with public taunts that 'Lebs' cannot swim. On 11 December 2005 about 5,000 young people converged on Sydney's Cronulla Beach, many wrapped in Australian flags, and attacked people of Middle Eastern appearance. The next day a group of young Lebanese Australians launched a reprisal attack. But the incident was portrayed by some media that it was instigated by the Australian Muslims rather than confining it to a squabble between Lebanese-Australians and local Cronulla boys (Kabir 2007).

In October 2006, during his Ramadan sermon at the Lakemba Mosque in Sydney, the Australian Muslim spiritual leader Mufti Sheikh Taj el-Din al-Hilali equated scantily dressed women with uncovered meat and blamed them for inciting men to rape. Although Sheikh al-Hilali subsequently offered an unreserved apology, saying that he meant to protect women's honour, his statement sparked a heated media debate, which continued for two weeks. Supporters of al-Hilali argued that the statement was taken out of context (Kabir 2008b).

In July 2007 an Indian-born physician Dr Mohamed Haneef was arrested and held in detention without charges and without the right to seek bail for 12 days in Brisbane. Haneef was alleged to have had a terrorist link with his cousin Kafeel Ahmed who had attempted to blow up Glasgow airport. The case against Haneef was later dropped due to a lack of evidence. In December 2010 Haneef was awarded compensation from the Australian government. In Dr Haneef's context, the fear politics was played by the Australian government (Kabir 2008a).

The contemporary events concerning Muslims in Sydney and Melbourne raised the 'Muslim question'. Though the participants of this study were based in Melbourne it was important to see if they were aware of these incidents, and felt connected to their broader collective Muslim identity. Similarly, in the USA, certain contemporary incidents (as discussed below) concerning American national security involved Muslims in America. In order to evaluate young American Muslims' identity and their connection to the broader collective Muslim identity, it was important to examine if the participants in Michigan were informed of those incidents, and if it impacted their identity. As discussed, identity involves emotion so when young Muslims see that their fellow Muslims are ridiculed or labelled as the 'Other', it can impact on their sense of belonging to their host country.

USA

In October 2009, Imam Luqman Ameen Abdullah was shot a total of 20 times (incurring 21 wounds, from which he died) during a raid by federal law enforcement agents on a warehouse in Dearborn, near Detroit in Michigan. A federal indictment alleged that Imam Luqman led a radical separatist mosque and conspired to sell stolen goods, and that he had open fired during a police raid on a stolen goods operation. However, Dawud Walid, executive director of the Council on American–Islamic Relations, Michigan, questioned the heavy-handedness of the law enforcement officers that, if Imam Luqman had been killed instantly, why he was found handcuffed? (Kabir 2014b: 96).

On 5 November 2009, Major Nidal Malik Hasan, a US Army psychiatrist, who was American-born of Palestinian-Muslim background, and who had counselled soldiers involved in foreign wars, open fired with two handguns on soldiers preparing for foreign deployment at the Fort Hood US Army post in Texas, killing 13 soldiers and wounding 30 others. It was a horrendous act of terrorism. Critics observed that there have been other acts of terrorism committed by non-Muslim Americans during the same period (discussed later in the chapter) but the media did not focus on those news as vehemently for several days as they did with Major Hasan news (Kabir 2014b: 123–33, 2017: 126–7).

On 25 December 2009, the 23-year-old Nigerian Umar Farouk Abdulmutallab (also known as the 'Underwear Bomber') attempted to blow up a Detroit-bound Northwest Airlines flight with explosives tucked in his underwear. Abdulmutallab was trained by Yemeni-based al-Qaeda in the Arabian Peninsula. Abdulmutallab pleaded guilty, and in 2012 a US federal court sentenced him for life without parole.

In this chapter, I have also asked the participants about Islamophobia (fear of the 'Muslim Other') since 11 September 2001, and their views on the media because these two ongoing contemporary issues have been impacting on some Muslims in Australia and the United States (Esposito and Kalin 2011; Kabir 2006).

Research Methodology

This chapter is a part of a broader research project on young Muslims in Australia and the US that was conducted in 2006–7 and 2009–11, respectively. The field research was approved by the ethics committees of two universities in Australia and the United States. The ethics committee of Edith Cowan University in Perth, Western Australia approved my field research for Australia, and the ethics committee at

Harvard University in Cambridge, Massachusetts approved my field research for the United States. In Australia, I conducted this research as a research fellow at the Edith Cowan University (2006–07), and in the United States, I conducted this research as a visiting fellow at the 'Islam in the West program' in the Center for Middle Eastern Studies at Harvard University (2009–11).

Participation in my research has been voluntary. I have approached several schools in Victoria and Michigan if their students and staff would like to participate in my study. For this study, two schools from these states agreed to participate. These two schools were located in socio-economically disadvantaged areas in Victoria and Michigan. The school in Victoria was located in the south-east from Melbourne; and the school in Michigan was close to Detroit.

For this chapter, I examine the life stories of 18 young Muslims (9 participants: 7 male and 2 female in a school in Victoria, Australia; and 9 participants: 4 male and 5 female in a school in Michigan, USA). The age groups of all 18 participants were: 11 participants: 15–17 years; 5 participants: 18 years; 2 participants: mid-20s. The interviews were in-depth, semi-structured and face-to-face for 40 minutes with each participant. The interview questions examined participants' life stories, including their early school memories, sporting activities, music, entertainment and cultural interests, contemporary events, together with their hopes, ambitions, and dreams. However, the main focus of this study was to find out how the participants defined their identity/identities, and how they perceived the contemporary events and issues discussed earlier.

I employed grounded theory method in this study. Grounded theory is a type of qualitative method (Glaser and Strauss 1967). It is a non-statistical method that describes a methodological approach that is about 'letting the data speak' and not imposing pre-formed hypotheses. The basic idea of the grounded theory approach involves reading through the data (interview transcripts) in order to pick up on consistent patterns and themes, which are then organized into thematic categories. The categories are then compiled and analysed manually in order to identify the similarities and differences on a particular concept, in this case, it is the 'Muslim question' in Australia and the USA. For anonymity, I have given the participants fictitious names.

Research Findings

The participants lived near their school's vicinity. All 18 participants lived with their parents in their own house. In Victoria, among 9 fathers of the participants: 5 were employed (engineer, public servant, IT staff and mechanic); 2 were self-employed (handyman and cab driver); 1 was a school teacher overseas; and 1 was retired. In Michigan, among 9 fathers of the participants: 7 were employed (car company, metal company, motor factory, electrician, non-government organization, and imam of a mosque); 1 was self-employed (taxi business/cab driver); and 1 dead. Among the mothers in both countries, 15 were stay-at-home mothers; in Australia, 1 mother was an engineer, and 1 a social worker; and in the US, 1 mother was a staff member in a school. In this study, 16 participants attended high schools while 2 participants (aged in their mid-20s) worked in schools.

All 18 participants were bicultural. They watched English-language TV programmes. They all spoke both English and their native language, although some participants were more fluent than others in their native language. Western and ethnic music were popular among 16 participants, and 1 listened to *nasheeds* (Muslim devotional songs). In Australia, the 7 male participants were more interested in sports (for example, Australian football, soccer, and cricket), and the 2 female participants were more into reading novels, watching television, and listening to music. In the US, 5 participants (including one female participant) spoke about sports, and 4 female participants discussed their love for music, television programmes, and online news. In both countries, some participants spoke about their respective cultural celebrations and Muslim *Eid* celebrations. For example, they spoke about *Eid ul Fitr*, the Muslim festival celebrated at the end of the month of fasting (Ramadan). On the *Eid* morning, boys wear their Islamic or ethnic clothes such as *shalwar* (trouser) and *kurta* (shirt), or *jilbab* (long dress), and girls wear beautiful *abayas* (long dress) or *shalwar* and *kurta*, and attend the *Eid* congregation with their family members. Generally, on the occasion of *Eid*, children get new clothes as gifts from their parents. Later, Muslims visit their relatives and friends on the *Eid* day. Some children also receive small cash gifts (known as *Eidee*) from their relatives.

With regard to current affairs or the 'Muslim question' in Australia, out of 9 participants, 6 participants had heard of the Cronulla riots in the news. Four participants had heard of al-Hilali's case in the news. Two participants had heard of Dr Haneef's case in the news. On the topic of the media, all 9 participants offered a critical view that the media is biased against Muslims. All participants were familiar with the 9/11 tragedy and its impact on Muslims. In the US out of 9 participants, 1 participant had heard of the Fort Hood shooting, and spoke on Imam Luqman's case, but all 9 participants had heard of Abdulmutallab's case. Most participants spoke of the impact of 9/11 on Muslims and racial profiling. Like in Australia, all 9 US participants had strong views on the media.

Muslim Identity and the 'Muslim Question'

The contemporary events and issues (discussed earlier) involved in the 'Muslim question' have impacted on the formation of some participants' identities. In other words, the 'Muslim question' and young Muslims' identity formation can be interlinked. The 'Muslim question' can single out the Muslims as the 'Other'. Therefore, it involves emotion which can impact on young Muslims' identity. However, some internal or external factors can impact on young Muslims identity. For example, sometimes their identity formation has been imposed by their parents and sometimes participants endorsed their Muslim identity through their personal journey.

Practising Islam

It is generally believed that Muslim identity is formed when children are born into a Muslim family. In the Muslim family environment children learn to believe in (and practice) the five pillars of Islam, which include *shahada* (belief in one God and Muhammad as His messenger); *salat* (five daily prayers); *zakat* (alms giving); *sawm* (fasting in the month of Ramadan); and *Hajj* (pilgrimage to Mecca). However, in a diaspora, some Muslim parents are keen that their children embrace their Muslim identity (Kabir 2016b; Rahman 2011). Sometimes, children endorse a Muslim identity by choice (for example, Muslim women choosing to wear *hijab* or when they confront some family issues).

AUSTRALIA

Ayesha, of Bosnian heritage, 17 years, who wears the *hijab*, identified herself as 'a Muslim Australian, Islam always comes first'. Ayesha said that she reads newspapers, books, and novels. About music she said, 'Nah, I don't listen to any music at all'. A few Muslims consider music *haram* (forbidden) in Islam.

Ayesha shared her journey to Islam. She said that her father was 'a really heavy drinker, he used to drink a lot, and he was abusive and stuff'. She continued, 'Then one man used to come over, he was *Masha'Allah* [God has willed] a really good brother, and he used to tell my dad, you have to stop. It's *haram* to drink and smoke and all this stuff'. Then Ayesha said, '*Al-hamdulillah* [Praise be to God] that brother guided my dad and that's how it all started happening ... Yeah my dad he goes a lot to mosque'.

Ayesha found that Islam had changed her father into a better person and a 'good Muslim'. This influenced her, and she was then comfortable with her Muslim identity in spite of all the media stereotypes against Muslims (Kabir 2016a: 11).

USA

Rabab, of West African background, age 15, identified herself as 'Muslim, African American'. She loved basketball and flag football (which is a version of American football). She supported the Cleveland basketball team and was a fan of its player LeBron James. Rabab's Muslim identity was imposed by her parents. Rabab said that she never felt confident about wearing the *hijab* in her former public school because she always encountered the 'Muslim question' ('Why do you do this?'). She says:

> When I was in 4th grade, my father told me to start wearing my hijab. I would make up excuses, I was so scared. So instead I wore the cap. People asked me, 'What's on your head?' And then it kept going. In the 5th grade, I will go in a room and pray. And then I wouldn't pray at school. I would just wait until I get home.
>
> When I was in 6th grade, I would fast during Ramadan. They'd go, 'Why are you not eating?' I'm like, 'I'm sick, I don't feel like eating'. Or when I don't eat pork, they go, 'Why don't you eat pork?' I'm like, 'I'm allergic'.

I actually started wearing my hijab last year. That's when my parents sent me to this [Islamic] school. I was very shy to be Muslim. But now I am confident, and now I wear my hijab. (Personal interview with the author)

Rabab was placed in a difficult situation. Her parents wanted her to endorse a Muslim identity through her *hijab*. But stereotypes against Muslims deterred Rabab from exhibiting her Muslim identity in public spaces. Later, in the Islamic school she was happy to wear her *hijab* and felt proud of her collective Muslim identity. On her hopes, Rabab said, 'I want to be a paediatrician and a motivational speaker in the media'.

Religiosity and Civic Behaviour

As discussed earlier that some contemporary events and issues in Australia (for example, the Cronulla riots) and the United States (Major Nidal Hasan's Fort Hood shooting incident) brought the 'Muslim question' to the fore. In the following section, through their diverse opinions, the participants showed that they were alert to the issues pertaining to the 'Muslim question'. It may have impacted on their Muslim identity formation. However, some participants did not specifically mention their Muslim identity but through their interviews, they demonstrated that they were vigilant of the contemporary issues concerning Muslims.

AUSTRALIA

Hashim, of Turkish heritage, 17 years old, identified himself as 'Muslim', and was also a *Hafiz-e-Qur'an* (memorized the Qur'an). He hoped to become an imam. On the Cronulla riots, Hashim said, 'I think the Lebanese people should become better Muslims. So if the teenagers aren't that good, they would also drink, they would always do these *haram* acts.' Then Hashim connected his Muslim identity to the broader *umma* (Islamic community transcending all national boundaries) identity when he said, 'Especially in Palestine and Iraq there are a lot of poor people. We should help them with money because we are their brothers in Islam.' Hashim considered mosques to be proper channels to send charity to the Muslim countries. Perhaps, Hashim was not aware that the 'Muslim question' has labelled some mosques as 'Other' institutions that are viewed with suspicion (Dunn, Klocker, and Salabay 2007: 565–9; Peucker and Akbarzadeh 2014: 152–5). While connecting his Muslim identity with the broader *umma* identity, Hashim brought to the fore the Australian and US foreign policy in the Middle East as a contemporary issue that can impact on the collective Muslim identity.

Another participant, Mateen of Tunisian background, age 16, identified himself as Australian-Tunisian, but his religiosity was exposed when he was critical of the Muslim rioters at Cronulla Beach, 'The riots there … it's quite disgraceful. I mean the Prophet (Muhammad, Peace Be Upon Him) always teaches to have restraint and to be a good believer and display the best of manners. If you do that kind of stuff you're only going to make the damage [to Muslim reputation] more.'

Mateen continued, 'Muslims have been put under the microscopes [by the media] quite a bit. I think as Muslims we should also be smart about it. I mean of course there is that negative media attention; however, for Muslims it's important that we are wise and just because if they look at us it's important that we display the best behaviour.'

On his hopes, Mateen said, 'My dream is to diminish poverty, study management and become a pilot'.

The next participant, Marium age 18, identity Australian-Albanian, observed that the territorial claim by Lebanese Australians and Anglo-Australians for Cronulla Beach had no logical basis, as Indigenous Australians were the original owners of the land. She explains, 'We're living in a multicultural country, we should all respect one another. We all came from different countries, no one owns this land besides the Aboriginals. So we should all be friendly and leave the past behind whatever has happened ….'

By holding the Australian flag Anglo-Australians and Cronulla residents claimed their exclusive territorial rights over the Cronulla space (see Figure 6.1). On the 'us–them' dichotomy that emerged in the conflict over the space at Cronulla Beach, Marium concluded that respect for one another should be the key, and we all should move forward.

On the al-Hilali issue, Erphan of Egyptian heritage, 17 years old, notes:

> I think what happened with the whole story behind what he said was that I find it is hard to translate something 100 per cent correctly from one language to another. There's always going to be a difference in the context. I think he meant only to say in a nice way, but it came out to the community in a wrong way, that's why everyone got offended. (Personal interview with author)

FIGURE **6.1**   Contestation over the Cronulla Beach space between Anglo-Australians and Lebanese Australians, December 2005
Reproduced with permission from: © Andrew Meares, *Sydney Morning Herald*. 11 December (2005). Fairfax Media Publications Pty Limited.

Erphan identified himself as Australian-Egyptian. Al-Hilali was of Egyptian heritage as well. So Erphan understood that sometimes the nuances of the Arabic language can be lost in translation. However, Mateen of Tunisian heritage also spoke Arabic at home, noted the importance of English language skills in Australia. He suggested that Muslim leaders should speak fluent English to counteract the misconceptions surrounding the 'Muslim question'.

USA

In America, Faizul of Bangladeshi heritage identified himself as, 'I am Muslim, a slave of Allah'. On his hope, Faizul said, 'My dream is to establish social order on this earth'.

Like the previous participant, Hashim in Australia, Faizul also included contemporary issues such as US foreign policy that can impact on the collective Muslim identity. While identifying himself as a Muslim Faizul did not confine himself to his own religious circle. He explains:

I consider myself a slave of Allah, working for Allah towards any human being … if there's an accident outside my road, or outside right now in the building, I'm not going to sit here and identify this individual as Christian or Jew, I'm going to identify them as human and that is why Allah has sent Prophet Muhammad (PBUH) to serve the humanity. (Personal interview with author)

By referring to Prophet Muhammad's acts to serve humanity Faizul embraced broader inclusive thinking, being willing to serve all people including Christians and Jews. At the same time Faizul expressed his ideological battle with the American system: the American media, the Federal Bureau of Investigation (FBI), American foreign policy, and American democracy. He elaborates:

If my ideologies or my beliefs come in contradiction of what American ideologies are, I'm sorry, I'm going to take my belief before my culture. American media is always negative on Muslims. For example, whenever they're allowed they would make fun of prophets and messengers but whenever you make a comment about Israel they're really mad and they're really scared … CNN [is] an example, Fox too. (Personal interview with author)

Further on the media, Faizul said, 'For example, look at what's going on at Guantanamo. There are so many tortures and oppression but none of it the media showed, nobody revealed it.' Faizul thought the American media did not report international news accurately, saying, 'Look what happened in Iraq, in Afghanistan. They always hide things, they always do undercover things. Why should I believe what they tell me about Fort Hood shooting?' Then Faizul spoke of FBI's raid on a Christian militia in March 2010 and compared it with the heavy-handedness of the FBI in Imam Luqman's case. He remarked, 'Well, hello! What happened to Imam Luqman? How come you guys (FBI) shot him down. Nineteen times, yes. It doesn't make sense. Logically, it doesn't make sense.'

Faizul questioned the selective reporting of the US media and law enforcement agencies on the subject matter of Muslims confined in Guantanamo Bay and the mysterious death of Imam Luqman (Kabir 2014b: 132–41, 165–74). Similarly, another participant in this study, Ata, was also bewildered by the mysterious death of Imam Luqman. Ata, 16 years, identified as, 'I'm Muslim first, African American citizen'. He hoped to do, 'Something in the medical field'. Ata spoke of Imam Luqman:

That was actually my imam. I used to attend his *masjid* [mosque] when we first moved here. So my family knew him. I knew him very well. *Al-hamdulillah*, he was a really loved and respected brother. I never witnessed or heard about him doing anything illegal. So the accusations they put against him, I didn't really believe them to be true. But Allah knows. (Personal interview with author)

In his book *The Muslims are Coming*, Kundnani discussed the heavy-handedness of the FBI agents who killed Imam Luqman. Kundnani observed that an indictment was issued against Imam Luqman the day before his raid, charging him with conspiracy to sell stolen goods, firearm possession, and alteration to a vehicle identification number (2014: 1–6). However, no terrorism-related charges were brought against him. The indictment only included claims based on the reports by the FBI-paid infiltrators of conversations in which Imam Luqman had advocated the spread of Islam through *jihad* against the US. The killing of Imam Luqman did not receive extensive media coverage (Kundnani 2014: 1–6).

The next participant, Iqra of Yemeni heritage, age 17, identified herself as 'Muslim, Arab American'. She hoped for a 'Good career, get married and be a good mother'. On the Fort Hood shooting case, Iqra stated, 'But what I read is that the man who was shooting was a psychologist. I think the only reason why he did it is because he just listened to too many depressed people and I guess he just couldn't take it anymore.'

Faizul endorsed a single Muslim identity and Iqra had multiple identities, but both were critical of American foreign policy, and were sympathetic to problems Muslims faced.

The Media Question

I have discussed earlier in the 'Contemporary Events and Issues section', that the rise of Islamophobia since 11 September 2001, and bias media representation of Islam and Muslims can bring at the fore the 'Muslim question' again—'Who are these people', 'What do they want', 'Will they ever integrate'? In the following section, participants in Australia and the US have shared their opinion on how some media can invigorate the 'Muslim question'.

Australia

Some participants discussed how the media has been keen to use Islamic words, and how it links perpetrators of crimes to Arabs or Muslims through names. For example, Erphan, of Egyptian heritage, observed that, 'There was one time I remember on the news they gave a completely wrong definition of *jihad*. As Muslims, we know that *jihad* is committing a sacrifice for the sake of Allah and that doesn't mean blowing up buildings or killing innocent people. Like when they claimed that September 11 was *jihad*, that's very incorrect'.

Academics such as Ramadan have observed that *jihad* is an Arabic word that has several meanings. It works on a spiritual level as well as on a broader level (2004: 113). On the very basic spiritual level, it means working on and managing one's self and ego and working towards positive things. On the social level, it is a struggle for justice and fair treatment, and against discrimination. On the political level, it is the defence of civil responsibilities and rights, on the economic level, it is action against neo-colonialism, and on the cultural level it is the promotion of human dignity and values. Erphan's perception of *jihad* focused on spirituality, for example, practising the five pillars of Islam. So he could not relate to the broader meaning of *jihad*. Erphan also noted:

> The media don't exactly say that Muslims did it. They'll start off as by saying 'these terrorists'. They'll claim first that they were terrorist attacks and slowly they'll build up that they were from an 'Arab' background or 'half Arab, half Australian' background so they emphasize too much that it's the 'Arabs' that they're picking on. And then maybe they'll say, okay nah this person's name was Mohammad, like Haneef, for example. (Personal interview with author)

Erphan made the point that some media immediately jumps to the conclusion that the perpetrator must be an Arab or a Muslim by naming them 'Mohammad' and 'Haneef'. He thought, with Dr Mohamed Haneef's name, people will immediately assume he is a Muslim.

USA

Sensational news reports about Muslims led some participants to believe in conspiracy theories.Iqra, age 17, identity Yemeni, believed that media stories about Muslims were a plot. She believes that, When somebody bombs a place, first they'll say it's a group of Muslim terrorists, or Arabs ... there might be a lot of Arabs and Muslims that do these stuff. But sometimes it just sounds like a plot ... it's like everything was planned. I don't like the media, I really don't.'

Similarly, Rabab of West African background age 15, identity Muslim African American thought that the news about Abdulmutallab (the 'Underwear Bomber') was not real. She observes:

> I watched the news ... The Christmas one, who put a bomb, I think in his pants. 'Boom, boom, boom, we saved the day'. Like, 'Oh, my God, this Muslim is about to do this, but we saved the day'. I'm starting to question, are these real? Are they setting up stuff to make a big scene, like in books and movies? 'We saved the day?' That's what I'm trying to understand. (Personal interview with author)

In the midst of so much media stereotyping about Muslims, Rabab thought that the reporting about Abdulmutallab also contained the conventional tone of 'We [the West] saved the day'.

Eliman, who identified herself as Yemeni American, age 26, worked in a school. However, she hoped to get a nursing degree. Eliman noted that the media has been keen to connect Muslim news with suspicion. She remarked:

> There is actually one incident that just happened very recently to somebody let's say neighbour from my own village. Her son was playing outside with a couple of kids. She takes perfect care of them. Her son fell off of the back porch and he fell on concrete. He had some trauma to his head, little swollen. He was taken to the ER (emergency department) of their local clinic. Eventually this kid passed away.
>
> I cannot forget how the media portrayed this incident. The police did a full investigation to make sure that if the boy was being abused. The three news stations were staked outside the house videotaping who goes in, who goes out, and at the end they found nothing and they just said it was just an accident.... The mother of the boy was about 28 years old, the media said that she was 18 in the news. I don't know why it's relevant to mention that she wears a full head *burqa*. (Personal interview with author)

This incident was also discussed by another participant of Bangladeshi heritage, Sami who lived in the same neighbourhood. He discussed how much anxiety some media can cause to Muslims who were already grieving the loss of a family member.

FIGURE 6.2   Homegrown terror
Source: *Muslim Observer* (15 March 2010).

Reproduced with permission from: © Khalil Bendib, http://www.bendib.com. All rights reserved.

There were three cases of homegrown terrorism in the US in 2009 and 2010 (as depicted in Figure 6.2). On 18 February 2010 Joseph Andrew Stack crashed a plane into the Internal Revenue Service building where 190 employees were working. On 4 March 2010 John Patrick Bedell shot and wounded two Pentagon police officers at a security checkpoint in the Pentagon station in Arlington County, Virginia. But the news media went overboard with Nidal Hasan's horrendous Fort Hood shooting incident in 2009 (Kabir 2014b: 123–41, 2017: 119–48).

Racial profiling, 9/11

In the Australian context, some scholars have observed that in times of local and national crises between Muslims and non-Muslims, for example, the Cronulla riots, the category of the 'Arab Other' shifts to the 'Muslim Other', from racialization to Islamophobia. Arabs (marked as 'Middle Eastern' appearance) and Muslims (marked through their Islamic visibility) are considered a political threat in the mainstream civic and media discourses (Johns 2015; Kabir 2007). In the Australian context (discussed as follows), the 'Muslim question' (the 'Other' or 'the immediate threat') can arise either with overt Islamic appearance or a Muslim-sounding name.

AUSTRALIA

Erphan recalled the impact of 9/11 on the Muslim community. He says:

> It had a big impact on our school. We had a lot of people come in to our school and threatening to kill us and threatening to plant bombs in our school and I was very young at the time, and it was a shock. Because our girl students they wear the *hijab* and there was a group of students that took the train and the train conductor didn't want them on the train. He kicked them off because he goes "I don't want terrorists on my train".
>
> But then the company contacted the school and they apologized on his behalf. They got rid of him. So it did cause a few problems, but *Al-hamdulillah* I think now Muslims are being accepted a lot more. (Personal interview with author)

Although Erphan identified himself as Australian Egyptian, when he said 'our girl students ... wear the *hijab*', his Muslim 'self' came to the fore.

USA

In the US context, some participants added 'racial profiling' to the 'Muslim question', for example, 'they [the Muslims] look different', 'their way of life is different', and 'they pose a security threat' so they should be treated as the 'other'.

Ayman, 16 years old, identified himself as African American. On his hopes and dreams, Ayman said, 'My goal is to be a better Muslim, a good job and make a lot of money'. Ayman's 'Muslim self' spoke of the challenges some Muslims faced even before 9/11. Ayman says:

> It was difficult before 9/11 because when you have to go to work and you have to pray, and everybody doesn't know what you're doing. They're looking at you, what is that guy doing and stuff like that.
>
> But after 9/11, I think it just got even harder, because now people are looking at us like we're the bad people, like we're terrorists. I don't think that's right. (Personal interview with author)

Ayman may have heard about Muslim prayer issues before 9/11 from his father but after 9/11 he faced similar experiences to Muslims viewed as the 'Other'. Mansouri and Wood observed that the Islamic totality that is associated with violence, oppression, and terror was construed in the western imagination well before 11 September 2001 (Mansouri and Wood 2008: 120).

Razzak, of Bangladeshi heritage, age 18, identified himself as 'more Bangladeshi', shared an incident that happened to his father at the airport. He elaborates:

> My dad was going to Hajj and he had a beard and a turban [*topi*—Muslim cap]. But when he was going they stopped him in New York and they searched him for three hours, they made him miss his flight … So he had to get back on track and get new flights and that cost him more than $500. (Personal interview with author)

The 'Muslim question' has generated concerns among some Muslims, leading Razzak to hope, 'I hope Islam and racial, ethnic background of Muslims is accepted in America very easily, just like the African Americans were accepted 50 or 60 years ago'. The next participant, Ata, age 16, identity African American, said that his 'biggest role model' was Malcolm X. Ata was proud of his Islamic heritage but he was distressed about his mother being racially profiled in public spaces because of her *hijab*. He remarks:

> My mother, she was going to take a trip to Washington, DC. And she was going through security check, her bags, they do the standard procedure. But then, they took her in the back to check her some more. And they actually told her to remove her scarf. Then she told her religion, you're not supposed to remove it for another brother. So they sent a female security. But that's like on my own personal experience … I've heard about other people's stories, but that's my own personal story. (Personal interview with author)

Some airports have introduced a full-body scanner, which some Muslim women who value the notion of conservative clothing or *purdah* find offensive. Duaa 18 years, identity Muslim, Bengali American, stated that, 'Honestly, I think manual checking with the metal detectors is enough … I heard a lot of people complaining … that's going too far was the body scanners. They practically look at you and practically strip you down. I think that's too much, like violation of someone's privacy'.

Later, Duaa connected racial profiling with race and religion stating:

I think they're just making Muslims look really bad. Making the non-Muslims hate us. Trying to slowly kick us out of their country. Yeah, I know this Bengali family. They were deported.

They were here for a couple years, and they had their papers and everything. A lot of people came, about 200 people, and they tried so hard to stay, but they got kicked out. They weren't citizens. They were trying to apply, but they wouldn't let them.

They are Muslims. That might be why. Because I believe that if it was someone from Bosnia or Albania, from a European country, that wouldn't have happened to them. Because that only happens very rarely to Europeans if they do something to get kicked out. But honestly, like Arabs, Bengalis, the Muslim races, even if you don't do anything and you're a good citizen, they'll find a reason to get you. (Personal interview with author)

Reflecting on the 'Muslim question', Duaa believed that Muslims were not seen as a desirable group of immigrants compared to Europeans. She equated Muslims to a 'race' who were susceptible to deportation because they were not considered ideal citizens. Duaa hoped 'To go to the university and become a registered nurse'.

Research has found that the lives of Muslims (and Arabs) in America have become exceedingly difficult because of the Patriot Act. It allows law enforcement agencies to use surveillance, and to search and deport people suspected of terrorism-related acts (Smith 2010: 186–8).

The next participant, Iqra, spoke of her mother's incident with the police. Her mother wore the *niqab/burqa* [head and face covering] and she thought that she was treated differently. She explains,

My mom, she covers her face, and when she drives around usually the police, if they're standing there, they'll pay more attention to her noticeably. She gets scared and asks us, "Hey, are you guys buckled up?" She's trying to check, "did I pass a stop sign or something?"

My mother got into an accident once on the highway, and it was a Mexican guy. Actually, he stopped and she came down. She starts writing his license number and she calls the police. And then when they're on their way, he runs away. But she did get his license plate number.

And then they [the police] took it and said, "We'll search and we'll find him". It's been about six months, and she's always calling them. I guess they just never cared to look for him … Because she was covered.

Like it was her fault. And it was actually the guy who crashed her from the back. (Personal interview with author)

Iqra's mother's story reveals that perhaps the police were concerned about security or they were not interested in the cases of people who looked culturally different. I have heard similar stories in Britain where a Somali participant said that the police were reluctant to attend to their cases because of their colour (Kabir 2012: 84).

Analysis and Discussion

The study for this chapter was conducted in two schools in Victoria (Australia) and Michigan (USA). Both the schools were located in socio-economically disadvantaged areas. Both places had different contemporary events and issues at different periods. For example, in Australia, the interviews were conducted in 2006–07, and in the US it was done in 2009–11. Yet the contemporary events generated concerns and emotions of the participants and that impacted on my participants' identity / identities. Common themes that came out of the 'Muslim question' in both places were Islamophobia, media stereotype, racial profiling, vilification of Muslim women, and excessive force of law enforcement agencies against some Muslims.

Therefore, the 'Muslim question' is imbued with misconceptions about Muslims that they are the dangerous 'other'. To counter the stereotypes of the Australian participants, for example, Mateen suggested that their fellow Muslims should exhibit their best behaviour and become model citizens. In the US, racial profiling was not only limited to immigrant Muslims but included African-American Muslims. In this context, for example, Ata spoke of his family's experience. The use of excessive force by law enforcement agencies, for example, in Imam Luqman's case created concerns in the Muslim community.

Young Muslims in both countries questioned government policies and the media's subjectivity on issues relating to Muslims. Some participants did not specifically mention their Muslim identity, but when they spoke of issues that were dear to them, their Muslim identity crystallized. Some participants, for example, Faizul were critical of their countries' foreign policy such as that relating to Iraq. But all participants expressed the critical view that the media did not represent Muslims fairly. Overall, the participants in both countries were not distressed over the 'Muslim question'. Through their bicultural skills, for example, the participants had a solid footing in their ethnic culture (native language) and Islamic culture (for example, *Eid* celebration), and mainstream culture (English language and sports).They appeared to be hopeful and have optimistic view of the future.

Studies by Melucci and Gregg demonstrate that bicultural individuals can shift identities between the cultural frames of in-groups and out-groups with relative ease (Gregg 2007: 210–11; Melucci 1997; see also Kabir 2014b: 210–11). That is, a bicultural identity caters for emotional tensions and creates a sense of adaptability (Gregg 2007: 19). Melucci observed that a (bicultural) self-identity becomes a dynamic system defined by recognizable opportunities and constraints (1997: 64). Identity is both a system and a process, because the field is defined by recognizable opportunities and is simultaneously able to intervene to act upon and restructure itself. Two crucial and perplexing questions arise here: the continuity of the self and the boundaries of the self. The question is one of deciding where the subject of action begins and where it ends and how a person is likely to adapt to a new culture. Mellucci (1197: 65) noted that an individual's (bicultural) identity floats within the primary bonds of belonging, like kinship or local and geographical ties (family, community, country of origin, and place of residence). Schwartz and Unger observed that fully bicultural individuals, for example those who have integrated their Hispanic and American cultural streams, reported the highest level of familial ethnic socialization. Individuals characterized as separated reported somewhat lower levels of familial ethnic socialization, and those characterized as assimilated with only one American identity reported among the lowest levels of familial ethnic socialization (Schwartz and Unger 2010: 28). Tadmor, Galanisky, and Muddux noted that at the professional level, working with the mainstream population, bicultural individuals have achieved higher promotion rates and more positive reputations compared with assimilated or separated individuals (2012). The participants in this study have allowed themselves to maintain their own culture and religion and also engage with the second culture, that is the mainstream American/Australian culture, for example, sports and other extracurricular activities, so their cross-cultural transition and adaptation, have assisted them to cope with the 'Muslim question' (see also Chen 2015; Kabir 2017).

Combating Terrorism and Islamophobia

The 'Muslim question' is an ongoing issue. With the advent of ISIL, Australian Muslims have been drawing more media attention. In August 2014 Australian Prime Minister Tony Abbott announced that the Australian government would introduce a series of counter-terrorism measures to give security agencies the resources and legislative powers to combat homegrown terrorism and to punish Australians who participate in overseas terrorist activities. The Muslim community denounced these proposed 'anti-terror' laws because giving excessive power to law enforcement agencies would be an infringement of civil liberties. Muslim leaders were also critical of Mr Abbott's divisive 'us' and 'them' comments when he said, 'Everyone has got to be on team Australia', and 'you don't migrate to this country unless you want to join our team' (Chen 2015).[1]

In the US, Islamophobic incidents have been happening in several states. On 20 March 2011, Terry Jones, pastor of a church in Gainesville in Florida, presided over a mock trial of the Qur'an inside his church where an assistant pastor burned a copy of the Qur'an. This incident led to a violent protest in Afghanistan, resulting in the deaths of 24 people (Kabir 2014b: 22). On 10 February 2015, three Muslim Americans were shot dead allegedly by their non-Muslim neighbour in North Carolina. Two victims wore headscarves (Kabir 2017: 147). In December 2015, during his election campaign the Republican candidate Donald Trump promised to ban all Muslims from entering the United States (Robbins 2015).

In June 2017, the US Supreme Court allowed a limited version of the Trump administration's Muslim ban executive orders. The ban prohibits migrants from six countries—Syria, Sudan, Somalia, Libya, Iran, and Yemen—from entering the country without an established, significant connection to the United States. The CAIR National Executive Director Nihad Awad commented, 'By arbitrarily dividing American Muslims

---

[1] *'Islamic Council Pulls out of Talks', The Advocate*, p. 15 (2014).

from their grandparents and other close relatives overseas, the Trump administration's new rules violate the Supreme Court's decision'. Awad said, 'These illogical rules must not stand, nor should any other part of the discriminatory and unconstitutional Muslim ban'. The CAIR National Litigation Director Lena Masri said, 'We call on the Trump administration to withdraw these irrational guidelines, as well as the entire Muslim ban. We can protect our nation without harming its values or reputation.' Masri further said, 'We will not hesitate to file a legal challenge to any violations of the court's decision'.[2]

On the other hand, since President Trump's election victory on 8 November 2016, there has been an upsurge of hate crime against some Muslim Americans.[3] CAIR's quarterly report indicated that the number of hate crimes in the first half of 2017 increased 91 percent compared to the same period in 2016, which was the worst year for such anti-Muslim incidents since the civil rights organization began its current documenting system in 2013. The number of bias incidents in 2017 also increased by 24 per cent compared to the first half of 2016. The most frequent type of incidents documented by CAIR in the second quarter of 2017 were harassment, in the form of a non-violent or non-threatening incident. The second type of bias incidents were hate crimes that have involved physical violence or property damage. Some attacks occurred through a trigger, for example, a Muslim woman's headscarf was a trigger in 15 per cent of incidents.[4]

While in Australia, the emergence of ISIL has increased Islamophobia, particularly attacks on visible Muslim women wearing *hijab*. In 2014–16, a Muslim woman reported that, 'they [the perpetrators] yelled out "ISIS B****""go back to where you came from" and snickered and said "shh or she'll behead you"'. The Muslim woman said, 'They followed me down the street. None of the train staff helped me out or stopped

---

[2] 'CAIR Decries Trump Administration's New "Muslim Ban" Guidelines, Promises Legal Challenge', 29 June 2017. Available at: https://www.cair.com. Accessed on 26 July 2017.

[3] 'CAIR Sends Letter to FBI Director Comey', *CAIR.com*. 28 November 2016.

[4] 'CAIR Report Shows 2017 on Track to Becoming One of Worst Years Ever for Anti-Muslim Hate Crimes', 17 July 2017. Available at: https://www.cair.com. Accessed on 26 July 2017.

them'. Another woman said she was nine months pregnant and pushing a pram with her daughter inside when a drunk man shouted at her 'Be careful!! She's going to bomb us!' (Begley 2017). A 2017 report on Islamophobia in Australia noted that the perpetrator were mostly Anglo-Celtic Australian males.[5]

Since the 'Muslim question' is surrounded by Islamophobia, media representation of Islam and Muslims, and divisive political rhetoric, young Muslim participants in this chapter have been vigilant about issues concerning their faith. However, under the current uncertain social and political climate when some Muslims are viewed with suspicion, and Islamophobic incidents have reached its record high both in Australia and the US, it is important to boost young Muslims confidence and self-esteem. Young Muslims should be provided opportunities for sports, music, debate, and intercultural dialogues. Schools should provide opportunities for dialogue between Islamic organizations and Muslim students. Some new Muslim immigrants experience culture shock when they migrate to the western countries, and impose cultural restrictions on their children (Kabir 2017: 66–118). Under the circumstances, Muslim parents should encourage their children to socialize with non-Muslim children for a better Muslim and non-Muslim understanding. Biculturalism should be considered cultural capital that is necessary for a cohesive society.

References

Ahmed, Zia. 2017. 'Islamophobia in Australia Report Launch', *Australian Muslim Times*, 20 July. Available at: http://www.amust.com.au. Accessed on 26 July 2017.

Australian Bureau of Statistics. 2017. 'Census: Religion', Media Release, http://www.abs.gov.au/ See Australian Bureau of Statistics, 2016 Census: Religion, 27 June 2017, Media Release. Available at http://www.abs.gov.au. Accessed on 26 July 2017.

Begley, Patrick. 2017. 'Women Bear the Brunt of Islamophobia: Charles Sturt University Report', *Sydney Morning Herald*, 9 July.

Burke, Daniel. 2015. 'Threats, Harassment,Vandalism at Mosques Reach Record High', *CNN.com*, 11 December 2015. Available at: http://edition.cnn.com. Accessed on 26 July 2017.

[5] 'Launch of first-of-its-kind Report on Islamophobia in Australia', 10 July 2017. Available at: http://news.csu.edu.au. Accessed on 26 July 2017.

Burke, Peter and Jan Stets. 2009. *Identity Theory*. New York: Oxford University Press.

Chen, Sylvia Xiaohua. 2015. 'Toward a Social Psychology of Bilingualism and Biculturalism', *Asian Journal of Social Psychology* 18, pp. 1–11.

Dunn, Kevin, Natascha Klocker, and Tanya Salabay. 2007. 'Contemporary Racism and Islamophobia in Australia: Racializing Religion', *Ethnicities* 7(4): 564–89.

Esposito, John L. and Ibrahim Kalin (eds.) 2011. *Islamophobia: The Challenge of Pluralism in the 21st Century*. New York: Oxford University Press.

Glaser, Barney and Anselm Strauss. 1967. *The Discovery of Grounded Theory: Strategies for Qualitative Research*. Chicago: Aldine.

Gregg, Gary S. 2007. *Culture and Identity in a Muslim Society*. Oxford: Oxford University Press.

Haddad, Yvonne. 2011. *Becoming Americans? The Forging of Arab and Muslim Identity in Pluralist America*. Waco, Texas: Baylor University Press.

Hall, Stuart. 1994. *Polity Reader in Cultural Theory*. Cambridge: Polity Press.

Jenkins, Richard. 2008. *Social Identity*. London: Routledge, 3rd edn.

Johns, Amelia. 2015. *Battle for the Flag*. Melbourne: Melbourne University Press.

Kabir, Nahid. 2006. 'Representation of Islam and Muslims in the Australian Media, 2001–2005', *Journal of Muslim Minority Affairs* 26(3, December): 313–28.

———. 2007. 'The Cronulla Riot: How One Newspaper Represented the Event'. In *Public Sociologies: Lessons and Trans-Tasman Comparisons*, B. Curtis, S. Mathewman and T. McIntosh (eds). TASA/SAANZ Conference, Department of Sociology, The University of Auckland, 4–7 December. Available at: https://www.tasa.org.au/wp-content/uploads/2008/12/268.pdf. Accessed on 26 July 2017.

———. 2008a. 'Globalised Islam: Does It Have any Impact on Australian Muslim Youth', *The International Journal of Diversity in Organisations, Communities & Nations* 8(2): 37–46.

———. 2008b. 'Media Is One-sided in Australia: The Muslim Youth Perspective', *Journal of Children and Media* 2(3): 267–81.

———. 2012. *Young British Muslims: Identity, Culture, Politics and the Media*. Edinburgh: Edinburgh University Press.

———. 2014a. 'Free Speech: Creating the "Us and-Them" Debate'. In *Freedom of Speech and Islam*, E. Kolig (ed.), pp. 163–86. London: Routledge.

———. 2014b. *Young American Muslims: Dynamics of Identity*. Edinburgh: Edinburgh University Press.

———. 2015. 'The Cronulla Riots: Muslims' Place in the White Imaginary Spatiality', *Contemporary Islam: Dynamics of Muslim Life* 9(3): 1–20.

———. 2016a. 'Muslim Women in Australia, Britain and the United States: The Role of "Othering" and Biculturalism in Identity Formation', *Journal of Muslim Minority Affairs* 36(4): 1–17.

————. 2016b. 'The Road to a Transcultural America: The Case of American Muslim Girls', *Journal of Intercultural Studies* 37(3): 250–64.

————. 2017. *Muslim Americans: Debating the Notions of American and Un-American*. London: Routledge.

Kundnani, Arun. 2014. *The Muslims are Coming! Islamophobia, Extremism, and the Domestic War on Terror*. London: Verso.

Mansouri, Fethi and Sally Wood. 2008. *Identity, Education and Belonging: Arab and Muslim Youth in Contemporary Australia*. Melbourne: Melbourne University Press.

Mohamed, Besheer. 2016. 'A New Estimate of the Muslim Population', Pew Research Center, 6 January. Available at: http://www.pewresearch.org. Accessed on 26 July 2017.

Melucci, Alberto. 1997. 'Identity and Difference in a Globalized World'. In *Debating Cultural Hybridity: Multi-Cultural Identities and the Politics of Anti-Racism*, Pnina Werbner and Tariq Modood (eds), pp. 58–69. London: Zed Books.

Peucker, Mario and Shahram Akbarzadeh. 2014. *Muslims Active Citizenship in the West*. London: Routledge.

Rahman, Shafiqur. 2011. *Bangladeshi Diaspora in the United States after 9/11*. El Paso, Texas: LFB Scholarly Publishing LLC.

Ramadan, Tariq. 2004. *Western Muslims and the Future of Islam*. Oxford: Oxford University Press.

Robbins, Liz. 2015. 'Queens Muslims Urge Trump, "Come Back Home"', *New York Times*, 9 December, p. A12.

Schwartz, Seth J. and Jennifer B. Unger. 2010. 'Biculturalism and Context: What is Biculturalism, and When Is It Adaptive: Commentary on Mistry and Wu', *Human Development* 53: 26–32.

Smith, Jane. 2010. *Islam in America*, 2nd edition. New York: Columbia University Press.

Tadmor, Carmit T., Adam D. Galanisky, and William W. Maddux. 2012. 'Getting the Most Out of Living Abroad: Biculturalism and Integrative Complexity as Key Drivers of Creative and Professional Success', *Journal of Personality and Social Psychology* 103(3): 520–42.

7

JAN A. ALI
DREW COTTLE

Islam–West Relations and the Rise of Muslim Radicalism and Global Jihadism

Muslim radicalism and global jihadism are borne out of a negative and destructive Muslim experience of Islam-West interaction. They are the consequences of past European colonial rule, expressions of the crisis of modernity and identity, and reflect a deep pervasive disenchantment and disillusionment with a material modernity. We argue in this chapter that Muslim radicalism and global jihadism are a reaction to the consequences of European colonialism and the way the West through its international relations and foreign policies presently treats Muslim nation-states and their impact on ordinary Muslims in the broader society.

Muslim radicalism and global jihadism are new phenomena in over fourteen hundred years of Muslim history. In the climate of European colonialism and imperialism, Muslim radicalism and global jihadism first began to ferment. Two hundred years later these forces catalysed in two momentous events—in the final decades of the twentieth century in the Iranian Revolution (Esposito 1990), and at the beginning of the twenty-first century with the calamity of 11 September 2001 (el-Aswad 2013).

Muslim radicalism and global jihadism are borne out of a negative and destructive Muslim experience of Islam-West[1] interaction. The era of European colonialism had a profound impact on the Muslim world and Islam-West relations. It carved out large Muslim territories governed by different Muslim empires into economically and politically weak Muslim territorial entities condemning them to remain under-developed corrupt authoritarian regimes (Owen 2002). The colonial powers steered away from the role of nation-building and the institutionalization of politics in the Muslim protectorates. European colonial history reveals a systematic exploitation of the Muslim protectorates and a 'divide and conquer' strategy which assumed an innate cultural superiority. The colonial powers were never concerned with the material lives of their Muslim subjects. Throughout the Muslim world from West Africa, North Africa and the Middle East to Central Asia and the islands of Indonesia, and the Southern Philippines, the various colonial state formations were structured to both maintain political dominance and to ensure the economic exploitation of the people and their natural resources. In the long period of decolonization after World War II, the emergent postcolonial Muslim regimes of the Third World were left with the mammoth task of nation-building. They inherited the legacy of the colonial state formation and faced the task of transitioning their societies from the condition of political subjection to a new Muslim or Islamic political paradigm.

These newly independent Muslim nation states had to endure or adapt to the experience of US global hegemony and the international politics of the Cold War. The US dominance in the Muslim world loomed large. Every national leader, government, or movement in Muslim majority countries were pressured, persuaded, or acquiesced into lending their support and allegiance to the US for the execution of its foreign policy ambition to either contain (as in Turkey, Iran, and Iraq) or confront and defeat (as in Afghanistan) the Soviet Union. In various major Muslim states throughout Greater Asia, American power

[1] The West primarily refers, despite their political diversity and minor social and cultural differences, to Western European, North American, and Australasian nationstates as a unified political and military coalition that functions particularly since the Second World War under the 'stewardship' of the United States.

was dominant but Washington failed to establish good governance in them (Fawcett 2005). In many cases, the US did the exact opposite: by supporting, for example, the Shah of Iran who ruled an authoritarian regime until the 1978 Islamic Revolution and in Pakistan where General Zia ul-Haq staged a military coup which ended its civilian-government.

The colonial subjugation of the Muslim world left generations of Muslims feeling that there was a continuous Western onslaught against their country, identity, culture, religion, and the way of life. Many, both in the Muslim world and the West, found European colonialism and American imperialism to have produced and sustained a clash between Islam and the Christian West. Muslims today see that European colonial powers attempted to totally transform their everyday life based on the Islamic religion to a way of life where secular principles replaced Muslim identity and culture with Western norms and values. European colonialism and its successor, American imperialism, have brought the Muslim world into a deepening state of crisis.

Muslim radicalism and global jihadism are the consequences of past European colonial rule and continuing American domination which have reproduced poor social and economic conditions where poverty and economic deprivation persist. The Muslim world is caught in a spiral of underdevelopment resulting from rapid change and modernization igniting disaffection and disorientation amongst its young who often constitute the largest sector of the population (Milton-Edwards 2000). These social reactions are understood by many Muslims as attempts to complete the process of self-determination and freedom from Western colonial subjugation. Muslim radicalism and global jihadism are expressions of the crisis of modernity and identity. They reflect a deep pervasive disenchantment and disillusionment with a modernity that reduces life to a reductionist calculus, as a transitional outcome controlled through rationality, science, and technology in which religion and the sacred have no place. Existentially, these twin social forces of Muslim radicalism and global jihadism are not merely the political responses to the poverty, illiteracy, disparity, repression, and disaffection of the Muslim world but also the perceived injustices, religious and cultural prejudices, and the expression of sympathy with victims of brutal regimes and disenfranchised and marginalized Muslims everywhere.

The emergence of Muslim radicalism and global jihadism are the creation of multifaceted and multidimensional problems that are deeply rooted in European colonialism. The consequences of colonialism had included decades of despotic regimes, religious oppression, and the segregation of religion and state politics in Muslim societies. Intervention in Muslim politics by European colonial powers and, later, by the United States saw one-sided Islam-West relations prevail. This chapter examines the rise of Muslim radicalism and global jihadism in the context of these one-sided Islam-West relations. The crisis of modernity also provides an important context for this chapter, with poverty, unemployment, illiteracy, prejudices, and marginalization feeding the roots of these phenomena. Islamist authenticity is the key to understanding the political aspirations of many in the Muslim world. The concept of Islamist authenticity refers to the shaping of social, economic, and political systems based on a Muslim country's ethico-moral structure, cultural traditions, and religious values. Muslim radicalism and global jihadism reveal how Islamist authenticity has entered into competition with Western development and economic achievement.

By adopting an unorthodox and perhaps even brutal redemptive methods, Muslim radicalism and global jihadism seek to rid the Muslim world of Western-style governments, corruption, social injustice, repression, and Western and secular values. Muslim radicals and global jihadists see themselves as saviours of their religion—Islam—and the *ummah* (community of believers). We argue that Muslim radicalism and global jihadism have no basis in any scripture-based religious practice. Instead Muslim radicalism and global jihadism are a reaction to the consequences of European colonialism and the way the West, through its international relations and foreign policies, presently treats Muslim nation states and their impact on ordinary Muslims in the broader society.

Islam-West Relations: From the Period of Early European Colonialism to the Present

The interaction of the West with the people of *dar al-Islam* (abode of Islam) has always been in essence exploitative, domineering, Othering, and 'Orientalizing' (Said 1978). Such practices have contributed in elemental ways towards the decline of the Muslim world (Esposito1983; Hunter 1988). Consequently, it inspired and prompted Muslim reaction to the situation, which over the years has been multifaceted and multifarious in nature. It has been a direct response to the challenges and experiences generated by Western influence and intrusion, particularly European expansion on Islamic life both within the Muslim-majority countries and in diaspora communities. The European conquests of Muslim territories which began in the sixteenth century gradually brought about fundamental changes in Muslim societies (Esposito 1983; Hunter 1988; Rahman 1982) through the introduction of processes of Westernization, secularization, and modernization (Bagader 1994) and effectively dismantled the Muslim political system embodied in Mughal, Safavid, and Ottoman dynasties. New Western ideologies, technologies, methods of economic management, social structures, and political systems were extensively introduced in Muslim societies during the colonial period. Muslim regimes from the twelfth century had been a formidable force in international relations. They had held empires which encompassed West Africa, the Middle East, Eurasia, and the Indian subcontinent. They were a global economic power which effectively forged a Muslim world. However, from the early nineteenth century this Muslim world felt the direct intrusions of European colonialism. Throughout the nineteenth century and into the twentieth century the existing traditional order of Muslim societies directly experienced these Western challenges and tribulations (Bagader 1994). Under Western dominance and colonial rule Muslim societies underwent widespread sociocultural, economic, and political reorganization (Rahman 1982) which impacted on traditional belief, norms, social relationships, and the established pattern of Muslim living causing a major crisis in religious authority, Islamic identity, and Muslim society broadly (Bagader 1994).

To counter the domination and exploitation of European colonial powers and secure Muslim independence, Islam adopted on a political dimension in the late nineteenth century in the *dar al-Islam* inspiring anti-colonial and nationalist movements. Notable Muslim figures such as Sayyid Ahmad Khan (1817–98) of India, Jamal al-Din al-Afghani (1838–97) of Iran, and Muhammad Abduh (1849–1905) of Egypt emerged to meet the modern challenges and embarked on a quest of forging a truly Islamic identity and establishing an Islamically oriented order. They came to the realization that the Muslim lack of representation in the modern world contributed to their failures and, therefore, they opted for redefining old ideas and exploring new concepts and in doing so encouraged the implementation of concepts such as nationalism, secularism, capitalism, and Marxist social radicalism. This was an attempt to 'modernize' Islam and subsequently restore the lost independence of Muslim societies.

Adopting Western Modernisation

This accommodationist vision saw many Muslim states adopt the political, economic, and educational institutions of the Western states that had colonized them. They embraced Western models of nationalism, parliamentary government, and economic and educational systems as ways to achieve independence. However, even though much of the Muslim World was decolonized and granted self-determination in the years after World War II, the colonial past left a lasting legacy. Esposito explains,

> Neither liberal nationalism nor the radical Arab nationalism/socialism of Gamal Abdel Nasser or the Baath party had succeeded. Problems of authoritarianism, legitimacy, and political participation continued to plague most Muslim countries ... corruption and the concentration of wealth persisted as twin pillars of Muslim society while poverty, illiteracy, and overpopulation galloped along unchecked.... The positive benefits of modernization seemed to benefit the few, while the lot of the masses remained relatively unchanged.
>
> (Esposito 1983: 12)

Similarly, Hunter notes that despite embracing of modernization and national development by the majority of Muslim states after independence, social and economic conditions did not improve for ordinary Muslims in general with many continuing to experience poverty, social inequality, and injustice (1988). The living standards of most ordinary Muslims barely changed. She argues that this was the result of incomplete modernization either because postcolonial Muslim states remained politically dependent or because the benefits of modernization were monopolized by traditional elites (Hunter 1988). A general feeling of decline and stagnation continued and the vast majority of Muslims finally realized that 'the paradigm of modernisation and the political elites associated with it have failed to avert the Islamic world's decline and end its state of political and economic dependency' (Hunter 1988: xii). Hunter also suggests that because of the specific nature of the process of modernization and the imposing way in which it was applied proved counter-productive and produced a widespread sense of despair and malaise (1988: xii). Instead of creating new cultural, social, and political attitudes and developing new and broad-based institutions with the ability to cater for the requirements of modernity, the focus centred exclusively on material modernization. By uprooting old social and political institutions and patterns of relationships based on tradition or religion this emergent material modernity created a void. The newly created social and political forces and other new demands were shunned or denied channels of expression. 'The result for the majority of people has been a growing feeling of psychological, social, and political alienation and disorientation' (Hunter 1988: xiii).

Furthermore, Sidahmed and Ehteshami note that 'Social dislocation resulting from or accompanying economic "development," rapid urbanization, destruction of traditional institutions, expansion of education, and social mobility had resulted in the growth of deep social tensions and discontent. This environment was compounded by the growing inability of the states to provide necessary services for their subjects as a result of mounting economic crises' (1996: 7). To a large extent, the top-down modern state-building project in the Muslim world proved a dismal failure because of limited socio-economic and political development in the new sovereign states. By the 1960s and 1970s the hopes and expectations of the expanding middle class strata suffered a severe blow as initiatives and programmes for social and economic opportunities and social advancement were severely curtailed by regimes which had become institutionally corrupt, nepotistic. and repressive. By the 1980s, the period of state-managed investment and development ended as many Muslim states adopted a policy of 'infitah', or openness to the global free market. These state failures engendered a sense of mass disenchantment, hopelessness, and unfulfilled expectations which was gradually transformed into a mounting rage and political discontent (Bennisaon 2002; Hakimian and Moshaver 2001).

The Young and Restless of the Modern Muslim World

Younger middle class Muslims were joined by their frustrated, despairing, more conservative and poorer counterparts gravitated to religious leaders who denounced the Westernization of their society and way of life as anti-Islamic and morally corrupt. This was a strange partnership but it demonstrated the intensity of disillusionment and disenchant-ment among the masses with the existing failures of the Westernized modern state-building project. The middle class saw their hopes and opportunities stifled or denied by the vagaries of state modernization whereas the alienated and conservative poor deemed modernization as harmful for Islam and Westernization morally corrupting. Their social fusion became the dynamic for Muslim radicalism and global jihadism (Kepel 2002; Roy 2006).

Muslim radicalism and global jihadism have emerged from this com-plex and vast cauldron of dissatisfaction and discontent. These social forces reveal a close nexus between Muslim radicalism, global jihadism, and Islam-West relations. In this complex nexus we see a process of mutual alienation where the West have always treated Islam and its adherents as inferior and subordinate to itself. Muslims have increas-ingly responded to this ideological construction by denouncing the West and its values as both anti-Islam and wicked. In the next section we will address the question of what Muslim radicalism is, as well as its roots and social meaning.

The Meaning of Muslim Radicalism

The question of what is Muslim radicalism demands critical analysis. There is one vital two-part question to be considered here: 'Is Muslim radicalism a phenomenon or a process and are they *real*?' The predomi-nance of the counter-radicalization narrative in recent years has become so widely and deeply, and often unquestioningly, ingrained in media, political, and social discourses that whenever a 'terrorist incident' occurs it immediately precedes a media investigation into what causes or what factors are responsible for the radicalization of its alleged perpetrators. The question whether radicalism or radicalization actually exists or not, which many experts such as Christopher Baker-Beall, Charlotte Heath-Kelly, Lee Jarvis (2015) question, is usually and conveniently ignored. What is of crucial importance is that radicalism has produced an epoch of reaction to and preventive governance of violent extremism. It can-not explain why there is a process of radicalization in operation. Many who study (academics and researchers), investigate and report (the media), and manage (the state) assume that radicalization inevitably results in terrorism. This has become the dominant singular explanation of violent extremism or terrorism. Other contending and alternative explanations are often rejected because they are not embedded in the established and existing sociopolitical hegemony where radicalism or radicalization are divorced from the social dynamics of poverty, unemployment, discrimination, injustice, grievances, alienation, disaffection, and disenfranchisement but is solely connected with ideology. It is only the received ideology that motivates and drives radicalism and leads to acts of terror. This intensifies suspicion of communities defined as 'problematic'. In the social panic of Western countries, it is Muslims who are seen as the ethnically and religiously 'Other', separated from the existing society. The dominant reductionist narrative of radicalism isolates the question of its political and terrorism management from the social problems of poverty, unemployment, illiteracy, disparity, repression, disaffection, injustice, and prejudice; the only explanation through this myopic focus is to 'explain' and view violent extremism as the outcome of a radicalizing ideology. The singular solution is the individualized process of 're-orientation' and 'de-radicalization' which will end any possible resurgence of violence.

Since the events of 9/11 it seems that we are suddenly in an epoch of radicalism yet the etymological analysis shows that radicalism is a phenomenon prevalent throughout human history (Baker-Beall, Heath-Kelly, and Jarvis 2015; Burnett and Whyte 2005). It is not the phenomenon but the overwhelming significance given to it through a political discourse that forms the principal basis for the understanding of terrorism which is new. The current Western political discourse of radicalism became dominant after the post-9/11 terrorist bombings in London, Madrid, and various other parts of the world. It has become the singular framework for the explanation for individuals seeking the path to terrorist activities. A fundamental question must be asked: does radicalism necessarily or inevitably lead to acts of violence or terrorism? This confusion in policy formulation and political discourse on radicalism exhibits the problematic nature of the term. Radicalism is now seen as a phenomenon in which the process of socialization enables individuals to engage in acts of terrorism. This idea forms the core in the explanation of terrorist activities through ideology. Explaining the process of socialization in this way is misleading. It assumes that the process of radicalization results in violent behaviour or acts of terrorism. Individuals who adopt radical beliefs and support radicalism may be construed as 'radical'. It does not mean that these individuals are 'violent' or will carry out acts of violence. In short, there must be a clear and fundamental distinction made between the self-identified sympathizers of radicalism and those actually involved in acts of political agitation and violence. Regrettably, such an intellectual task is often never considered.

In the post-9/11 'War on Terror' era, 'radicalism' is solely linked to Islam and Muslims and, ideologically reduced to a religious and a Muslim phenomenon. In this framing, radicalism has been given an unquestioned notoriety in the research areas of global jihadism and countering violent extremism by Western policymakers, politicians, journalists, and academic 'experts'. In most arenas of public discourse the now 'taken for granted' concept of radicalism is often passionately debated but rarely analysed or understood. Its links to Islam and Muslims are never delineated or questioned.

Radicalism and various theories about its processes and causes have become critical analytical tools for understanding the issues of global jihadism and 'home-grown' violent extremism, particularly in the West (Amghar, Boubekeur, and Emerson 2007; Silber and Bhatt 2007). A specific solipsis pervades such Western understanding. The assumption is that the growing problem of narrow-minded radical, young Muslims can only be understood and interpreted through the popular discourse of an undefined radicalism. In this scenario, radicalism is generally defined, at least in theory, as a process through which an individual is gradually socialized into an alien body of 'extreme' ideas and beliefs which will potentially lead to political action of a destructive or violent nature. By isolating this form of radicalism from its social and intellectual context, it is seen a great threat to national security sanctioning the agencies of the state to undertake surveillance and contain the social threat posed by the identified radical perpetrators. The unquestioned discourse on Muslim radicalism leads to the neoliberal ideas of governmentality and 'risk management' exercised by the state (Dean 1999; Rose 1999) and renders such radicalism an ongoing political problem.

Understanding Global Jihadism

Jihad is one of the fundamental concepts in Islam and plays a prominent political role in the Muslim society. However, it is steeped and mired in recent Orientalist controversy because Westerners and Muslims in general both understand jihad exclusively as armed struggle or 'holy war' often associating jihad with violence and fanaticism. This is a narrow and limited understanding of jihad which is often misleading. Jihad has a much broader meaning. How jihad is defined, understood, and practised has wide-ranging implications relating to inter-Muslim relations, Muslim and non-Muslim relations, intercontinental relations, dispute resolution, and global perception of Islam. In classic Islamic thinking, much of the discussion of jihad has principally been the purview of the *fuqaha* (jurists) (Martin 2003). In the modern period, however, with the disappearance of Muslim central authority,[2] compartmentalization and consequent diminution of juristic authority and role, and subsequent emergence of a plethora of Muslim scholarships and legal authorities, discussion of jihad and its construction are very much an individual enterprise. When comparing modern Muslim constructions and expressions of jihad with the more classic constructions, especially among the jurists, sharp and multi-variant understandings of jihad emerge (Mir 1991). In modernity competing constructions and understandings of jihad have emerged battling for authenticity and legitimacy. These constructions and understandings have been greatly influenced by the existing social, economic, and political situations in many Muslim societies. In contemporary context, for example, the broader acceptable thinking is to construct jihad around the idea of warfare. By equating jihad solely with warfare the subjects of jihad and warfare are now and always considered as one. This is analytically problematic. There are two logical explanations why these concepts of jihad must be considered and discussed independently.

Firstly, the meaning of jihad is not simply a 'holy war' or warfare. Secondly, the principle of warfare is found in the Qur'an without any reference to jihad.

Jihad is an Arabic term derived from the word *jahd* or root *j-h-d*, meaning effort, exertion, strive, struggle, or application. The term jihad appears repeatedly in the Qur'an, often in the idiomatic expression *al-jihad fi sabilillah* ('striving in the cause of Allah'). According to Ibn Rushd (1126–98) there are four kinds of *jihad fi sabilillah*:

---

[2] By central authority we are referring to an established state structure such as a caliphate.

   i. *jihad bil qalb/nafs*(jihad by the heart/soul) which is concerned with struggling or fighting against evil and is considered to be a greater jihad—*al-jihad al-akbar,*

   ii. *jihad bil lisan* (jihad by the tongue) or *jihad al-qalam* (jihad by the word) is connected with speaking the truth and preaching Islam with one's tongue,

   iii. *jihad bil yad* (jihad by the hand) is about doing what is right and fighting against evil, injustice, corruption, and oppression with action, and

   iv. *jihad bis saif* (jihad by the sword) which is concerned with armed struggle or physical fighting in the cause of God. (Peters 1996)

Scholars of Islam emphasize two forms of jihad: *al-jihad al-asghar*—a lesser outer jihad such as a military struggle or warfare as a physical struggle against the enemies of Islam, and *al-jihad al-akbar*—a greater inner jihad such as spiritual struggle, the struggle of personal moral self-development against wicked desires which takes a non-violent form. *Al-jihad al-asghar*, a military struggle or a physical struggle against the enemies of Islam, according to Fatoohi (2004), is a temporary measure or a momentary reaction against armed hostility from an enemy and when the hostility is over jihad ceases too. Robert Spencer, in *Islam Unveiled*, takes an opposite view stating that 'The Jihad that aims to increase the size of the Dar al-Islam at the expense of the Dar al-Harb is not a conventional war that begins at a certain point and ends at another. Jihad is a "permanent war" that excludes the idea of peace but authorizes temporary truces related to the political situation' (2002: 145). Jihad is a contested concept. A variety of interpretations and constructs of the term jihad exist. This is the case because the interpretations and constructions of jihad are shaped by prevailing social, economic, and political conditions in different contexts. Jihad as war in its military sense is permissible in Islam. It can be declared by a legitimate and authorized body such as the government for a struggle to defend human rights and to protect the freedom of people and the freedom of faith. When human rights and freedom are violated and people are subjected to oppression, mounting a defense—jihad—is fundamental and it becomes obligatory as the following Qur'anic verses attest:

> Fight in the way of Allah those who fight you but do not transgress. Indeed, Allah does not like transgressors (Al-Baqarah: 190);

And kill them wherever you overtake them and expel them from wherever they have expelled you, and fitnah is worse than killing. And do not fight them at al-Masjid al- Haram until they fight you there. But if they fight you, then kill them. Such is the recompense of the disbelievers (Al-Baqarah: 191);

Fight them until there is no [more] fitnah and [until] worship is [acknowledged to be] for Allah. But if they cease, then there is to be no aggression except against the oppressors (Al-Baqarah: 193);

They ask you about the sacred month—about fighting therein. Say, 'Fighting therein is great [sin], but averting [people] from the way of Allah and disbelief in Him and [preventing access to] al-Masjid al-Haram and the expulsion of its people therefrom are greater [evil] in the sight of Allah. And fitnah is greater than killing' (Al-Baqarah: 217);

Permission [to fight] has been given to those who are being fought, because they were wronged. And indeed, Allah is competent to give them victory.[They are] those who have been evicted from their homes without right - only because they say, 'Our Lord is Allah' (Al-Hajj: 39–40);

And what is [the matter] with you that you fight not in the cause of Allah and [for] the oppressed among men, women, and children who say, 'Our Lord, take us out of this city of oppressive people and appoint for us from Yourself a protector and appoint for us from Yourself a helper?' (An-Nisa: 75)

Without having recourse to Qur'anic exegesis, the term jihad only appears thirty-six times and only ten of these 'can be unequivocally interpreted as signifying warfare'(Landau-Tasseron 2003: 35). Other explanations are open to different interpretations but some of them definitely signify effort or struggle such as the following, 'The believers are only the ones who have believed in Allah and His Messenger and then doubt not but strive with their properties and their lives in the cause of Allah. It is those who are the truthful' (Al-Hujurat: 15). 'In sum, there are only ten places in the Qur'an where *j-h-d* definitely denotes warfare. Nevertheless, there are verses in the Qur'an that attest to other significations' (Landau-Tasseron 2003: 35). For instance, 'And strive hard in God's cause with all the striving that is due to Him' (Al-Hajj: 78) and 'And as for those who strive hard in Our cause, We shall most certainly guide them to paths that lead to Us, and, behold, God is indeed with the doers of good' (Al-Ankabut: 69).

Importantly, jihad is not the main term with respect to warfare in the Qur'an. The term *qital* (kill) or the root *q-t-l* is used in the Qur'an but the warlike meaning of jihad has become predominant in modern discourse as *qital* has been glossed by jihad giving jihad, in a sense, a legal definition. Shahrour (2008) and Donner (1991) have constructed different arguments relating to war in Islam and differ in their thoughts on whether war is permissible in Islam or not, however, they both are in concordance that the Qur'an treats jihad and *qital* differently where *qital* no doubt is exclusively connected with *harb* (war). Also, the use of the Qur'anic phrase *jihadfi sabili llah* ('struggle in the cause of God') alongside another Qur'anic phrase *qitalfi sabili llah* ('armed struggle in the cause of God') seems to have contributed to equating *j-h-d* with holy war or warfare. Shahrour sheds some light on this arguing that *jihad fi sabili llah* in particular is a struggle to secure justice and ensure the protection of freedom of religion and the freedom of speech for the entire humanity from different persuasions of faith (2008). The terms jihad and *qital* apparently cannot be used interchangeably because while *qital* specifically means killing and is used in the Qur'an in specific reference to armed struggle or war, jihad has a much broader meaning than simply killing.

Islam-West Relations and Muslim Radicalism in Perspective

This analysis of the interrelated topics of Islam-West relations, the rise of Muslim radicalism, and global jihadism is guided by a series of sociological and political questions. We have attempted to historically outline the colonial and imperial roots of the relations between Islam and the West. Before the intrusion of Western colonialism in the early nineteenth century, the Muslim world, in its different historical expressions had been a dominant power. From this period, the Muslim world underwent profound economic, social, and political changes wrought by Western colonialism. The Muslim world was re-constituted into colonial states, protectorates, or dependencies of the West. The colonial impact on the Muslim world was profound andlong-lasting. Western ideas, political and economic institutions, and forms of exploitation and oppression were imposed onto the existing Muslim societies. The religion of Islam was confined to the religious realm where once it had been dominant in traditional Muslim societies. Western imperialism reduced the Muslim world to a state of colonial dependency. Western powers saw Islam and Muslims as weak, backward, and inferior (Hodgson 1974: 241–2). 'They were convinced of the necessity of their "civilizing missions" in the Muslim lands' (Knysh 2017: 382).

From the end of World War II, the Western colonial empires crumbled as the peoples of the Asia and Africa won their independence either by force or resigned consent by the former overlords. In this period, regimes in the Muslim world embarked on new forms of modern state-building. By the 1980s most of these national projects had failed to remove the burden of their colonial legacy. Although some Muslim states attempted to industrialize, urbanize, and modernize, all were deeply divided by wealth and poverty, nepotism, corruption, and repression. Western modernization brought few social or economic benefits to most Muslims. The Muslim world was integrated into the circuits of the Western globalized economy. Many Muslims migrated to selected Western countries to form diaspora communities. From the end of the Cold War, Western powers directly invaded Muslim countries for the first time since the end of the colonial period. Muslims in their heartlands and diasporas were angered and bewildered by these Western military actions. Throughout the Muslim world, after the combined failures of secular Arab nationalism, state building, the advent of Western neoliberal globalization, and the series of Western military operations, Muslims turned to Islam for answers and solutions. Specific variants of a politicized radical Islam arose and spread through the Muslim world and its diaspora. For an acute minority of usually young, Westernized, disaffected, disillusioned, and disconnected Muslims Islamic radicalism, its various permutations, was a mark of their alienation from both the traditions of Islam and their rage against Western globalization. Awan notes in the context of western European Muslims that:

> One of the potential consequences of socio-economic deprivation, political disaffection, and the gradual lack of identification with minority and majority cultures …, is the manifestation of a state of anomie. This absence of values and standards, with the concomitant feelings of alienation and purposelessness, are not necessarily alleviated by the recourse to TREs [Transitional Religiosity Experiences]. Instead, the individual turns to the espousal of radical Islamism, which serves as an emphatic rejoinder to the banality and inane humdrum of daily life. In its stead, this new world view provides, perhaps for the first time, a sense of being part of an elite group that compensates for the shortcomings of one's own petty existence. (2008: 16)

These disparate forms of Muslim radicalism sometimes metamorphosed into global jihadism or Islamist internationalism where social groups of Muslims through the Muslim world and its Western diaspora sought to mobilize an ideological and military war against the Western powers and Muslim states. In this relation Knysh notes, 'many areas of the Muslim world witnessed popular uprisings against the European "benefactors" waged under the banners of *jihad* (italic in original)' (2017: 382). Muslim radicals fight for identity, recognition, and a place for themselves in the complex mosaic of larger society with the intention to make Islam relevant and a foundation for success in the modern world. They start by setting up boundaries, identifying the enemy, seeking out converts, creating and maintaining institutions in an attempt to comprehensively recreate the society. Muslim radicals neither intend to artificially impose old practices and lifestyles nor to simply return to a sacred past or a golden age—although such a desire always lingers in the thoughts of radicals. Instead, renewed religious identity forms the exclusive and absolute basis for a reinvented political and social system which has its focus on the future and not the past. Muslim radicalization can be either violent or nonviolent and there are multiple pathways which lead to the process of radicalization. Their politicization has nothing in common with the faith and practices of Islam. Their war is a rage against the failures, disappointments, frustrations, corruption, and weaknesses of the benighted Muslim world which is powerless against the depredations of the West. Many Muslims may share this anger against the existing Muslim state order's complicity in its ruination by the West, but few of even the young are drawn into the impossibilities and futility of a global jihad. Yet, global jihadism creates an extensive international security concern in view of occasional small-scale assaults conducted by the jihadists minority in the name of Islam. Such events have been discussed to be contributing globally to unfavourable attitudes towards Islam and Muslims as enemy 'other'.

In the West, the protection of society against danger and any form of attack whether from within or without has become the heart of the discourse of Muslim radicalism and the way to manage it. The discourse of managing Muslim radicalism is embodied in securitization which involves regulating spatial exclusion and inclusion of Muslims by concentrating on the individual—person's identity and socio-religious background—to establish his or her spatial appropriateness. Securitization renders migrant Muslims as a transnational social category for the purpose of scrutiny, surveillance, and policing resulting in them conceptually separated from their particular social, political, and national settings but at the same time produces a discourse in which diverse Muslim communities are collectively considered as dangerous and a social and political threat.

We have attempted to examine and explain historically and socio-logically the inter-connections between Islam-West relations, the rise of Muslim radicalism, and global jihadism. Unless the impact, experience, and legacy of Western colonialism and imperialism on the Muslim world are explored the contemporary rise of Muslim radicalism and global jihadism cannot be understood. Or worse, since the events of 11 September 2001 in America, Muslim radicalism and global jihadism are reduced to external or internal threats to the national security of Western states.

The Muslim world was devastated by the predatory nature of Western colonialism and imperialism. Forms of state control and eco-nomic systems were imposed. The centrality of Islam as a faith and way of being had no place in these colonial constructions. Responses to these Western impositions and denials sparked both social and intel-lectual struggles in the Muslim world. When the colonial and Western powers left or were driven out of these newly emerging states after World War II, their legacy had blighted the Muslim world, where weak corrupt, dependent, repressive often illegitimate regimes maintained power. The experiments in postcolonial state making in the Muslim world largely failed. Their economies were integrated into the circuits of Western power. Muslims in these social orders and the diasporas witnessed or lived through these state failures. Islam had only a nomi-nal place in this new state-dominated Muslim world. Generations of Muslims were alienated, disaffected, and oppressed in this new social reality. Many looked to their faith for answers and solutions. Their existing reality radicalized them. Some, usually the young, saw the West as the despoiler of the Muslim world. For a minority of those radicalized only a global jihad against the West could save or rebuild the Muslim world. Only when there were random symbolic terrorist attacks on the West were Islam and Muslims seen as violent radicals bent on the West's destruction. Muslims and Islam became a question of internal and external security for Western powers. The colonial and imperial past and its impact on the Muslim world were never consid-ered. Muslims were seen as violent unstable fanatical outsiders. The meanings of radical and radicalization became euphemisms in popular and much scholarly discourse for Muslims and Islam. The meanings of jihad were reduced to cry for war by radicalized Muslims. Our research has attempted to critically analyse the unknown, fraught, and contested interconnections between Islam-West relations, the rise of Muslim radicalism, and global jihadism.

References

Ali, Abdullah. 1938. *Roman Transliteration of Holy Quran with Full Arabic Text*. Lahore: Sh. Muhammad Ashraf.

Amghar, Samir, Amel Boubekeur, and Michael Emerson (eds). 2007. *European Islam: Challenges for Public Policy and Society*. Brussels: Centre for European Policy Studies.

Awan, A. 2008. 'Antecedents of Islamic Political Radicalism among Muslim Communities in Europe', *Political Science and Politics* 41(1): 13–17.

Bagader, A. 1994. 'Contemporary Islamic Movements in the Arab World'. In *Islam, Globalization and Postmodernity*, A. Ahmed and H. Donnan (eds), pp. 114–26. London: Routledge.

Baker-Beall, Christopher, Charlotte Heath-Kelly, and Lee Jarvis (eds). 2015. *Counter-Radicalisation: Critical Perspectives*. London: Routledge.

Bennisaon, A. 2002. 'Muslim Universalism and Western Globalization'. In *Globalization in World History*, A. Hopkins (ed.), pp. 74–97. London: Pimlico.

Burnett, J. and D. Whyte. 2005. 'Embedded Expertise and the New Terrorism', *Journal for Crime, Conflict and the Media* 1(4):1–18.

Dean, Mitchell. 1999. *Governmentality: Power and Rule in Modern Society*. London: Sage.

Donner, F. 1991. 'The Sources of Islamic Conceptions of War'. In *Just War and Jihad: Historical and Theoretical Perspectives on War and Peace in Western and Islamic Traditions*, J. Kelsay and J. Johnson (eds), pp. 31–69. New York: Greenwood Press.

el-Aswad, el. 2013. 'Images of Muslims in Western Scholarship and Media after 9/11', *Digest of Middle East Studies* 22(1): 39–56.

Esposito, John. 1990. *The Iranian Revolution: Its Global Impact*. Florida: Florida State University Press.

————. (ed.). 1983. *Voices of Resurgent Islam*. Oxford: Oxford University Press.

Fatoohi, Louay. 2004. *Jihad in the Quran*. Kuala Lumpur: A.S. Noordeen.

Fawcett, L. (ed.). 2005. *International Relations of the Middle East*. Oxford: Oxford University Press.

Hakimian, Hassan and Ziba Moshaver (eds). 2001. *The State and Global Change: The Political Economy of Transition in the Middle East and North Africa*. Surrey: Curzon Press.

Hodgson, Marshall. 1974. *The Venture of Islam*. Volume 3, Chicago: Chicago University Press.

Hunter, S. (ed.). 1988. *The Politics of Islamic Revivalism: Diversity and Unity*. Bloomington: Indiana University Press.

Kepel, Gilles (trans. by Anthony Roberts). 2002. *Jihad: The Trail of Political Islam*. London: I.B. Tauris.

Knysh, Alexander. 2017. *Islam in Historical Perspective*. 2nd edition, New York: Routledge.

Landau-Tasseron, Ella. 2003. 'Jihad'. In *The Encyclopedia of the Qur'an*, Vol. 3, Jane McAuliffe (ed.), pp. 35–43. Leiden: Brill.

Martin, Richard. 2003. 'Discourses on Jihad in the Postmodern Era'. In *Islamic Ethics of Life: Abortion, War, and Euthanasia*, Jonathan Brockopp (ed.), pp. 155–72. Columbia: University of South Carolina Press.

Milton-Edwards, Beverley. 2000. *Contemporary Politics in the Middle East*. Cambridge: Polity.

Mir, Mustansir. 1991. 'Jihad in Islam'. In *The Jihad and Its Times*, H. Dajani-Shakeel and R. Messier (eds), pp. 113–26. Ann Arbor: Centre for Near Eastern and North African Studies: University of Michigan.

Owen, Roger. 2002. *State, Power and Politics in the Making of the Modern Middle East*. 2nd edition, New York: Routledge.

Peters, Rudolph. 1996. *Jihad in Classical and Modern Islam*. Princeton: Marcus Wiener.

Rahman, Fazlur. 1982. *Islam and Modernity: Transformation of an Intellectual Tradition*. Chicago: The University of Chicago Press.

Rose, Nikolas. 1999. *Powers of Freedom: Reframing Political Thought*. Cambridge: Cambridge University Press.

Roy, Olivier. 2006. *Globalized Islam: The Search for a New Ummah*. New York: Columbia University Press.

Said, Edward. 1978. *Orientalism: Western Conceptions of the Orient.* London: Routledge.

Shahrour, Mohammad. 2008. *Tajfif Manabi al-Irhab* [Draining the Sources of Terrorism]. Damascus: al-Ahali.

Sidahmed, A. and A. Ehteshami. 1996. 'Introduction'. In *Islamic Fundamentalism*, A. Sidahmed and A. Ehteshami (eds), pp. 1–15. Boulder: Westview Press.

Silber, Mitchell and Arvin Bhatt. 2007. *Radicalization in the West: The Home Grown Threat.* New York: New York Police Department.

Spencer, Robert. 2002. *Islam Unveiled: Disturbing Questions about the World's Fastest Growing Faith.* San Francisco: Encounter Books.

8

THIJL SUNIER

Engaging with Islam, Engaging with Society

The Participation of Muslims in Dutch Society

Terrorist attacks in Europe, allegedly committed by Muslims, not only led to a further securitization of society, but also heated up the debate about the loyalties of Muslims and their positioning in Western societies. This is certainly not a new issue—the orientation of Muslims and their alleged lack of loyalty to European societies has been one of the main issues in the public debate since the 1990s. Anxieties were further exacerbated after 9/11. Suspicion of Muslims has obviously resulted in growing Islamophobia in Europe, and the increase of forms of societal exclusion. In all European countries, anti-Islamic parties are gaining support. Muslims are increasingly being racialized and excluded on the basis of their religion (De Koning 2016). It is a question not only of loyalty, but also of the alleged existence of parallel societal structures and networks that circumvent control by the state and strengthen international networks. This image has been strengthened by occasional or systematic attempts by foreign powers to intervene in domestic issues. A case in point here is the mobilization of Turkish citizens in Europe by Turkey's President Erdoğan in advance of the Turkish referendum and his calling upon all Muslims in Europe to resist assimilation.

Many Muslims still react to Islamophobic attitudes by 'closing ranks' and considering all non-Muslims as potential adversaries, but an increasing number of Muslims in Europe do not buy into the idea, promoted by right-wing populist politicians as well as by some militant Islamic movements and spokespersons, that there is a gulf between Muslims on one side and non-Muslims on the other. They reject the exclusionary political rhetoric of nationalist politicians as much as the call by militant Muslims to completely disengage with Western society.

In this chapter I will address the situation in the Netherlands.[1] A growing number of young Muslims challenges the religious interpretations of terrorists and militants. They argue that Islamic concepts and principles have been 'hijacked' by terrorists. They want to 'reclaim' Islamic principles and demonstrate that being Muslim does not mean disengaging from society. Most of these young Muslims were born and raised in their country of residence. They want to be recognized as equal citizens but with a specific cultural or religious background.

A number of highly visible initiatives has been taken by young Muslims to emphasize this claim. The international social media initiative called *Not in my name*, instigated by Muslims to protest against terrorists committing attacks in the West in the name of Islam, resonated well with Muslims in the Netherlands. But other recent initiatives are also relevant and important in this respect. In the summer of 2016, a demonstration took place in the city of Amsterdam under the banner *Every1#*. The event was organized by a successful and popular Dutch-Moroccan

---

[1] In 2015 in the Netherlands, there were almost one million people with an Islamic background, comprising about 6 per cent of the total population. Turkish Muslims constitute the largest group (372,000), followed by Moroccans (335,000), Surinamese (45,000), Pakistanis (50,000), Iraqis (45,000), Afghans (38,000), and Iranians (30,000), with the remainder coming from Somalia and some other African countries. There is also a relatively small number of Muslims from Indonesia—about 10,000 according to estimations -- —and a small proportion from other East Asian countries. There are about 12,000 converts to Islam in the Netherlands. Nominally, Islam constitutes the second largest religious denomination in the country (CBS 2016). An estimated 50 per cent of people generally identified as Muslims are practicing.

movie actor with the aim of showing that Muslims and people of non-European origin have been as shocked as other citizens by the terrorist attacks in several cities in Europe. They wanted to protest against the ever increasing polarization of society, the growing gap between citizens of different backgrounds, and the inflammatory speech that dominates the public debate. The demonstration was also a reaction against the growing support for populist parties who stir up anti-Muslim sentiment among the rest of the population. The participants argued that they too are part of society and consider the Netherlands their country, and they too are worried about what is happening.

The event and the message behind it is reminiscent of an earlier initiative called *Wij Blijven Hier* (We Stay Here) that was launched in 2005 by a group of young Muslims in the Netherlands to counter the hatred for Muslims that emerged after the assassination of filmmaker Theo van Gogh in 2004 and the call by right-wing politicians for Muslims to leave the country. By giving the initiative this name, the founders wanted not only to express their intention and willingness to be an integral part of Dutch society, but also to state that in fact they already were.

All these initiatives lay bare an intriguing development in Dutch society that has been taking place for some time now. In many policy documents, Islam is still predominantly portrayed as a 'migrant religion', as something that comes from abroad. Consequently, the position of Muslims in society is primarily considered an integration issue (Sunier 2014). The growing emphasis on cultural assimilation in integration policies in European countries in the past decade has not only generated an increasingly culturalist underpinning of citizenship (Duyvendak and Scholten 2011), with concomitant participatory practices but it also favours only one specific conception of how individuals are connected to society, and how and through what channels, networks and trajectories they engage with society and identify with the common good. This is generally linked to a set of core values that are presumed to constitute society. Forms of engagement that do not fit these assumptions are deemed irrelevant or even counterproductive and are virtually delegitimized in the dominant integration discourse. However, this 'mono-cultural approach to societal engagement' that can be observed in policy documents ignores, and even rejects, the increasing diversity within society and the complex dynamics at play.

The initiatives described above are thus not just a protest against exclusion and discrimination; they reveal an intriguing demand that is being made of Dutch society. The organizers of and participants in these events and initiatives want to demonstrate that there are multiple ways of being a Dutch citizen and of engaging with different sections of the population. In other words, these initiatives should not be perceived as another multiculturalist demand for equal rights. The message is more sophisticated and compelling. As one of the organizers of the *Every1#* event stated: 'We too are citizens of this country, but we articulate and perform that citizenship on our own terms.' They reject the idea that they cannot fully participate in society while at the same time adhering to their religious or cultural specificities.

The current associational landscape among Muslims in Europe constitutes the point of departure for newly emerging forms of engagement. A gradual shift can be witnessed among young Muslims from a 'politics of cultural and religious recognition' to one that advocates a new mode of inclusion and focuses on the multiplicity of ways in which citizens relate to the common good. This is an important stage in the process of taking root in society and may be observed not just in the type of activities they engage in, but also in the ways Muslim identity is being reformulated and reshaped.

Muslims and the Common Good

There is an extensive body of literature dealing with civil society and religion, notably Islam.[2] Most of these studies deal with the political dimensions of civil society and the state and analyse how faith-based organizations are a constitutive part of civil society and how they contribute to the institutionalization of democratic structures. Many authors critically engage with the assumption that there is only one single public sphere and concomitant civil society and only one way to democratic formation (cf. Kamali 2001). Some studies concentrate on the relationship between civil society and secularism and how secular states impose certain normative frames upon society, thereby

[2] For example, Chambers and Kymlicka 2002; Casanova 2001; Hann and Dunn 1996; Casanova 2001; Tonkiss et al. 2000; Chambers and Kymlicka 2002; Turman 2004.

legitimizing some forms of societal and organizational activity and delegitimizing others (Mahmood 2015; Turam 2004). Most of these studies focus predominantly on nation-building and the political implications of civil society.

An issue that has not yet been explored very extensively is the role of civil society networks and associations in the distribution of welfare and diverse conceptions of the 'common good' (cf. Salvatore and Eickelman 2004). The retreat of the neo-liberal state in most Western countries has generated a discussion about the so-called 'participation society', a society that depends more on private networks and local initiatives than on the state. Citizens, it is argued, can no longer rely on state support in times of scarcity and crisis at the level to which they have become accustomed. In some European countries where the recent economic crisis has hit particularly hard, such as in Greece, citizens have been forced to develop their own local level networks of relief and support (Dalakoglou 2016).

Here, we might observe a paradoxical development. If we are to accept the retreat of the central state and the emergence of participatory initiatives to be developed by citizens motivated by new modes of solidarity and reciprocity, it should be accompanied by a reconsideration of what compassion entails and an acceptance in principle of the diverse ways and diverse motivations with which people engage with society as a whole. In every society there exists a multiplicity of conceptions of 'the good', of what social engagement entails, what factors generate compassion, and what motivates citizens to contribute to society. In other words, there is no one social texture, no one civil society, just as there is no one public sphere. However, alternative modes of engagement and commitment, particularly when they are to be developed by citizens with 'other' religious and cultural backgrounds, are increasingly delegitimized. Charitable and voluntary work carried out by Muslims, for example, is depicted as undesirable because it is assumed that they serve other than purely humanitarian goals.

Scholarly work has been done on conceptions of the common good in countries with a Muslim majority (Salvatore and Eickelman 2004), but hardly any research has been conducted about notions of social engagement among Muslims in Europe. Participation is a social practice. A thorough assessment of the multiplicity of ways in which citizens participate in and engage with society is necessary in order to fully understand how migrants, minorities, or religious communities become embedded in society. Two aspects are important here. First, contemporary European nation states have different historically grown legal arrangements for how religion is positioned vis-à-vis the state. This produces socially, politically, and culturally specific arrangements and ways in which citizens are engaged with society. Second, nation states develop particular notions of which practices are legitimate and desirable, and which ones are in fact illegitimate and not in line with the dominant self-image of the nation state. In the Netherlands the history of pillarization is particularly relevant in understanding the place of religion in society.

Associational Life and Communal Networks among Muslims in the Netherlands

The formal and legal equality of all religious denominations, in conjunction with the absence of the legal principle of religious recognition, constitutes the central element in the relationship between state and 'church' in the Netherlands (Sunier and Sengers 2010). Formally speaking, Islam is constitutionally equal to Protestantism or Catholicism. Although the origin of this equality principle dates back to the beginning of the century, the thorough revision of the Constitution in 1983 gave a new impetus to this principle. Formally, all financial relations between the state and the church were broken off (Hampsink and Roosblad 1992: 9). Since then, all religions have been considered legally equal (including 'new' religions such as Islam and Hinduism). 'Non-recognition' is nowhere explicitly stated in the law, but does constitute an important element in the Dutch version of religious equality. It actually implies that religious denominations can never, from a legal perspective, acquire a privileged position vis-à-vis other religious denominations. In practice, however, there are of course privileged positions and implicit differences.

The current position of religion can be subsumed under three legal principles:

1. equality of all religious denominations,
2. freedom of religion, and
3. separation of church and state.

The first principle implies that all religions, irrespective of their historical link to the Dutch state, are equal and should be treated accordingly. This may sound trivial, but the principle of equality produced intriguing discourses about the special position of religious minorities. The second and third principles imply that the state should not interfere in religious affairs and should consider religion a private pursuit.

Constitutional principles interfere with the Dutch history of pillarization. Dutch society was organized along confessional lines, from the 1920s till the 1960s. Dutch society consisted of so-called 'pillars'— corporate religious communities or blocs that dominated the political landscape. The Dutch pillar system is one of the more complicated aspects of Dutch political history. During those 40 years, there were two confessional pillars—a Catholic one and a Protestant one. In addition to that there was a Socialist movement and a so-called Liberal sphere. The two confessional pillars comprised more than 50 per cent of the Dutch population and ran through all social classes. They had their own political parties, trade unions, schools, universities, media, and all kinds of other associations. The churches were at the heart of these pillars. The Socialist movement, though not a pillar in the literal sense, was actually organized as one, although it had its political base mainly in the working class. These three blocks were organized from top to bottom and exerted a great influence on their rank-and-file. The ruling elite of the Liberal sphere was economically the strongest fraction in society, but from a social-organizational point of view it was the weakest. It was mostly composed of people who were not affiliated with one of the three other blocks and it adhered to the principles of the liberal Constitution of 1848.

An important characteristic of the system was the strong emphasis on sovereignty of religious communities. The two confessional pillars especially demanded no state interference whatsoever in matters that were related to the daily life of the rank-and-file. Although these kinds of politico-ideological divisions were not unique for Europe, the way in which the system almost completely shaped and determined political relations in the Netherlands during that period is unique. It was also the political (to some critics rigid) stability that was so characteristic. This generally accepted stability rendered the system its seemingly 'natural' character. Despite the dividedness there was a strong feeling of belonging to one nation, which was not yet the case in the nineteenth century. The blocks were principally considered equal and balanced to one another. Social conflicts were pacified and neutralized by closely cooperating ruling elites at the top of the four blocks. Due to the rigidity of the system political developments were extremely slow in the Netherlands between the 1920s and 1960s. The system continued to shape political relations for a considerable period of time even after the Second World War.

Towards the 1960s the system lost its function and in most sections of civil society a breakdown of the pillar structure took place, but the principle that all religious denominations should be treated equally is still valid. It is through this principle that Muslims can claim equal treatment, such as in the right to found religious schools. The level of religious autonomy that existed in the heyday of pillarization, however, has been replaced by strict top-down government control of the provision of public services and welfare since Second World War (Sunier 2004).

Although the current situation can in no way be compared to the religious pillarization in the inter-war period, that system is often invoked as an example of local-level solidarity and reciprocity. Whatever the ramifications of a participatory system of mutual help will be in the long run, proponents of a participation society envision a social texture that consists of relatively independent self-regulatory collectivities, a stronger dependence on voluntary initiatives, and also a stronger role for private initiatives, with 'smart government' as the buzzword.

With regard to the participatory practices and conceptions of the common good among Muslims, the question that emerges here is how the role of faith-based organizations and networks, particularly Islamic ones, is generally understood. To understand their position in contemporary Dutch society, apart from these historical and legal aspects, two observations are relevant. Firstly there is the continuous association of Islam with migration and foreignness. Organizations of Muslims are consistently and continuously treated as organizations of migrants. Despite the constitutional freedom of religion and the legal provisions that pertain to the state–religion relationship, Muslim associations are at the same time perceived as 'coming from abroad'. The persistence of such organizations is seen as proof that integration has still not been fully accomplished. In the 1980s, Dutch governmental integration policies dealt with the question of how newcomers, minorities, and migrants participate in society and how integration actually takes place. In much of the extensive body of literature on Islam in Europe, Muslim organizations are predominantly perceived as the structural organizational imprint of migration, the visible proof of the presence of a minority. Local associations, national umbrella organizations, and transnational networks pertain to the organizational activity of a religiously defined community (Sunier 2010).

The perception of Muslims coming from abroad, despite the fact that the majority of people with an Islamic background are born and raised in the country, also generates a fundamental suspicion about their intentions and loyalties (Silverstein 2005). The 'foreignness' of Muslim associations is a source for suspicion about their alleged links with radical networks and lack of loyalty to the Dutch nation state. This suspicion has increased tremendously in recent years.

Second, we can observe a development in all European countries with a sizable Muslim population referred to as the culturalization of citizenship and the shift to more assimilationist integration policies (Duyvendak and Scholten 2011). This development has exacerbated the negative image of Muslim organizations, as being concerned only with their 'own' community. In 2014, I published a report, commissioned by the Dutch Ministry of Social Affairs, about the Turkish Islamic organizational landscape in the Netherlands. The Ministry's request was motivated precisely by these concerns about the emergence of a so-called parallel society (Sunier and Landman 2014). 'Parallel society' is a term that has gained international reputation of late. In Europe, it mainly refers to the idea that many Muslims with a migration background hardly participate in mainstream society, but instead live almost exclusively in networks, associations, and societal structures that function relatively independently from society and are controlled by community leaders, religious leaders, and organizational structures that are largely beyond the control of the state. The more services and support these networks provide to their constituency, the more dependent upon them individual Muslims become, and the more they tend to live in isolation from the rest of society. Not only does this kind of dependency hinder individuals to exert their agency in societal matters and to take their own decisions, so the argument goes, but it also makes integration into society (in this case of Muslims) increasingly difficult.

The rationale behind this assumption about the growth of a parallel society is that apparently inwardly oriented activities, denoted by Putnam as bonding (1994), may be instrumental in forging inner bonds and contribute to community building, but they do not engender outwardly-oriented networks (bridging) and they do not build trust (cf. Herbert 2000). A general conviction is gaining ground that the very existence of such organizations and their activities are undesirable, tout court. This is based on the impression that they lack transparency and do things that are counterproductive and sometimes dangerous, particularly when it concerns Islamic organizations and networks. Islamic activities must be monitored in order to prevent radicalization; apart from that, they should in any case be considered not very productive for building societal cohesion.

The following case illustrates the concerns of policymakers beyond the regular suspicion about questionable ideas and convictions. It illustrates the dilemmas faced by policymakers and community leaders alike. I recently witnessed a discussion between a representative of an umbrella organization of Turkish Muslims in the Netherlands and a local politician about the concerns raised by Dutch politicians about the apparent emergence of parallel societal structures among Turkish Muslims.

During the discussion, the politician expressed his worries about the activities of local Islamic associations, which may publicly express their willingness to participate in mainstream society, but in fact spend most of their energy and time in religious activities for their own community, which, according to the politician could not possibly be considered as very integrative. Instead of stimulating young people to socialize with non-Muslims, to take part in society, and to develop their own opinions, they lock them up in a socially and discursively closed community. They teach them all about Islam but do not in any way prepare them for society at large. According to this politician,

> Muslim organizations should put much more energy in teaching young people to be part of Dutch society, but what I see happening is that although they express all kinds of intentions and good will in that direction when I meet them either in my office or in their organizations; at the end of the day they continue to care exclusively for their community. I see no positive development here. (Author's notes from fieldwork)

The representative of the Turkish organization tried to explain that 'being in this world' and actively engaging with the surrounding society is of course the duty of every good citizen, but it is also the duty of a virtuous Muslim, ordained and sanctioned by God. He explained that care for the needy, doing charitable work, voluntary activities, building local networks, and actively engaging with society are all essential aspects of being a good Muslim and constitute a moral obligation. In other words, the representative expressed an alternative conception of the common good and social justice. Thus according to this representative, a volunteer in the association:

> God has ordained that a good Muslim should always take care for fellow people, whether Muslim or non-Muslim. This neighborhood is our neighborhood so we are part of this larger community consisting of people with different backgrounds. This is what we teach our young people. This is what Islam teaches us. (Author's notes from fieldwork)

This religiously phrased argument did not impress the politician in any way. In general, Dutch policymakers take hardly any interest in the activities of Muslim organizations, especially when they are branded as religious. Religious activities are by definition inwardly oriented activities and so do not contribute to cohesion beyond one's own community. The politician expressed the general opinion felt by politicians. 'Religious activity' is a broad generalizing and unspecific policy category used in policy reports to denote those activities that pertain to religion and which should therefore be separated from activities considered 'secular' and societal. 'Religious activities' are in principle not eligible for subsidy because of the separation of religion and state, but the depiction of Muslim organizations and institutions as being in reality migrant organizations adds another element to the argument. Even if religious activity is constitutionally permitted, it is considered problematic because it may hamper integration.

Engagement and Compassion

There is a widely held belief that Muslims are less willing than other citizens to participate in charitable work. This was an issue during the relief work for refugees that took place in several locations in 2015, when relatively large numbers of refugees entered the country. There was an impression that Muslims were in general less willing to participate in all kinds of initiatives set up by local inhabitants to help out. Two authoritative government advisory boards, the *Central Office for Statistics* and the *Social Policy Office*, substantiated this impression and produced figures that would indeed demonstrate the lower levels of voluntary participation of Muslims.[3] Although these figures are problematic in many respects, they contribute to the general image that Muslims are concerned with themselves rather than with society.

The unwillingness on the part of the politician to accept the explanation of the representative, as discussed above, about their religious motivations may partly be explained by the continuous depiction of Muslim associations as migrant organizations and by the concerns about the separation of church and state, but there is yet another factor at play. Muslims have the constitutional right to engage in associational activity, but Islam is not considered an inherent element in the Dutch nation. An underlying argument against Muslim conceptions of the common good is rooted in the assumption that adherence to Islam is by definition not a constituent part of the Dutch imagined community.

This implies that the religious motivations of Muslims to express and act out societal engagement, unlike those of Christians, are not considered very valid. To the extent that they do engage socially, it is assumed that they engage mainly with fellow Muslims and are predominantly inwardly motivated. By implication, charity activities by Muslims for needy people with an Islamic background are proof of the argument.

However, compassion is about social relations and is shaped by the multiple ways in which people are situated in society. Charity, reaching out, and other forms of engagement are always culturally informed and motivated. To consider charity as something pertaining to the autonomous inner self ignores this embeddedness. As Mauss has argued in his seminal *Essai sur le Don* in 1923, there is no unconditional one-way free gift. Every human act is conditional and culturally informed and implies reciprocity. The way in which we conceptualize the moral underpinnings of this reciprocity is thus also culturally embedded. For virtuous practicing Muslims, charity, engagement, and compassion are inextricably linked with Islamic ethics. Being in the world cannot be separated from moral imperatives formulated in Islamic sources. Apart from the well-known examples such as the *zakat* (alms giving, one of the pillars

---

[3] See website SCP: https://www.movisie.nl/feiten-en-cijfers/feiten-cijfers-vrijwillige-inzet (assessed 20 December 2016)

of Islam), there are numerous references in the Islamic sources to compassion and engagement.

In his research into Muslim societal engagement in the city of Amsterdam, Yar argues that, besides the more legalist language of duties and obligations that operates in Islam, in which a concept like *maslaha* refers to the notion of public interest, there are several references to concepts such as *ehsan* (referring to an inner spiritual motivation) that deal with the ethical underpinnings of being with and in the world.[4] But also, in the mystical dimensions of Islam, there lies the idea that the quest for God contributes to the moral improvement of the practitioner. In the Gülen-movement, the ideal of a golden generation precisely captures this idea of a morally good person actively engaging with the world.[5] I am neither taking a normative position about the moods and motivations of individual Muslims, nor am I judging the effectiveness of their activities. I am arguing that these principles should not been considered as simply normative frames imposed upon Muslims, but rather as a referential category, a moral register.[6]

To substantiate this argument, let me give an account of a discussion I observed in a mosque in the city of Rotterdam some 25 years ago. It is a good example of how engagement was framed as an Islamic moral imperative in novel circumstances. The discussion was about a pressing issue that was emerging at that time. The chairman of the board of the Turkish mosque, a young man who was a socially very active resident of the local neighbourhood, proposed organizing a small event in the mosque around the *iftar* (a collective breaking of the fast in the holy month of Ramadan). He suggested turning the ritual into a

---

[4] In his current research in progress on social engagement among Muslims in the Netherlands, Yar shows how active volunteers in mosque associations legitimize and motivate their engagement by referring to an Islamic ethical frame of reference.

[5] The Gülen-movement, founded by the Islamic teacher Fethullah Gülen, is an originally Turkish organization. The movement has built up a world-wide network of schools and educational institutions. They promote an attitude that combines a pious Muslim life with an active engagement with the contemporary world.

[6] The website *Productive Muslims* provides interesting examples of how voluntary work is connected to ethical principles. See http://productivemuslim.com/benefits-of-volunteering/.

meeting were the local community and a number of key players in the neighbourhood would be invited. The mosque discussion provides an intriguing insight into the central theme of this special issue and leads into the question I want to dwell upon in this chapter.

The mosque was located in an area of the city that was in the middle of a thorough urban renewal process. For the successful accomplishment of the reconstruction process it was vital for the local municipality to include all residents in the proceedings and to have an optimal communications platform. For mosque associations, it was a time of political opportunities and openings, but also of challenges and predicaments. Some local mosque representatives regarded the quickly changing circumstances as an important opportunity to improve their position in the neighbourhood and also to negotiate a better location for the mosque. They would become important interlocutors for the municipality, and they could also improve relations with local authorities and neighbourhood institutions. The 1980s were successful for mosque associations in terms of growth, but relations with the rest of the local (predominantly non-Muslim) community were tense. There was minimal contact. The urban renewal process had the potential to turn this tide. But there was much more at stake. It was a time when a new generation of Muslims who had grown up in Europe was becoming increasingly visible on the Islamic landscape. They questioned the established associational status quo and the strong orientation of mosque associations towards the countries of origin. Many of these new activists considered that becoming more rooted in the local community was more important than the maintenance of strong networks with the countries of origin (Sunier 1996).

It was in these circumstances that some local mosque associations were thinking about the question of how to accomplish this. The aforementioned Turkish mosque was one of them. Until then, organized activities between mosque associations and the local population were confined to the regular mutual visits between mosques and churches, the so-called dialogue meetings. Most of these encounters consisted of the usual exchange of information about religious traditions and practices, drinking tea, and expressing warm words about religious freedom and tolerance.

To invite non-Muslims to the very intimate ritual moment of the *iftar* was a daring initiative. Today, such meetings are common practice in many mosques in Europe, but in those days it was a novelty. As a regular visitor to the mosque for a number of years, I had previously attended the ritual, even though I am not a Muslim. For those who had doubts about allowing non-Muslims to observe these sacred Islamic occasions, my presence was acceptable only if I kept a low profile. However, the chairman's proposal was of a different nature. He was considering opening up the ritual and making it a public event, or he at least intended to invite a limited number of people to attend the ritual and the subsequent meal at the mosque. The motive behind this initiative was to create more understanding about Muslim rituals and norms, but also to emphasize that the mosque and Muslims in general were an integral and cooperative part of the neighbourhood. Some weeks before the discussion in the mosque took place; he had raised the idea and shared it with some of his associates to learn what they thought of it. It was decided that it should be discussed with the old members and the previous board.

During the discussion with the larger group of associates it turned out that some were vehemently against the idea. Others had serious doubts, not just about the practicalities of such an initiative and about the reactions of the regular visitors to the mosque, but also about the implications of the idea. Those who were against inviting non-Muslims to the ritual end of Ramadan argued that Ramadan was a renewed engagement with the ethical underpinnings of Islam. Introspection and ethical reflection emanating from the physical impositions of the food regime generate ethical sensibilities that tend to wane under ordinary everyday conditions. Some of the participants in the discussion referred to Ramadan as an ethical realm that by definition must remain exclusive and extraordinary. One of the participants said, 'We have to teach our children what the important aspects of Islam are. How can they appreciate that when we consider everything accessible for everyone? You take part in Ramadan when you want to become a good Muslim, not because it is an obligation.'

Those who initially came up with the plan admitted that it took considerable time, doubt, and ambiguity before they arrived at the conclusion that it was neither a breach with Islamic principles, nor a compromise with requirements of the non-Muslim environment, as some opponents would argue. It was, in their words, an ethical choice completely in accordance with the 'true meaning of Islam'. At some point the discussion revolved around the question of timing. The transition from the end of Ramadan to the beginning of *Eid-ul- fitr* (end of Ramadan festival) constitutes a clear moment of passage. During Ramadan, Muslims go through a month of contemplation, introspection, and sometimes physical endurance by not eating or drinking from sunrise to sunset. The beginning of *Eid-ul-fitr* marks the end of this period of effort and is an explicitly festive and joyful event. It is an occasion for inviting friends and family, to prepare an abundance of good food, and to look forward to the coming year. To share this joy with people outside the Muslim community is a regular practice.

The opponents of the initiative argued that, if non-Muslims were allowed in it would seriously infringe upon these very crucial moments of religious experience, and, more importantly, it would lead to ethical neglect. Those in favour of admitting non-Muslims argued that this was not at all against the rules of Islam or against the deeper meaning of fasting. Bridging the gap between Muslims and non-Muslims by including them in ritual activities was not a violation of religious norms. On the contrary, they argued, sharing deeply felt convictions and practices with non-Muslims, or performing these practices amidst people who do not fast, reinforces the quality of fasting as a conscious virtuous act. In fact, some argued, isolating intimate religious practices from the outside world is an easy way to fulfil religious duties. It is not in accordance with the deeper meaning and it is actually not very sincere. But, on the other hand, it was also a virtuous act because it would make Islam an inclusive religion. 'This is precisely how the Prophet built the earliest religious community', one participant argued.

Multiple Ways of Being in the World

In his work on Italian and American civil society, Putnam has applied the conceptual pairing of 'bonding and bridging' (1994, 2007). He shows in his study how individuals are linked to state and society through informal networks and organizations. Community-building, organizational development, and the existence of social networks are necessary conditions for the functioning of a democracy. Bonding and bridging refer to seemingly opposing modes of engagement. Bonding refers to the degree to which individual citizens form part of their own networks and organizations, while bridging refers to the ways links with the wider society are developed and maintained. Putnam argues that active citizenship comes about predominantly through informal networks and organization. It is the most common way in which citizens establish contacts and arrange things and connect to the formal institutions of the state. He introduced the concept of this civic community. The closer the networks of organizational relationships are, the stronger this civic community becomes. Putnam argues that participation in society is dependent on the degree of confidence that individual citizens develop towards the state. In situations where citizens are hardly or not at all connected to informal networks and organizational relationships, a fundamental trust in the functioning of the state cannot be developed and so they are tempted to turn away from society (Putnam 1994, 2007).

Putnam's thesis has been applied to analyse the level of participation of migrant communities (Fennema and Tillie 1999). However, both Putnam and those authors who applied his conceptual scheme have adopted a rather fixed understanding of what kinds of activities pertain to bridging and what to bonding, which is the mainstream dominant perception of participation and engagement. This 'post-multicultural' or 'mono-cultural' approach to societal engagement creates an intriguing paradox. Not only does it delegitimize alternative forms of engagement, but it also makes Muslims who take part in general initiatives of social engagement, such as voluntary work, suspicious in advance. To put it differently: 'if a Muslims does voluntary work, there is probably a double agenda at work'. This is not just a matter of formulating criteria about participation, engagement, and commitment to the common good. It touches implicitly, and in many cases explicitly, on what is considered sincere and unconditioned dedication. By implication it in fact delegitimizes other forms of engagement and reciprocity.

What I propose here is to reconsider the otherwise useful concepts of bonding and bridging and to take on board different underlying conceptions of compassion and different ways of understanding the common good. This implies finding different conceptions of what pertains to bonding and what to bridging. For a country like the Netherlands, with its history of pillarization, this is historically common ground. In the heyday of the pillarization structure, society was deeply divided at the level of everyday interaction, but different ways to the common good were acknowledged and political leaders worked together. Along with the secularization that took place after

World War II and the growth of centralized welfare states, the system disappeared almost completely, but what remained is what I would call a 'pillarization register' among a part of the population in the Netherlands. The organizers of the demonstration I referred to at the beginning of this chapter tapped into this register. They wanted to demonstrate that there are multiple ways of being part of society and identifying with society. If these kinds of initiatives could be analysed more rigorously, it might lead to a reconsideration of what bridging actually entails.

References

Casanova, J. 2001. 'Civil Society and Religion: Retrospective Reflections on Catholicism and Prospective Reflections on Islam', *Social Research* 68(4): 1041–80.

Centraal Bureau voor de Statistiek. 2016. *Jaarrapport Integratie 2016*. Den Haag: CBS

Chambers, S. and W. Kymlicka (eds), 2002. *Alternative Conceptions of Civil Society*. Princeton: Princeton University Press.

Dalakoglou, D. 2016. 'Anthropology and Infrastructures: From the State to the Commons', Inaugural lecture. Free University Amsterdam.

De Koning, M. 2016. '"You Need to Present a Counter-Message"—The Racialization of Dutch Muslims and Anti-Islamophobia Initiatives', *Journal of Muslims in Europe* 5(2): 170–90.

Duyvendak, J.W. and P. Scholten. 2011. 'Beyond the Dutch Multicultural Model', *International Migration and Integration*, 12, pp. 331–48.

Fennema, M. and J. Tillie. 1999. 'Political Participation and Political Trust in Amsterdam: Civic Communities and Ethnic Networks' *Journal of Ethnic and Migration Studies* 25 (4): 703–26.

Hampsink, R. and J. Roosblad.1992. *Nederland en de islam*. Nijmegen: KUN.

Hann, C. and E. Dunn. 1996. *Civil Society: Challenging Western Models*. London: Routledge.

Herbert, D. 2000. 'Faith, Trust and Civil Society'. In *Trust and Civil Society*, F. Tonkiss, A. Passey, N. Fanton, and L. Hems (eds), pp. 52–72. Basingstoke: Palgrave McMillan.

Kamali, M. 2001. 'Civil Society and Islam: A Sociological Perspective', *European Journal of Sociology* 42(3): 457–82.

Mahmood, S. 2015. *Religious Difference in a secular Age*. Princeton: Princeton University Press.

Mauss, M. 1923. 'Essai sur le don. Forme et raison de l'échange dans les sociétés archaïques', *L'année Sociologique* 1: 30–186.

Putnam, R. 1994. *Making Democracy Work.Civic Traditions in Modern Italy*. Princeton: Princeton University Press.

———. 2007. 'E Pluribus Unum: Diversity and Community in the Twenty-First Century. The 2006 Johan Skytte Prize Lecture', *Scandinavian Political Studies* 30(2): 137–74.

Salvatore, A. and D. Eickelman (eds). 2004. *Public Islam and the Common Good*. Leiden: Brill.

Silverstein, P. 2005. 'Immigrant Racialization and the New Savage Slot', *Annual Review of Anthropology* 34: 363–84.

Sunier, T. 1996. *Islam in Beweging*. Amsterdam: Het Spinhuis.

———. 2004. 'Naar een nieuwe schoolstrijd?' *BMGN* 119(4): 552–76.

———. 2010. 'Assimilation by Conviction or by Coercion? Integration Policies in the Netherlands'. In *European Multiculturalism Revisited*, Alessandro Silj (ed.), pp. 214–35. London: Zed Press.

———. 2014. 'Domesticating Islam: Exploring Academic Knowledge Production on Islam and Muslims in European Societies', *Ethnic and Racial Studies* 37(6): 1138–55.

Sunier, T. and E. Sengers (eds). 2010. *Religious Newcomers and the Nation State: Political Culture and Organized Religion in France and the Netherlands*. Delft/Chicago: Eburon.

Sunier, T. and N. Landman, 2014. *Turkse Islam. Actualisatie van kennis over Turkse religieuze stromingen en organisaties in Nederland. Een literatuurstudie in opdracht van het Ministerie van Sociale Zaken en Werkgelegenheid*. Den Haag: Ministerie van Sociale Zaken en Werkgelegenheid.

Turman, B. 2004. 'The Politics of Engagement between Islam and the Secular State: Ambivalences of "Civil Society"', *British Journal of Sociology* 55(2): 259–81.

PART THREE

FAITH AND IDENTITY

9

TEREZA HYÁNKOVÁ

'Muslims in the Modern Sense'

Kabyles Negotiating Religious Identity in the Czech Republic

Prior to 1980s, there was little or no interest in social scientific research towards Muslim populations in Europe (Kepel 1997: 48). This situation however has change over the last 10 years, due to the growth in the Muslim presence—one which has drawn an increasing interest in scholarly, political and media circles, notwithstanding their representation in simplistic and inaccurate terms, particularly as they continue to be portrayed as a homogenous group. At the same time, immigrants from predominantly Muslim countries are often automatically categorized as Muslims. Drawing on the example of the Kabyle immigration to the Czech Republic, I demonstrate that such an essentialist perspective proves to be highly problematic.

Kabyles are Berber-speaking inhabitants of North-East Algeria. The Kabyle migration to the Czech Republic started after the fall of Communism as a result of opening the borders of European countries previously inaccessible as migration destinations due to iron curtain.[1]

---

[1] In fact, there was a fraternal cooperation between socialist Algeria and communist Czechoslovakia. Young Algerians studied in the Czechoslovakia and Czech doctors and engineers worked in Algeria. In this sense, it is possible

The migration experience represents a significant part of Kabyle collective memory. Overseas migration from rural Kabylia was the result of social and economic upheavals produced by the French colonization. The Algerian immigration in France is well-known. Even though Algerians continue to migrate to France, other countries became significant targets of Algerian migration.

Canada, the USA, and Western Europe countries still represent for various reasons—such as the economic situation, the standard of living, and asylum opportunities—more attractive migration destinations than the Czech Republic. However, even in the Czech Republic there is already a small community of Kabyle immigrants. This group is composed almost exclusively of young single males coming from the rural areas of Kabylia.

In this chapter, I examine the Kabyle immigrants' religious practice and their perception of Islam. I argue that a specific combination of multiple historical, social, and political factors have induced an ambivalent relationship with Islam and a weakened religious activity. I subsequently analyse the most important factors that have shaped Kabyle immigrants' religiosity, that is, (*i*) colonial and post-colonial politics of Algeria; (*ii*) specific type of migration; (*iii*) Islamophobia in the Czech Republic.

The Immigrants' Religious Discourse and their Practice: Interpreting Ethnographic Data

In 2003 when I visited my friends in Biskra, a town in the Arab-speaking region of Algeria, we undertook a pilgrimage to Sidi Okba[2] with five women of the family and two other female friends. In the mosque, my friend asked me if I did not want to pray there. Since everybody knew

---

to speak about the process of migration. Nevertheless, it concerned a limited number of people and the migration was only temporary.

[2] Sidi Okba (also Sidi Uqba) is a pilgrimage locality with the tomb of the famous Arab conqueror of the Maghreb, Okba ibn Nafi. He defeated Byzantine troops, occupied the cities of Fezzan and Ifriqya and founded the city of Kairouan. He died in 683 AD in a battle against Berber tribes in the Aurès mountains. For this reason, he is nowadays perceived by Arabs as a hero, and by Berbers as an aggressor.

that I was not a Muslim, I found it strange to pray in the Muslim way. At the same time, it seemed absolutely inappropriate at such an important and sacred place for Muslims, to kneel down, cross myself, and recite the Lord's prayer in Czech. Hence I refused. Till now I do not know how the suggestion should have been understood.

In Biskra, I spent a lot of time discussing religion. Zohra—an eight-year-old girl—asked me complicated questions about tri-unity that I was obviously unable to answer. After I had showed her the Christian way of praying, she declared her willingness to convert to Christianity since she considered this kind of prayers less complicated and more comfortable than the Muslim ones. My friends and the friends of my friends explained me the spirituality, the morality, the rightness, and the depth of Islam and at the end of my stay told me how much they appreciated me; there was just one think that surprised them: how little I spoke about God. They assured me that they would pray for me so that I find one day that Islam is the right religion for me.

In Kabylia, religion was never a topic of conversation evoked by my friends. In comparison to Biskra, Batna, Annaba, Constantine, or Algiers, it was more usual to see young men drinking alcohol and rare to see a woman wearing *hijab*. Moreover, the girls wearing *hijab* in Kabylia were sometimes targets of severe looks and objects of ridicule by their compatriots. With my friends in Kabylia, we often spoke about Kabyle linguistic rights as an ethnic minority and about the repression of Berbers by the Algerian state. All this is far from establishing that all Arab-speaking Algerians are practicing and are much attached to religion while all Kabyles have distant attitude to Islam. Nevertheless there are some obvious differences in the presence, the perception, and the representation of Islam in Arab-speaking regions of Algeria and in Kabylia. In conversations with Kabyles, Arabs were often portrayed as uncritically attached to Islam and outdated traditions; while in conversations with Arabs, Kabyles were described as bad Muslims and bad Algerians. This specific situation resonates in the immigration.

The parents and grandparents of the Kabyle immigrants in the Czech republic observed Islam in all of its forms. Apart from a minority including men working as immigrants in France, they did not drink alcohol and respected Muslim alimentary taboo. Of interest Kabyle immigrants in their country of origin of Algeria, especially young ones, rarely observed fundamental elements of Islam. Most of them did not go to the mosque, did not pray five times a day, and some of them did not observe Ramadan, yet many of them participated in Muslim celebrations. Observance has been connected to local community activities; celebrating Muslim feasts meant to participate in the village life. Thus, one may interpret it as a mostly social rather than religious act. Hamid told me,

> I am not observing and I never was. I am not a Muslim. The religion interests me from the spiritual angle. I think religion is a personal thing. When I was in Algeria, I remember how in the morning, *adhan*[3] bothered me. I always put the blanket over my head so I could hear nothing and keep sleeping. I never observed any rules. When there was L'Aïd de mouton[4] and my brothers helped my father with the lamb and all people celebrated it, I always went away.

In a follow-up discussion with Hamid's brothers and their reaction to his basis of his perception, they offer little but sharp criticism for his behaviour, not because of his refusal to participate in a Muslim celebration, but because of his individualism and his lack of support to the family. According to his brothers' narratives, Hamid was never described as a bad Muslim. In a sense they seem to share with him an attitude of distance towards Islam. Indeed, Hamid was dispraised as a man unable to fulfil his role as the first son, being 'lazy and asocial'.

A majority of Kabyles in the Czech Republic do not observe Islam at all and continue to drink, ordinarily, alcohol and eat pork. I noticed only one exception—Salah. During his first year in the Czech Republic, he did not observe Islam and intended to marry a Czech woman as most Kabyles in the Czech Republic do. Despite his intensive effort, he did not succeed. He therefore decided to marry a Kabyle woman and take her to the Czech Republic.

Since his future Kabyle wife was the daughter of an *imam*,[5] he started to observe Islam carefully. Despite his plan to take his newly married

---

[3] *Adhan* is the Islamic calling for prayer, usually carried out from minaret.

[4] By *L'Aïd de mouton* Hamid refers to *Aïd al-Kabīr*, an important Muslim feast. It is the commemoration of Ibrahim agreement to sacrifice his son Ismail. At that day, the lamb is sacrificed and divided to be distributed to people.

[5] An *Imam* is the leader of a mosque and/or the spiritual leader of a community.

woman to the Czech Republic after the wedding took place in Algeria, the couple did not leave Algeria and Salah abandoned the idea of re-emigration to the Czech Republic, because of the insistence of the bride and her parents.

Mouloud embodies another exceptional case. Even when his parents observed Islam attentively, he never did. The first time I conducted an interview with him, he criticized Islam a lot, but simultaneously declared himself as being 'culturally Muslim'. After some time, he met a Czech Catholic woman he would later marry. He told me that at the beginning he went to the church just to make her happy, but that he later discovered the real Christian message. Nowadays he speaks about his conversion to Christianity as about 'finding the right path, goodness and light'. He got married in a Catholic church and decided to change his name to a Christian-Czech one.

Salah's and Mouloud's stories are unusual; most Kabyles in the Czech Republic do not observe any religion. Whilst they adamantly express their reservation towards Islam, some of them declare themselves to be true Muslims, others do not. The decision is highly individual; neverthe-less there is a clear convergence between the commitment to 'Berber cause' and the perception of Islam. The immigrants who prove to be the most eager in their fight for Kabyle political rights criticize Islam the most. Those declaring themselves as Muslims feel always a need to explain their own perception of Islam. I noticed the expression 'Muslim in the modern sense' repeatedly.

One of those who fit this category is Malik; he told me:

S: My family is very observing, namely my mother; my father since he returned to the country. My grandparents are also very, very observing.

T: Your father started to observe Islam when he returned from France?

S: Yes, he began to observe. The way I see it, I got over this state, I cannot be observing Islam - nor in the past, neither in the future. I cannot be practicing; I can be only practicing in accordance with my everyday acts.

When I asked him what is meant by, 'practicing in accordance with his everyday acts', he spoke about moral rules: to be generous, to be kind to other people, not to steal, and not to be violent. To him, 'Muslim in the modern sense' meant to have Muslim parents and to follow aforesaid moral prescriptions. No rituals, no feasts, and no alimentary regulations were mentioned as the elements of 'Modern

Muslim' identity. In the interviews, God was never pointed out; while talking about moral values, the responsibility or duty towards Him were not part of the discourse. Islam was defined by Malik and others in terms of cultural heritage and morality expressed by non-religious vocabulary. All Kabyle immigrants without exception considered religion as a private matter; they criticized the interconnection of politics and Islam and spoke about the secular political model as the most suitable one.

In brief, Kabyle immigrants in the Czech Republic do not observe Islam and have a distant relationship towards Islam. While some of them declare not being Muslims, others define themselves as 'modern Muslims'. In this case their 'Muslim-ness' is understood as sharing a concrete moral code and a cultural inheritance. The religious identity of Kabyle immigrants is ambiguous, changing, and—till some extent—open to potential conversion. This situation reflects both the theory and the practice of young Kabyles living in Algeria. The reasons for their ambivalent relationship to Islam lie in the colonial and postcolonial politics implemented in Algeria.

Colonial and Postcolonial Politics of Algeria: Production of the Difference

The Entrapment of the Kabyle Myth

In contemporary Algeria, the polarization between Arabs and Kabyles is present not only in politics, but also in discourses of 'ordinary' people on both sides. Arabs are perceived by Kabyles as oppressors, while Kabyles are seen as incessant grumblers and as a threat for Algerian unity. But the Berber-Arab cleavage as it exists today, was absent in precolonial times. The boundaries of collective identities were based on completely different foundations—namely the locality and the inclusion in extended families, clans, tribes, and Muslim brotherhoods.

Since the colonization, Algerians have been described by French through the lens of the Berber-Arab opposition. Despite this long-standing perspective, some authors consider that Algeria's Berber and Arab populations may have more similarities than differences due to their adherence to Muslim faith and related ways of organizing family structures and gender relations (Goodman 2005: 4–5). Nevertheless, because of the multiple processes of colonial and postcolonial politics, Arabs and Berbers see each other as significantly different.

Up until the beginning of the French colonization, Kabyles did not have a good reputation in France (Ageron 1960: 312, 315). Islam was not seen as savage, rather as a 'backward and imperfect civilization' entrapped in its 'feudal' and 'aristocratic' past (Silverstein 2004: 47); it was also feared as a potential unifying political force (Lucas and Vatin 1975: 34). The creation of the positive Kabyle stereotype was inspired by the colonial strategy of 'divide and rule' and by the idea of assimilation (Ageron 1960). There were two premises that fuelled the Kabyle myth: (i) Arabs were perceived as the conquerors of North Africa, therefore Berbers could be presented as the real indigenous people; (ii) because of their history, they were supposed to be akin to French civilization (Ageron 1960: 317). The Kabyle myth reached its climax somewhere between 1871 and 1892 (Ageron 1960: 320). Even after 1892, when Kabylophilia declined, the resonance of this imaginary persisted not only in the colonizer's mind, but also in Algerian collective memory. Ethnic stereotypes were adopted by Arabs as well as by Kabyles.

Several arguments were advanced to show that Kabyles are entirely different from Arabs and as suitable candidates for assimilation, were numerous. One of these was associated with their history; their supposed origins and their way of life.[6] By using Latin sources, the French colonial ethnographers of the end of nineteenth and the beginning of twentieth century claimed that Kabyles were related to Romans (Silverstein 2004: 63). Berbers were seen as the inheritors of the Roman civilization, and as examples of the *homo mediterraneus* (Silverstein 2004: 64). They were thus deemed close to French. It was also believed that they were of Celtic origin.

Noteworthy, prior to the arrival of Arabs, a significant part of Maghreb was Christian, French portrayed Kabyles as 'ancient Christians, Muslims as little as possible' and as having a predisposition to a 'complete return to Christianity' (Warnier as cited in Ageron 1960: 317). Arabs were largely seen as religious 'fanatics'; it necessarily hindered their potential

---

[6] For detailed studies on the Kabyle myth, see Ageron (1968), Colonna (1976), Lacoste-Dujardin (1984) and Lorcin (1995).

assimilation. Although Kabyles were Muslims; they were seen as less 'fanatical' in their religious practice. The Kabyle social organization was described as democratic, secular, and egalitarian[7] and thus close to the French. Berbers were represented as sedentary diligent peasants in opposition to nomadic Arabs. 'Arab nomadism' was meant to provoke political disorganization and instability, and therefore embodied the very opposite of modern civilization (Lorcin 1995: 37–40). The industriousness of Kabyle land workers was celebrated in contrast to the 'Arab laziness'.[8] Although the nomadic/sedentary dichotomy did not reflect any social reality—in precolonial Algeria, there lived sedentary Arab-speaking populations as well as nomadic groups of Berber-speaking population (Touareg people)—this distinction was supposed to confirm the Berbers' ability to adopt the civilization process.

Neglecting Kabyle traditional laws that grant less inheritance rights to women than *sharia* (Lacoste-Dujardin 2005: 136)[9] and forgetting that Arabs and Kabyles have a similar attitude towards family and gender, French scholars portrayed Kabyle men as respectful of women, thus relating closer to 'civilized' Europeans and further distancing them from Arabs. A strong argument for this attitude was Kabyle 'traditional'

[7] The main reason was the existence of an institution called *jemaâ* (sometimes transcribed also as *djemaâ*). This assembly of male villagers took decisions concerning the elaboration and the application of customary laws and the village life (feasts, celebrations, assistance, and conflicts). All participants could speak at the assembly and the decisions were submitted to vote (Lacoste-Dujardin 2005: 44). According to Goodman, when French characterized Kabyle social organization as secular, they neglected the important social phenomenon present in Algeria—the relationship between "ordinary" Kabyles and *marabouts* (that is, people belonging to a sacred lineage) (Goodman 2005: 10). For more information on the Kabyle 'traditional' social organization, see Brett and Fentress (1996); Camps (1987); Hanoteau and Letourneux (2003); Mahé (2001).

[8] One of the most influential examples was Daumas (1853).

[9] While according to *sharia* a woman inherits the half of the male inheritance, in pre-colonial Kabylia, women were completely excluded from inheritance. Lacoste-Dujardin (2005: 136) stands that this customary prescription dates probably back to the half of eighteenth century, while the period before was more egalitarian as far as gender was concerned.

monogamy (Ageron 1960: 317) and the absence of veil amongst Kabyle women—in opposition to their Arab counterparts.[10]

Even though Kabyle culture was represented as oral in opposition to Arab written culture, Kabyles were not debased as 'primitive'.[11] The Berber language and culture became scholarly objects and thus gained historical legitimacy (Chaker 1998: 31). Kabylia was a frequent place chosen for ethnographic researches. Under the influence of ethnographic approaches and methodology, works on Kabyle culture almost never alluded to the local written tradition. Examining Bourdieu's ethnographic work, Hammoudi interprets the lack of interest in written texts as the result of a division of work between ethnographers and Orientalists (Hammoudi 2009: 201, 231). Whereas French viewed Arabs through the lens of religion,[12] they saw Berbers through the lens of culture (Goodman 2005: 5).[13] This differentiated approach deeply influenced the (self) perception and (self) representation of Arabs and Kabyles and had a clear resonance in Algerian postcolonial politics.

Building Algerian National Identity

French colonization cannot be the only key to the contemporary antagonism betwen Arabs and Kabyles. The construction of Algerian national identity and Algerian postcolonial politics played a very important role in the escalation of their rivalry. Algerian nationalism was formed in the colonial context. Sayad writes:

---

[10] Lacoste-Dujardin also contrasts *marabout* women that were veiled and did not work outside with Kabyle laic women (Lacoste-Dujardin 2005: 226).

[11] Silverstein notices also the reduction of Arab civilization to Islam by military scholars (Silverstein 2004: 50).

[12] Bourdieu proves to be a significant example. As Hammoudi correctly noticed, in his Kabyle ethnography, Bourdieu (Bourdieu 2000 [1972]) does not mention religious brotherhoods (Hammoudi 2009: 204), although they played a very important role in the 'traditional' Kabyle culture. Phenomenon such as marriages, the sense of honour, or Kabyle houses is described without being framed in the Islamic context (Hammoudi 2009: 234).

[13] *Umma* means 'the community of believers', today it is used also for denominating a 'nation'.

Today's Algerian nationalism is sick, insecure, confused, disoriented, without clear direction and prospect. The reason is losing its partner which constituted it. [...] All references which Algeria can refer to are considered as degrading. The only exception in their eyes is (except negation and denouncement of the past) in referring to mythic Arabo-Islamism.

(Sayad 2002: 75–6).

Stora (2002) emphasizes the point that oblivion is synonymous with future in Algeria. He and other like-minded scholars explain that the Algerian way of national building is inspired by the Jacobin idea of a nation state united by a single language and culture (Chaker 1998: 22–3; Goodman 2005: 15, 55; Stora 2002: 14). Chaker draws attention also to another inspirational belief, namely the mythic model of Islamic *umma*[14] (Chaker 1998: 22–3). Since the independence, the Algerian national identity has been intended, planned, and defined as Arabo-Islamic (Chaker 1998: 22; Stora 2002: 19). Islam was declared as the religion of the state and Arabic as the only official national language. The term 'Arabization' was proclaimed in reaction to colonialism, as a way to put an end to the domination of a colonial language. Therefore anybody, who impugned Arabization, became suspected of colonial inclination.

Arabization especially altered the public space, the administration, and the educational system. The educational programme clearly omitted the real Algerian sociolinguistic situation. Teachers from the Middle Eastern countries were invited to teach Arabic language despite the obvious differences between Algerian and Middle Eastern versions of Arabic. The Algerian school system of the 1960s and 1970s shaped Berber identity in a significant way (Goodman 2005: 33). The Berbers experienced the repression of their mother tongue in schools, but at the same time valued it. Even when their language was repressed, the school system inscribed in them the idea that national identity and language are closely related (Goodman 2005: 36).

---

[14] Concretely, it concerns the FFS and the RCD. The FFS, *Front des Forces socialistes* (The Socialist Forces Front) was founded in 1963 by Hocine Ait Ahmed. The party promotes strongly democracy and secularism (*laïcité*) and its orientation is social democratic. The RCD, *Rassemblement pour la Culture et la Démocratie* (The Rally for Culture and Democracy) was founded in 1989 by Saïd Sadi. The party promotes democracy and secularism as well and can be considered as liberal.

Goodman rightly claims that Berber language was, after independence, positioned with the regard to Arabic just like Arabic was to French during the colonization: Berber was portrayed by Algerian system as unable to express modern notions and scientific idioms and classified as a dialect, not language. Therefore Kabyles were portrayed as lacking culture (Goodman 2005: 56).

Influenced by the ideology of French colonial politics and Algerian post-independent politics, Kabyle identity has been focused on its pre-Islamic past, language, 'traditions', and 'culture' whose significant phenomenon (such as poetry, music, and material objects) have been represented in the folkloristic, ethnographic, and museological way independently on the Islamic context. In the contest for prestige gain, they have focused on their 'indigeneity' presenting themselves as the 'real Maghrebians', population that was present in North Africa before the Arab conquest.

The demands for their political rights have been often expressed in French, since most Kabyle intellectuals often master French better than Arabic and since Arabic is, unlike French, perceived as a threat for their ethnic identity. The Kabyle regular usage of French is by their Arab counterparts interpreted as a clear sign of Kabyle pro-colonial inclinations and as a lack of national pride.

The increased Islamization of Algerian society intensified Kabyle requirement for secular democracy. The Kabyle political parties[15] criticized the 'obscurantism' of Algerian political system claiming that the modern democracy of European style as model suitable for Algeria. In consequence they are charged as 'enemies of Islam' (Maddy-Weitzman 1999: 41).

From this analysis one can see how a spectrum of stereotypes about Arabs and Kabyles have accrued and led to antagonism between them, and used to by French colonial politicians and the Algerian post-independent regime in an adverse manner. In the name of anti-colonialism, colonial thoughts have been often replicated. The Algerian national identity was constructed based on the Jacobin idea of nation, where there is no place for linguistic diversity. Kabyles have been portrayed as detrimental to national unity and as bad Muslims. Further Kabyles have associated themselves with pre-Islamic Maghrebian history, principles

---

[15] The difficulties concern especially the problem of gaining legal status, further low salaries, and high rents.

of secular democracy and 'culture' and 'traditions' that have been interpreted independently on Islamic context. In the interviews conducted with Kabyle immigrants in the Czech Republic, it is possible to identify clearly the echo of this complex situation whether it concerns immigrants' reserved attitude towards Islam, their focus on 'culture' and 'cultural heritage' or the appreciation of modern secular democracy.

Specific Type of Migration: The Advantage of Being Unknown

Due to the difficulties new Kabyle immigrants faced in the Czech Republic,[16] a sizable majority opted to re-migrate from the Czech Republic to different countries of Western Europe. What triggered a lifelong decision and how they judged their decision to leave after certain time and if/how their lives changed will be presented herewith.

The story of Sofian is telling. After legislation changes in 2000 that aggravated the situation of many immigrants in the Czech Republic, he experienced tremendous stress. His chances to gain legal status seemed to be hopeless; therefore he decided to migrate from Prague to the Great Britain. Few weeks after his migration to London, he started to speak about the Muslim hospitality, the spirituality of Islam, the importance to 'live in the right way' and the idea to observe Ramadan. I was surprised, since in the Czech Republic he expressed rather reserved attitude towards Islam and did not practice. Therefore I was interested in the cause of this change. I found out how Sofian's cousins who were living in London at that time had a major influence on his decision. Soon after his arrival in London, they provided him with housing and helped him find a job. They communicated to him that upon their arrival to England, the only help they received was from the local mosque—a place where Muslims helped one another. Of interest, as soon as Sofian gained independence in London, he decided not to observe Islam. Such a scenario is unlikely to occur in the Czech Republic.

---

[16] The statistics are highly problematic. According to the Czech Statistical Office, 3,358 people identified their religion as Islam in the 2011 census (Český statistický úřad). The estimations of Ministery of Interior from 2007 speak about 10 thousands (Ministerstvo vnitra České republiky) and Topinka et al. (2014: 245) about 20 thousand Muslims living in the Czech Republic.

As noted earlier, there is a clear trend due to French colonial politics and construction of the Algerian national identity, that Kabyles may have a reserved attitude towards Islam. I showed also that the Kabyle immigrants' religious identity in the Czech Republic is fluid and open to changes. Nevertheless the majority of Kabyle immigrants do not practice and express their distance towards Islam. I argue that there is a specific configuration of factors that does not fuel the positive re-interpretation of Islam. The decisive role play reasons for emigration, gender, presence / absence of powerful Muslim solidarity connected to mosque network in the immigration country, and size of immigrated population.

Characteristics of their Migration

The Kabyle immigration to the Czech Republic is almost exclusively a male migration. It concerns young single men coming from rural region of Kabylia, from families of farmers or semi-skilled and non-skilled workers. In Algeria, they worked as semi-skilled workers or were unemployed. Their emigration is designed as permanent. Even when their practice has often proved the continuity, in their narratives, they focused strongly on rupture with Algeria. In their biographical stories, they often mentioned desire to escape not only the complicated social and economic situation of young Algerians and the Algerian despicable political system, but also the social control of their community—family and village. Algeria is represented in their notions by the imperative to live for others, by oppressive *communautarisme*, and boredom—everything they wanted to escape. They affirm their willingness to live the 'Western' lifestyle. The migration is thus seen as liberation and completion of lifestyle change.

'Western' lifestyle is often perceived mainly as sexual freedom and by intermarriage with Czech women. Since the immigration concerns almost exclusively young single men, community social control concerning their chastity is absent. They also prefer not to identify themselves as Muslim in their search for a successful intermarriage. Generally low awareness of the Berber community amongst the Czechs is the main factor of maintaining a neutral to positive stereotype about them in the Czech republic. Consequently, the immigrants' religious identity that could be till some extent open to conversion is not exposed to the influence that would induce such change.

Unlike the situation in Great Britain, there are fewer wealthy mosques supported by oil-rich Middle Eastern states which provide tangible assistance and encouragement to fellow Muslims. Also, compared to many Western European countries, Muslims immigration to the Czech Republic is insignificant.[17]

Islamophobia in the Czech Republic at Present

In last 10 years, Islam has become an important 'hot' political topic evoked frequently in various European countries. After World War II it projected and encouraged a legitimate identity for immigrants (Werbner 2004: 481). At the same time, the public visibility of Islam in 1950s, 1960s, and 1970s in Europe was considerably smaller than nowadays.[18] This changed with the general raise of Islamic fundamentalism and politicization of Islam at the end of 1970s. The Middle Eastern politics influenced the situation in Europe, when the oil-rich states began from diverse religious, charitable, and political reasons to invest petrodollars into the Muslim infrastructure in Europe, especially through the financing of mosques and other Muslim organizations (Grillo 2004: 863). Islam was made visible by the *fatwa* of Ayatollah Khomeini and book burning in Bradford by Muslims in 1989, both reactions to publication of Salman Rushdie's *Satanic Verses* (1988). The events were followed with great interest by media. Islam became in Europe gradually a sign of opposition (Werbner 2004: 481).

The situation escalated after 9/11 when it was discovered that many members of Al-Qaeda involved in the preparation of New York's twin towers attacks, had permanent residence in different Western European countries. Since 2001, there has been a long list of events that have nourished the Islamophobic tendency in Europe: Madrid train bombings in March 2004, murder of the Dutch filmmaker Theo van Gogh in 2004, London attacks in 2005 known as 7/7, Jyllands-Posten Muhammad

---

[17] Grillo (1985, 2004: 863) also mentions that in his own research on immigrants in France in 1970s, Islam while not irrelevant to their lives was not at the forefront of their concerns.

[18] Kepel (2003) interprets the raise of fundamentalist Islam and politicization of Islam (as well as of Christianity and Judaism) as the reaction to disillusion from secular ideologies and utopias at the beginning of 1970s.

cartoons controversy in Denmark with its international resonance, Chechen female suicide attacks in Moscow subway in 2010, and suicide bombings in Russia's North Caucasus republic of Dagestan. Even the riots in Paris suburbs in 2005 were interpreted by the Czech press as the problem of 'Muslim presence in Europe' and 'Islamic threat'. An attack at the Paris office of French satirical magazine *Charlie Hebdo* in January 2015, November Paris attacks in 2015, Brussels bomb attacks in March 2016, a cargo truck attack at the promenade of Nice in July 2016, and many smaller attacks of Islamists in Germany, France, Belgium, the UK, and Denmark significantly strengthened Islamophobia in Europe. Important role in strengthening Islamophobia plays also the European refugee crisis and associated fear of uncontrolled movement of people who may be linked to the Islamic state.

On the international level, conflicts in Palestine, Chechnya, Kashmir, the nuclear confrontation between India and Pakistan, the wars in Afghanistan, Iraq, and Syria, and especially the existence of Islamic state (IS) have contributed to the negative image of Islam. Even when each conflict is unique and has very different historical, political, and social background, this global situation evokes the simplistic interpretation of the type 'where are Muslims, there are conflicts'. At the same time, Muslims in Europe identify with their 'brothers' in Palestine, Syria, Iraq, and Afghanistan and feel being beleaguered both locally and globally (Werbner 2004: 482). In contemporary Europe, it is difficult to be a Muslim and pass unnoticed. Muslims evoke suspicions and are therefore often stigmatized. Anti-immigrant and Islamic populist policy became part of the political scene in Europe. The most visible symbols of this policy are Geert Wilders of the Netherlands and Marine Le Pen of France.

Even when the number of Muslims living in the Czech Republic is still very small, the fear and antagonism towards them is quite strong. This is manifested by public protests against construction of mosques, amount of internet pages with Islamophobic content and frequently Islamophobic discourse of Czech people, and also of Czech President Miloš Zeman, who quite openly expresses his extreme anti-Islamic attitudes. According to Zeman, Islam is a religion of hate, compares it to Nazism and calls it 'anti-civilization'. Integration of Muslims into Czech society is, as he says, almost impossible. The Islamophobia in the Czech Republic can be explained on one hand by general xenophobia of a nation state that is ethnically and culturally very homogenous and that was isolated during Communism, on the other hand by the all-European media image of Islam. Nevertheless such a negative image and strong Islamophobia did not exist during the Cold War period. Many Arab states were socialist and presented as 'our friends' in the opposition of 'evil West'. The situation changed after the fall of Communism when borders started to be open for immigration and when media brought news about conflicts in the Middle Eastern without Marxist interpretation and reports about the 'problems' with immigrants in Western European countries.

For Kabyle immigrants it is therefore a very advantageous strategy to emphasize their Kabyle / Berber identity and to present themselves as the victims of Arab nationalism and Muslim fundamentalism.

A Nuanced Understanding of Islam

The majority of Kabyle immigrants in the Czech Republic do not observe Islam. The factors that have shaped their religious practice and their perception of Islam are the colonial and postcolonial Algerian politics, the specific type of migration and the Islamophobia in the Czech Republic. The French colonial scholars and politicians created the rivalry between Arabs and Kabyles presenting them as significantly different. In addition, the postcolonial Algerian national identity building based on Arab language and Islam and the repressions of Kabyle political rights, added considerably to the enmity. As the consequence, Kabyles have been perceiving Arab language and sometimes also Islam as a threat for their ethnic identity. The young generation of Kabyles has therefore a reserved attitude towards Islam. The Kabyle migration to the Czech Republic has been motivated not only economically, but it has been also perceived as a liberation from social control and thus as the achievement of a lifestyle change. The life in a predominantly atheist environment does not fuel the Kabyle religious activity. In the Czech Republic, there is not a solid network of wealthy mosques providing help to immigrants, which could lead to a positive reinterpretation of Islam amongst Kabyles. Moreover, due to the general mistrust and hostility towards Islam in the Czech Republic, to present oneself as a victim of Arab chauvinism and Muslim fundamentalism proves to be an efficient strategy to escape stigma and gain sympathy. The Kabyle immigrants who do not declare themselves as Muslims are the ones that are the most critical of the Algerian repressive politics towards Kabyles, and consequently the most critical of Islam as well. When other Kabyle immigrants declare being 'Muslims in the modern sense', their main references are a concrete moral code expressed in profane terms and the Kabyle cultural heritage. The Muslim identity symbolizes for them a spiritual bond with their family and their origin.

References

Ageron, Charles-Robert. 1960. 'La France a-t-elle eu un politique kabyle?', *Revue historique* 223: 311–52.

———. 1968. *Les Algériens musulmans et la France (1871–1919)*. Paris: Puf.

Bengio, Ofra and Gabriel Ben-Dor (eds). 1999. *Minorities and the State in the Arab world*. Covent Garden: Lynne Rienner Publishers.

Bourdieu, Pierre. 2000[1972]. *Esquisse d'une théorie de la pratique précédé de trois études d'ethnologie kabyle*. Paris: Édition du Seuil.

Brett, Michel and Elisabeth Fentress. 1996. *The Berbers*. Oxford: Blackwell Publisher.

Camps, Gabriel. 1987. *Les Berbères. Mémoire et identité*. Aix-en-Provence: Collection des Hesperides.

Chaker, Salem. 1998. *Berbères aujourd'hui*. Paris: L'Harmattan.

Colonna, Fanny. 1976. 'Du bon usage de la science coloniale (1830–1962)', *Le mal de voir, Cahier Jussieu* 2 (10/18): 221–42.

Daumas, Eugène. 1853. *Moeurs et coutumes d'Algérie*. Paris: Librairie de L. Hachette et Cie.

Goodman, Jane E. 2005. *Berber Culture on the World Stage: From Village to Video*. Bloomington: Indiana University Press.

Grillo, Ralph. 1985. *Ideologies and Institutions in Urban France: The Representation of Immigrants*. Cambridge: Cambridge University Press.

———. 2004. 'Islam and Transnationalism', *Journal of Ethnic and Migration Studies* 30, pp. 861–78.

Hammoudi, Abdellah. 2009. 'Phenomenology and Ethnography: On Kabyle Habitus in the Work of Pierre Bourdieu'. In *Bourdieu in Algeria: Colonial Politics, Ethnographic Practices, Theoretical Developments*, Jane E. Goodman and Paul A. Siverstein (eds), pp. 199–254. Lincoln & London: University of Nebraska Press.

Hanoteau, Adolphe and Aristide Letourneux. 2003 [1872–73]. *La Kabylie et les coutumes kabyles*. Paris: Bouchene.

Kepel, Gilles. 1997. 'Islamic Groups in Europe: Between Community Affirmation and Social Crisis'. In *Islam in Europe: The Politics of Religion and Community*, Steven Vertovec and Ceri Peach (eds), pp. 48–55. Basingstoke: Macmillan.

———. 2003 [1991]. *La Revanche de Dieu: Chrétiens, juifs et musulmans à la reconquête du monde*. Paris: Édition du Seuil.

Lacoste-Dujardin, Camille. 1984. 'Genèse et évolution d'une presentation géopolitique: L'imaginerie kabyle à travers la production bibliographique de 1840 à 1891', *Connaisances du Maghreb* 257–78. Paris: CNRS.

———. 2005. *Dictionnaire de la culture berbère en Kabylie*. Paris: La Découverte.

Lorcin, Patricia M.E. 1995. *Imperial Identities: Stereotyping, Prejudice and Race in Colonial Algeria*. London: I.B. Tauris.

Lucas, Philippe and Jean-Claude Vatin. 1975. *L'Algérie des anthropologues*. Paris: Maspero.

Maddy-Weitzman, Bruce. 1999. 'The Berber Question in Algeria: Nationalism in the Making?' In *Minorities and the State in the Arab world*, Ofra Bengio and Gabriel Ben-Dor (eds), pp. 31–52. Covent Garden: Lynne Rienner Publishers.

Mahé, Alain. 2001. *Histoire de la Grande Kabylie aux XIXe et XXe siècle, anthropologie historique du lieu social dans les communautés villageoises*. Paris: Editions Bouchène.

Sayad, Abdelamalek. 2002. *Histoire et recherche identitaire suivi de Entretien avec Hassan Arfaoui*. Saint-Denis: Bouchène.

Silverstein, Paul A. 2004. *Algeria in France: Transpolitics, Race, and Nation*. Bloomington: Indiana University Press.

Stora, Benjamin. 2002. *Algérie, Maroc. Histoires parallèles, destins croisés*. Paris: Maisonneuve et Larose.

Topinka, Daniel, Tomáš Janků, Lenka Linhartová, and Jan Zadina. 2014. 'Muslimové imigranti v České republice: Etablování na veřejnosti.' In *Fenomén moci a sociálne nerovnosti. Zborník príspevkov z nultého ročníka konferencie doktorandov a mladých vedeckých pracovníkov*, Lukáš Bomba, Estera Köverová, and Martin Smrek (eds), pp. 238–73. Bratislava: Univerzita Komenského v Bratislavě.

Werbner, Pnina. 2004. 'Pakistani Migration and Diaspora Religious Politics in a Global Age'. In *Encyclopedia of Diasporas, Volume II: Diaspora Communities*, Melvin Ember, Carol R. Ember, and Ian Skoggard (eds), pp. 475–91. New York: Kluwer Academic/Plenum Publishers.

10

PAUL MITCHELL
HALIM RANE

Faith, Identity, and Ideology

Experiences of Australian Male Converts to Islam

Background

In recent years, Western Muslim converts have been exposed to significant media attention and scrutiny. For this 'minority within a minority', the decision to embrace a religion which has come to embody the 'other' in Western discourse can lead to significant societal obstacles and challenges. While religious conversion is undoubtedly a deeply personal journey, it is often also a journey through discrimination and social marginalization, emanating from both the Muslim and non-Muslim communities. Despite this potential for marginalization, there are suggestions that converts may have the ability to play a vital role in bridging the gap between Muslims and non-Muslims in Western societies—a notion which appears to be supported by many converts themselves.

How do converts learn about and practice their new faith, and what kind of ideologies and interpretations of Islam do they embrace? How do they navigate social and community rejection and acceptance? To what extent can they serve as a bridge between Muslim communities and wider society? Based on in-depth, phenomenological interviews, this chapter examines the varying experiences of Australian male converts to Islam and considers how they build and maintain new identities in contemporary Australian society.

In recent years, Western Muslim converts have been exposed to significant media attention and scrutiny (Brice 2010; Rayment 2006). For this 'minority within a minority' (Brice 2010), the decision to embrace a religion which has come to embody the 'other' in Western discourse (Haddad, Smith, and Moore 2006: 31) can lead to significant societal obstacles and challenges. While religious conversion is undoubtedly a deeply personal journey, it is often also a journey through discrimination and social marginalization, emanating from both the Muslim and non-Muslim communities (Brice 2010: 21–2). Despite this potential for marginalization, there are suggestions that converts may have the ability to play a vital role in bridging the gap between Muslims and non-Muslims in Western societies—a notion which appears to be supported by many converts themselves (Brice 2010; Soutar 2010).

Conversion to Islam

Over the past decade, a growing body of literature has sought to understand the phenomenon of conversion to Islam throughout the Western world, with a substantial proportion of the recent scholarship being focused on the experiences of female converts (McGinty 2006; Soutar 2010; van Nieuwkerk 2006). Such attention is arguably due to widespread perceptions of an inherent gender inequality within Islam, and the resulting confusion over why a woman would choose to convert to a religion which seemingly subjugates women (Barlas 2002: 2; Haddad, Smith, and Moore 2006: 41). In contrast, few studies have sought to explore this phenomenon from a male perspective (Rao 2015). As gender is believed to represent a crucial element of the conversion process (van Nieuwkerk 2006:1–2), it is necessary to consider the male experience in order to approach a more comprehensive understanding of this deeply complex phenomenon.

While there are a variety of approaches to defining and analysing the phenomenon of religious conversion (van Nieuwkerk 2006:1–2), it is generally understood that this involves an individual's newfound commitment to a particular faith or religious movement (Halama 2015).

Lewis Rambo asserts that religious conversion may be defined as 'a process of religious change that takes place in a dynamic force field of people, events, ideologies, institutions, expectations and orientations' (1993: 5). This process is not uniform and religious converts are not a homogenous group. As Rambo elaborates 'there is no one cause of conversion, no one process, and no one simple consequence of that process' (1993: 5). This view is supported by Halama, who asserts that 'there is agreement that no standard way of conversion exists and that there are significant differences in the ways that people convert' (2015: 186).

Self–Other Relations

For many converts, the most significant challenges of the conversion process are often the impacts on self-other relations (Brice 2010; King 2013; Köse 1996). By adopting Islam, converts may encounter confusion and rejection from friends and family members, discrimination from segments of the wider public, as well as difficulty being accepted by born Muslims. In his study on British converts, Brice found that the majority (66 per cent) of his participants had experienced negative reactions and hostility from family members following conversion (2010: 21). While the attitudes of family members often improved over time, in some cases conversion did lead to permanent alienation from loved ones (Brice 2010: 21; Zebiri 2008: 71). In her study on female converts, Turner found that participants had remained 'in the closet' for sustained periods of time following their adoption of Islam, due to their fear of negative reactions and rejection from family and friends (2010: 39–40).

Negative perceptions of Islam and Muslims among the wider public may also lead to societal barriers for converts at a broader social level. Exploring the relationship between conversion and national identity in Sweden, Jensen (2008) found that by adopting Islam, converts were viewed as 'traitors' by segments of the Swedish population. Several studies have also examined processes of racialization which Caucasian converts are subjected to following conversion. Alam found that in an Australian context, 'the act of conversion is one that racialises white Muslims, removing the privilege of racial invisibility' (Alam 2012: 124). The author found that visible markers of a convert's Muslim identity (such as traditional forms of clothing) superseded phenotypical attributes, imposing upon them a racial 'foreignness' (Alam 2012: 124). As a result, converts were subjected to 'not just Islamophobic slurs but clearly racist slurs' (Alam 2012: 130). Alam's findings were echoed in studies by Moosavi and Galonnier on the experiences of Muslim converts in Europe and the United States (Galonnier 2015; Moosavi 2015). In terms of engagement with 'born' Muslims, socialization into this new religious community is considered to be a vital step in the conversion process (Köse 1996: 132; Suleiman 2016). For many converts, however, integration into the existing Muslim community can prove to be challenging. Converts may encounter difficulties in being accepted by local Muslim communities (Zebiri 2008: 62), while also experiencing disappointment with the behaviour of born Muslims (Roald 2006). It is important to note, however, that such obstacles are not experienced by all converts, many of whom report high levels of acceptance and positive engagement with local Muslim communities (Brice 2010: 27).

While Western converts may be exposed to a number of social obstacles, there is also a belief they may be particularly suited to act in the capacity of 'intercultural interlocutor' (Soutar 2010: 14); Zebiri 2008: 82). According to this perspective, converts' groundings in both the Muslim and non-Muslim 'worlds' make them uniquely qualified to facilitate intercultural communication and contribute to greater levels of social cohesion. Research indicates that this view is also shared by many converts themselves. Participants in a number of studies (Brice 2010; Soutar 2010; Suleiman 2016) have expressed both a desire and willingness to contribute to intercultural and interfaith dialogue in an attempt to bridge the gap between Muslims and non-Muslims in the West, and to improve understanding between these communities.

The Australian Context

While there is an expanding corpus of literature on Western conversion to Islam, research on this phenomenon in an Australian context remains limited. To date, a mere handful of studies have explored conversion within Australia, predominantly focusing on the experiences of female and Indigenous converts. Currently, little in-depth research has specifically addressed the conversion experiences of Australian male converts. Among the existing body of scholarship, works by Turner (2010), Woodlock (2010), and King (2013) have considered various aspects of female conversion, including overall conversion narratives, engagement with local Muslim communities, and processes through which female converts articulate and express their Islamic identities. Several studies have also examined the motivations and experiences of Indigenous Australian converts and the relationship between Islam and Indigenous culture (Onudottir, Turner, and Possamai 2013; Stephenson 2010, 2011). Examining motivations for adopting Islam, Stephenson found that perceptions of a 'cultural convergence' between traditional Indigenous beliefs and the fundamentals of Islam have made the faith particularly appealing to Indigenous converts (2011: 265). Stephenson also found that the biography of Malcolm X (Lapidus 2002: 807)[1] had been an influential factor in the adoption of Islam by Indigenous men, with Malcolm X's struggles with racial inequality, prejudice, and cultural appropriation in the United States strongly resonating with the experiences of Indigenous converts (2010: 244). While these studies represent valuable contributions to understandings of conversion to Islam in the Australian context, the deeply complex and contextual nature of conversion necessitates a broader, more comprehensive approach to its study.

Methodology

This chapter is a modest attempt to contribute some insight into the experiences of Australian male converts, based on in-depth interviews with 10 Australian males of various ages who have converted to Islam. We used a qualitative approach as this allowed us to 'explore human experiences in personal and social contexts, and gain greater understanding of the factors influencing these experiences' (Gelling 2015: 43). Specifically, we utilized descriptive phenomenology as this method aligned with our objective to gain insight into the lived experiences of converts in relation to the phenomenon of conversion. Both a philosophical movement and method of scientific inquiry, phenomenology is underpinned by the belief that human experience, as perceived by the individual, should be the subject of scientific research (Lopez and

---

[1] Malcolm X (1925–1965) was a prominent leader of the North American organization Nation of Islam, which represented a fusion of Islam and black nationalism. Malcolm X and the Nation of Islam are considered to have been highly influential in the adoption of Islam by significant numbers of African Americans throughout the twentieth century.

Willis 2004: 727). According to proponents of the descriptive phenomenological approach, by 'bracketing' assumptions and preconceptions
about a given phenomenon, researchers may uncover its true essences,
or 'eidetic structures' (Lopez and Willis 2004: 728).

A snowball method was used to identify our interviewees. We
began by contacting Muslim convert groups and individual converts
to Islam within our social networks. On completion of each interview,
which generally lasted between one and two hours, the interviewees
were asked if they could recommend other converts who might be
willing to be interviewed. This method was found to be an efficient
way of recruiting participants as it built on the trust and rapport that
was established with each interviewee. Interviews were conducted
between July and October 2016. The 10 interviewees ranged in age
from 27 to 73 years. They had converted to Islam at different ages and
had been Muslim for varying periods of time, ranging from 6 months
to 48 years, with an average of 19 years since conversion. All interviews were conducted face-to-face, with the exception of two which
were conducted via Skype due to the interviewees being overseas at
the time of data collection. Follow-up questions were conducted via
telephone.

The qualitative data analysis software program NVivo Version 11
was utilized in the coding process, in order to systematically catego-
rize the interview data. Interview transcripts were uploaded to NVivo,
with significant statements identified and assigned to 'nodes'. Data was
then subjected to a process of nomothetic analysis, which involved the
identification of common themes and experiences among participants,
in order to arrive at the 'essences' or 'eidetic structures' of the phenomenon (Lopez and Willis 2004: 728). In order to protect the anonymity of
our interviewees, pseudonyms were used throughout the data analysis
process and within this chapter.

Motivations for Conversion

Before considering the impacts that converting to Islam has had on the
lives of our interviewees, it is essential to first consider their motivations for embracing the faith. In line with van Nieukwerk's assertions
that conversion to Islam often involves both 'rational' and 'relational'
factors, we found that the path to conversion was, in most cases,

influenced by a combination of positive personal encounters with practicing Muslims (relational factors) and a spiritual or intellectual attraction to the Islamic faith (rational factors) (2014: 673). While the journey to Islam is different for each convert, personal encounters with Muslims are often considered to be crucial in introducing individuals to the faith (Haddad 2006: 27). Personal interactions with practicing Muslims were influential in the conversion journeys of the overwhelming majority of the men we interviewed, although the nature of these encounters varied.

After initial encounters with Islam and Muslims, many future-converts enter a period of 'learning' as they strive to understand more about the Islamic faith (King 2013: 33). This process may also include experimentation with Islamic practices such as praying and fasting. Almost all of the converts we interviewed underwent processes of investigating Islam prior to taking the step of converting to the faith. For these men, a variety (and combination) of pedagogical tools were used throughout this learning process. Resources which the men relied on included books, academic courses, new Muslim friends and family members, and the internet. Many used a combination of these resources as they set about learning Islamic beliefs and practices. The Qur'an was one of the primary sources which the men utilized throughout the learning process, with this sacred, foundational text of Islam acting as not only a source of information, but also as a symbol of the 'truth' of Islam.

Further considering interviewees' motivations for converting to Islam, eight of our interviewees cited specific aspects of the faith which strongly resonated with them, and which they considered to have played an important role in their decision to convert. These included the holistic nature of Islam, the logic and clarity of the religion, as well as the Qur'an itself. The sacred text of the Qur'an was cited by several interviewees as being one of the primary features which attracted them to Islam. For Joseph and Jacob, for instance, the 'unaltered form' of the Qur'an was particularly appealing. Joseph felt that while other religious texts, such as the Christian Bible, had been altered over the centuries, the Qur'an had remained in its original form. This view of the Qur'an was also reflected in the men's perceptions of Islam itself. There was a belief that while other major faiths, such as Christianity and Judaism, had deviated from their original paths, Islam had 'stayed true' to its original message. In Jacob's view, Islam had 'stayed sincere and true to its original teachings. Whereas in Christianity, I think it changed over time according to what people's opinions are'.

For Ibrahim, Islam provided clear answers to a number of questions which he felt Christianity had not resolved. It was this 'logic' and 'sense' which made Islam particularly appealing to him:

> Well it made sense. And it does make sense. The more that you study into it, the more believable it becomes, and it resolved many issues that, for instance, exist among some Christians, who might say that, if God is all good, then why is there so much evil in the world? But in Islam that is explained in that God created everything, and he created the potential for good and for evil. But he sent down guidance, through messengers and revelations, to guide people. (Extract from a personal interview with Ibrahim, Brisbane, August 2016)

The structure and holistic nature of Islam were particularly appealing to Adam, who felt that Islam provided not just a belief system, but a 'way of life'. He explained that 'They say it's a *din*—a way of life—not a religious creed. It's a total way of life. And it really is. To the point where … going to the toilet is accounted for'.

For Adam, a perceived compatibility between Islam and Indigenous culture was also an attractive aspect of the faith. He explains, 'I'm an Aboriginal person, and we see things in a very holistic way. We're all connected. And Islam preaches these same things, that's why it was easy for me to resonate with the Qur'an. Aboriginal people, we look at nature, we look at the environment, trees—we see everything as being interconnected'.

Adam's views resonated with the findings of Stephenson's 2010 study, which found that perceptions of a 'cultural convergence' between Islam and Indigenous culture were particularly appealing to Indigenous Australian converts (Stephenson 2010: 265–7).

The conversion narratives of interviewees demonstrate that the 'path' to Islam is a complex process which is unique to the experience of each convert. In the majority of cases, both 'rational' and 'relational' factors contributed to converts' initial interest in, and eventual acceptance of the Islamic faith. These findings align with van Nieuwkerk's assertion that conversion to Islam often involves both 'rational' and 'relational' aspects (2014: 673).

Ideology and Identity

In constructing their individual interpretations and 'expressions' of Islam, the men underwent processes of what may be described as a form of *ijtihad*[2] (Kamali 2008: 171) or independent reasoning, as they explored various Islamic traditions and sources in a search for meaning in their own individual contexts. These individualized expressions of Islam were most visibly reflected in the types of Islam which converts identified with, as well as in changes to name and physical appearance. Our findings aligned with those of studies by McGinty (2007) and King (2013) who asserted that the female converts whom they interviewed engaged in processes of *ijtihad* throughout the conversion process, undertaking an 'independent, rational search for meaning' in Islamic texts and discourses (McGinty 2007: 483).

In terms of the specific interpretations of Islam with which converts identified, interviewees displayed a significant level of diversity. While four men identified with specific branches of Islam, such as Sunni Islam or Sufism, others avoided denominational labels, expressing concern that this led to divisiveness among the global Muslim community (*ummah*). Adam explained that while he had initially been trained in the Sunni Hanafi *madhab*[3] (Rane 2010: 83–4) he had come to identify broadly with three of the four Sunni jurisprudential schools of thought. He noted that racial and ideological divisions he had witnessed within his local Muslim community had motivated him to explore other perspectives, finding that the Maliki and Shafi'i *madhahib* (*madhab*—singular, *madhahib*—plural) practiced by many African Muslims strongly resonated with him. Adam also felt that while many Muslims were reluctant to identify with a particular school of thought, the *madhahib* demonstrated the diverse nature of Islam and Muslims. He explains, 'A lot of people won't wade into the *madhab*. I think the beauty about the whole universe is that greatness can be articulated in so many ways. And that we don't just have one way in Islam, but there are different

---

[2] *ijtihad* (independent reasoning) is a concept generally used in relation to the interpretation of Islamic texts by religious scholars.

[3] *madbhab* refers to a legal school of thought. There are a number of *madhahib* (pl.) within the Sunni and Shi'a traditions.

ways of expression ... I think that's the beauty. So for me, I like to be across it all'.

Ibrahim had recently come to identify with the Sunni Hanafi *madhab*, 'after being a *Shafi'i* Muslim for about forty years'. He explained that after completing his Master's degree in Islamic Civilization and working closely with *Hanafi* scholars, he had come to the conclusion that the *Hanafi* approach more closely aligned with his own personal views and understanding of Islam.

Unlike Adam and Ibrahim, Michael identified only as 'mainstream Sunni', stating that he had avoided joining particular groups or adopting specific ideological interpretations of Islam. Mark identified as 'just Muslim', expressing a belief that identification with specific interpretations or branches of Islam led to division within the global Muslim community. Joseph associated with a Sufi interpretation of Islam, explaining that although some Muslims may not accept Sufism as a legitimate expression of Islam, the Sufi emphasis on spirituality strongly aligned with his personal views and conception of Islam. Jacob did not identify with any one particular interpretation of Islam, instead choosing to draw upon the teachings of various branches of the faith, saying, 'I don't think I identify myself as either Sunni or Shia. But I believe both Sunni and Shia are very valid forms of expressing Islam. I don't really believe in choosing a camp. I learn from both. I try to practice virtuous teachings from both schools. And Sufism has had a very big impact on my expression of Islam.'

The significant level of diversity displayed in the 'types' of Islam which interviewees identified with demonstrates the heterogeneous nature of converts and suggests that these men continue to engage with new discourses and develop their understandings of Islam long after the initial period of conversion. Furthermore, interviewees did not uncritically accept notions of what constitutes 'correct' Islamic practice or behaviour. In some cases, interviewees questioned the beliefs and attitudes of fellow Muslims (for example, on issues such as homosexuality), further highlighting processes of *ijtihad*, or independent reasoning, which converts undertake as they develop their individual understandings of Islam.

In addition to the particular interpretations of Islam which converts identify with and practice, changes to name, dress and physical appearance may also be used to articulate and reflect converts' 'Muslim' identities. Zebiri asserts that the adoption of a new 'Muslim' name is a 'highly symbolic act' for converts, which serves to 'strengthen both the new identity and the sense of belonging to a group' (2008: 111)—in this case, the Muslim community. Taking a new 'Islamic' name following conversion is often strongly encouraged, although this is not something which all converts choose to do (Zebiri 2008: 111). The men interviewed for this study reported varying attitudes towards taking on new names to reflect their new religious identities. While some men had legally changed their names following conversion, others only used these names in certain social and religious contexts. Others still had resisted suggestions to adopt a Muslim name, feeling that this was not a necessary step and that it did not fit into their own personal journey. Overall, seven of the 10 men we interviewed had adopted 'Islamic' names in some capacity.

For Michael, taking on a new 'Muslim' name had largely been the result of his conversion taking place in Singapore, where this was a requirement due to the nation's dual legal system. Upon returning to Australia, he continued to use both his given and 'Muslim' names. Ibrahim, who also adopted Islam while in South East Asia, took on a new name soon after becoming Muslim and has since legally changed his name to reflect this. Ibrahim noted that while the decision to adopt a new name should be entirely voluntary for converts, it was a meaningful step in his conversion journey.

Mark and Adam have both taken Muslim names, while continuing to use their original given names. In these cases, both men used their Muslim and given names in different, specific contexts. Mark and Adam discussed their close relationships with their mothers, explaining the influence of familial bonds on their decision to maintain their given names. Adam explained:

> I was really reluctant to change my name. And I haven't changed it officially. In Islamic circles, I'll be referred to by my Muslim name. Because that's etiquette and protocol....My mother still calls me Adam. Professionally I'm called Adam. All the brothers at the masjid will call me Uthman. But for me, it was like...you hold your mother sacred. And we've been through a lot together. She gave me this name, and I want to make my mother happy. (Extract from a personal interview with Adam, Brisbane, July 2016)

While it was important for Mark to maintain both his given and Muslim names, alternating between the two had proven to be difficult on occasion. He noted that at times, 'I've gotta turn up for an appointment and I don't know what I've introduced myself to the person as'. While most interviewees had adopted Islamic names in at least some capacity, Jacob, Ryan, and Joseph had not. Jacob explained that while he had been strongly encouraged to change his name during the early period of his conversion, he had resisted such suggestions, feeling that this was not a necessary step.

The adoption of traditional 'Islamic' clothing and other changes to physical appearance may also represent a means for converts to express their new identities as Muslims and/or create distance from their former selves. For male converts, the adoption of traditional forms of clothing[4] and the growing of beards can also represent a means of 'emulating' the Prophet Muhammad. While such steps are encouraged by many in the Muslim community, this is not something which all converts choose to do. Interviewees in this study largely saw such changes as voluntary, although for some, these were viewed as meaningful steps in the construction of their Muslim identities. Overall, eight of the 10 men had adopted forms of traditional 'Islamic' clothing in some capacity.

Adam explained that during the early stages of his conversion, changing his appearance had been a way for him to establish a new Islamic identity, while creating distance from his former life. While he initially embraced traditional forms of 'Islamic' clothing, Adam came to the conclusion that this created unnecessary social barriers:

> When I first became a Muslim, I grew my beard straight away. Shaved my head. And wore Islamic dress all the time. But once my obligation became more apparent to me, what I needed to do, I realized what a strict Islamic garb meant. It alienated more people than it brought close to me. So I had to make the decision—is my Islamic identity, is the nature of my religion based upon what I wear? (Extract from a personal interview with Adam, Brisbane, July 2016)

Today, Adam continues to wear traditional forms of 'Islamic' clothing, but this is generally in specific social and religious contexts, such as when attending a mosque. The tendency to wear traditional forms of clothing in a predominantly religious context, primarily for attending mosques and religious events, was evident in the stories of most interviewees.

---

[4] Traditional 'Islamic' forms of clothing worn by some Muslim men include full length robes (*thawb*) and skull caps (*taqiyah* or *kufi*).

Mark explained that although he had initially been shocked at seeing himself in traditional robes, he had come to adopt such forms of clothing, largely in specific religious and social contexts. Jacob noted that while other Muslims had encouraged him to wear traditional robes, he generally only did so when attending a mosque.

Of the 10 interviewees, Joseph and Sam were the only men not to have adopted forms of traditional clothing, even in specific religious contexts. While eight of the 10 men had adopted certain forms of traditional Islamic clothing in specific contexts, none had altered their dress wholly. These findings aligned with those of Köse, who found that only a minimal number of male converts in his study (6 per cent) had 'changed their dress completely' (1996: 131). In terms of growing beard, four of the 10 men had done so since becoming Muslim. In Jacob's view, while wearing traditional Islamic clothing was a choice, the growing of a beard was not, saying, 'I believe that is something that Muslim men have to do. There's no question about it. The Prophet was very direct and clear about the fact that the Believers, ever since the first prophets, all the men grew beard as a sign of their covenant. So I've tried to grow my beard'.

The degree to which our interviewees are influenced by pressures to conform to appearance-related aspects of 'Islamic' identity and are convinced of it as a requirement of Islam's teachings, seemed to decline the longer an interviewee had been Muslim, and whether their conversion was more recent. Those who had converted more recently (after the year 2000), appear to be more exposed to ideological and identity issues than those who converted decades earlier. This suggests that the time-period and social context of conversion have at least an initial influence on the type of Islam to which a convert adheres.

Society and Social Relations

Conversion involves not only internal, spiritual transformations, but also has a variety of social implications and effects. As Zebiri notes, 'identity is not just about the individual, but also about the relationship between the individual and society' (2008: 89). In terms of the impact of conversion on existing relationships with friends and family, six of the 10 men reported that their decision to adopt Islam had resulted in minor concern or hesitation from loved ones. For most of our interviewees who became Muslim prior to 9/11, reactions from their friends and family had not been overtly negative. In these cases, while there was some initial concern or hesitation, their loved ones soon accepted their decision to embrace Islam. Ibrahim believed this was a result of the socio-political context in which he converted, noting that during this period, Islam was viewed more as a 'curiosity' than a threat. Faisal, who converted in 1968, recalled that his atheist parents had been largely indifferent to his adoption of Islam, telling him that 'if you want to be stupid and believe in God, that's up to you'. Ibrahim's experience was similar, noting that while his parents didn't embrace his decision, they 'didn't really have any objection'. Michael, who converted in 1999, recalled that his parents had been 'very apprehensive' when he first revealed that he had converted. Michael's parents soon embraced his decision, something which he credited to introducing them to his Muslim wife.

For Adam and Mark, who converted in 2002 and 2012 respectively, acceptance from family members hadn't posed any major challenges. Adam's mother was shocked when he first revealed to her that he had become a Muslim. Her initial response was 'are you gonna become a terrorist? Are you gonna blow yourself up?' She quickly came to accept his decision, however—something which he believed was due to the positive behavioural changes which he had undergone since becoming a Muslim. Eventually, Adam's mother and stepfather (with whom he previously had a very strained relationship) both converted to Islam. The news of Mark's conversion was not met with any significant concern or hostility from friends or family members. Echoing Adam's experience, Mark's mother soon came to adopt Islam herself—something which he credits to the positive behavioural changes he underwent after conversion.

For Jacob and Joseph, the response from friends and family members was decidedly more negative. For Joseph, who had converted to Islam only six months before being interviewed, the reaction of his family and friends had been 'mostly negative'. His conversion to Islam had resulted in the breakdown of his relationship with his biological mother and he experienced rejection from many friends and family members. While he had intended to wait before revealing the news to his loved ones, a close friend in whom he had confided made this public via social media, an experience which Joseph likened to being 'outed'.

Jacob's family, who he described as 'devout Catholics', did not react positively to news of his conversion. He recalled that immediately after taking the *shahadah* (testimony of faith), he had rushed home to inform his parents. Upon hearing this news, Jacob's mother broke down, 'thinking that I'd done something terrible'. Jacob's father likened Islam to 'devil worshipping' and warned him that he was 'going to go to hell'. This period was particularly difficult for Jacob, who was living with his parents at the time:

> They told me that I wasn't allowed to go to the mosque. Every Sunday they forced me to go to church with them, and every second night I'd have intense bible study where a priest would come in and try to tell me that Islam is wrong, this is why Muhammad's a false prophet and you have to come back to Christianity. And when I'd try to say my prayers at home, I'd get beaten or stuff would be thrown on top of me. (Extract from a personal interview with Jacob, Brisbane, September 2016)

While still experiencing difficulties with members of his extended family, Jacob's immediate family have begun to accept his decision. He narrates, 'They started coming around, as they realised if they kept doing that, they would lose their son, which none of us wanted because we were a very close family. So they came around, but they still don't understand everything properly'.

While relations with his family have improved, Jacob no longer associated with many friends from his pre-conversion life. Many of those whom he socialized with prior to becoming a Muslim were devout Christians and had not accepted his decision to embrace Islam.

Four interviewees also reported encountering discrimination and prejudice at a broader social level. By becoming a Muslim, Australian converts challenge complex notions of cultural, ethnic, and national identity (Alam 2012; King 2013). As such, reactions to conversion may be influenced and informed by negative perceptions of Islam which link the religion to terrorism, fundamentalism, and misogyny. For the men involved in this study, experiences with members of the Australian public varied according to the sociopolitical context in which they converted to Islam, while also being linked to converts' 'visibility' as Muslims.

Faisal, Ibrahim, and Michael did not report any significant difficulties in being accepted by the Australian public. The men, who had each converted prior to 2001, felt that the sociopolitical context of their conversion period may have played a role in this, with public perceptions of

Islam becoming increasingly negative following 11 September 2001. As Ibrahim explained, 'I converted over forty years ago. And at that time, there weren't any issues really about Islam. The only sort of negative aspects were a hangover from the Middle Ages, when in European society there was a bit of a fear of Islam. And that was combated by sort of denigrating Islam, and denigrating the Prophet'.

Furthermore, each of the men had spent significant amounts of time living in Muslim-majority nations following their conversion, which afforded them the time and space to develop and somewhat refine their Muslim identities.

Half of our interviewees converted to Islam at various points over the past 15 years. These men reported the most negative and prejudicial reactions from the wider Australian public. For Adam, Mark, and Jacob, antagonistic encounters with members of the Australian public had been largely linked to their 'visibility' as Muslims, with these men experiencing the most hostility while wearing traditional forms of Islamic clothing. Adam converted to Islam in 2002, and had experienced discrimination and hostility from members of the Australian public on a number of occasions. He described his initial period of conversion as being particularly difficult:

> Those early stages of being a Muslim, right at the start, accepting Islam after 9/11 was hard, mate. Especially travelling away on planes. I still get hit with those tests every time I go through the bloody airport I'm hit with a random bomb test. People look at you walking down the corridor, the aisle of the plane, and they're thinking 'shit, don't let him sit next to me'. My wife is Aboriginal. She wears a scarf, the hijab. And people swear at us and tell us to go back to our country. (Extract from a personal interview with Adam, Brisbane, July 2016)

Jacob, who converted to Islam in 2009, had experienced both physical and verbal abuse from members of the wider public, primarily when wearing traditional Islamic clothing in public spaces. He considered acceptance from society as the biggest obstacle of his conversion journey:

> Sometimes you get people yelling out 'terrorist' or 'you filthy Muslim'. Or I've had people spit on me. There was actually an old lady—she was walking past and she turned around and spat at me...I've been attacked. If it's time for me to pray and I'm outside, I get very scared. I need to find somewhere to pray where no-one's gonna see me. There have been a few times when I've had to say my prayers in a park or something, and you

have people coming up and attacking you from behind. (Extract from a personal interview with Jacob, Brisbane, September 2016)

While Mark had also experienced hostility and discrimination from members of the Australian public, he felt that Muslim women often bore the brunt of such behaviours. Michael expressed a similar view, noting that 'the women get it because they wear the *hijab*, it's more obvious'. The views of Mark and Michael mirrored those of male converts in Suleiman's study, who expressed a view that female converts faced greater social challenges following conversion as a result of their greater 'visibility' as Muslims (Suleiman 2016: 4).

Despite the social obstacles they faced, interviewees continued to feel that engagement with non-Muslims was crucial to improving negative perceptions and understandings of Muslims within Australia. Half of our interviewees expressed a belief that converts were well-equipped to act in this capacity, and could assist in educating non-Muslim Australians on Islam. Furthermore, Jacob felt that converts could also assist in addressing negative views of non-Muslims among the Muslim community. Our findings in this respect are consistent with those of Brice, who found that the majority of British converts surveyed supported the notion of converts acting as cultural bridges (2010: 30). Like multigenerational Australian-born Muslims (Rane, Amath, and Faris 2015), Australian converts to Islam have the potential to act as a bridge between cultures. This builds on Amath's (2015) work on social cohesion which identifies the role of Muslim civil society organizations as potential bridges between Muslim communities and various governmental and non-governmental sectors of the wider society. However, in light of other research that contends that longer established communities and those oriented towards and invested in building bridges with the wider society are more likely to succeed in social bridging activities (Allen 2010), further research is needed into the types of Islam adopted by converts, and Muslims more generally, and the extent to which they advocate coexistence and cohesion with the wider society.

In considering the social aspects and implications of conversion, it is also crucial to examine converts' relationships and interactions with other Muslims. Engagement with other adherents of a convert's new faith is considered to represent a vital component of the conversion journey (Köse 1996: 132), and while many converts to Islam report positive engagement and interaction with members of local Muslim communities (Brice 2010: 27), in some cases, integration and acceptance can prove challenging (Brice 2010).

For the male converts in this study, engagement with Muslim communities had been largely positive. Born Muslims were consistently cited as sources of support and knowledge, and the majority of men had successfully established new social networks and relationships among their local Muslim communities. Five of the men also reported active engagement with Muslim organizations such as charities and community groups, in local and international contexts.

Despite these generally positive experiences, four of our interviewees had experienced or observed behaviours and attitudes among born Muslims which they considered to be problematic. For Adam, 'total acceptance' from born Muslims had been elusive. Adam explained that while born Muslims had initially been very welcoming after he first converted to Islam, this had only extended so far. In his view, there was a perception amongst some in the Muslim community that converts were 'tainted goods', as they had not been raised within the faith. He said that while Muslim families may 'invite you over to dinner ... they won't marry their daughters to you'. Adam's concerns over 'total acceptance' among born Muslims echoed those expressed by male converts in Suleiman's study on conversion to Islam in the United Kingdom (Suleiman 2016: 10).

Adam also felt that converts faced pressures from some born Muslims to conform to what they viewed as 'correct' Islamic behaviour and practice. Adam noted that he had encountered difficulties with some members of his local Muslim community who had expected him to behave in a certain manner. He explained that 'if the way that you articulate and express yourself is outside those realms, it puts you at odds with these people'.

This issue was also acknowledged by Ibrahim, who noted that 'sometimes our fellow Muslims can be obstacles'. Ibrahim explained that some born Muslims had a tendency to be overly critical of converts, particularly in the context of performative rituals such as prayer.

Socialization into new religious communities may also expose points of tension between elements of religious doctrine and converts' existing personal beliefs. While Jacob was highly positive regarding the strong support he had received from members of his local Muslim community, he expressed concern over negative attitudes towards homosexuality which he felt were prevalent within Brisbane's 'very conservative' Muslim community. In Jacob's view, there was no incompatibility between being gay and being Muslim. He believed that negative views of homosexuality were linked to cultural attitudes, rather than having any basis within Islam itself.[5] Joseph also raised the issue of homosexuality, explaining that while he understood that this was a contentious issue for Muslims, he nevertheless continued to support social causes such as same-sex marriage. The attitudes of Jacob and Joseph towards homosexuality provide an interesting contrast to those of male converts in Suleiman's study, in which all participants expressed a strong belief that homosexuality was forbidden in Islam (Suleiman 2016: 11–12). Our findings in this regard further demonstrate processes of *ijtihad* which converts may undertake as they critically engage with, and in some cases, challenge, Islamic discourses and beliefs, in their quest to articulate their individualized interpretations of Islam.

Experiences of Conversion

This chapter is a modest attempt to provide insights into the experiences of Australian males who have converted to Islam. By becoming Muslim, converts are confronted with a number of challenges in terms of their own identity, relations with family and friends, and how they are perceived by segments of the wider Australian society. It seems from our interviews that Muslims over time have increasingly placed emphasis on outward manifestations of an 'Islamic' identity, which has significantly contributed to the othering of converts and the negativity some have experienced from family, friends, and the wider society.

While twentieth century converts to Islam seem to have experienced less hostility in response to their decision to convert, and also seem to have experienced less pressure to adhere to outward manifestations of 'Islamic' identity, twenty-first century converts have been negatively impacted by their desire to adhere to such norms and by the pejorative connotations family, friends, and other members of the wider society associate with

---

[5] As Zebiri (2008: 164) notes, 'according to the vast majority of scholars (both Muslim and non-Muslim), the Quran condemns homosexuality and upholds male-female sexual relation (within prescribed legal relationships) as the norm'.

certain expressions of Islam. This raises important questions concerning the priorities of Islam in the twenty-first century and whether an emphasis on a distinct identity not only creates unnecessary distress for converts but ultimately distracts from and undermines the positive aspects of Islam which converts are potentially well-placed to showcase within the wider society.

We hope that this chapter may provide non-Muslims with some insight into the people behind the beard and robes. They are Australian men who have been inspired by a set of ideas about human existence and how to live a more fulfilling life. In the experiences of our interviewees, Islam has imbued their lives with meaning and purpose, and they are happy with their decision. Most of our interviewees, particularly those who have been Muslim longest, are not naive and have a more nuanced understanding of Islam relative to the Islamist ideological strain that sees Islam as an all-encompassing answer to everything. They are still Australian, bear no malice against their fellow Australians and desire to maintain positive relations with family and friends.

References

Alam, Oishee. 2012. 'Islam is a Blackfella Religion, Whatchya Trying to Prove? Race in the Lives of White Muslim Converts in Australia', *La Trobe Journal* 89: 24–139.

Allen, Richard. 2010. 'The Bonding and Bridging Roles of Religious Institutions for Refugees in a Non-Gateway Context', *Ethnic and Racial Studies* 33(6): 1049–68. doi: 10.1080/01419870903118130.

Amath, Nora. 2015. *The Phenomenology of Community Activism: Muslim Civil Society Organisations in Australia*. Carlton: Melbourne University Press.

Barlas, Asma. 2002. *'Believing Women' in Islam: Unreading Patriarchal Interpretations of the Qur'an*. Austin: University of Texas Press.

Brice, Kevin. 2016. *A Minority within a Minority: A Report on Converts to Islam in the United Kingdom*. London: Faith Matters. Available at: http://faith-matters.org/images/stories/fm-reports/a-minority-within-a-minority-a-report-on-converts-to-islam-in-the-uk.pdf. Accessed on 1 November 2016.

Galonnier, Juliette. 2015. 'The Racialization of Muslims in France and the United States: Some Insights from White Converts to Islam', *Social Compass* 62(4): 570–83. doi:10.1177/0037768615601966.

Gelling, Leslie. 2015. 'Qualitative Research', *Nursing Standard* 29(30): 43–7.

Haddad, Yvonne. 2006. 'The Quest for Peace in Submission: Reflections of the Journey of American Women Converts to Islam'. In *Women Embracing Islam: Gender and Conversion in the West*, Karen van Nieuwkerk (ed.), pp. 19–47. Austin: University of Texas Press.

Haddad, Yvonne, Jane Smith,and Kathleen Moore. 2006. *Muslim Women in America: The Challenge of Islamic Identity Today*. Oxford: Oxford University Press.

Halama, Peter. 2015. 'Empirical Approach to Typology of Religious Conversion', *Pastoral Psychology* 64: 185–94. doi: 10.1007/s11089-013-0592-y.

Jensen, Tina. 2007. 'To Be "Danish", Becoming "Muslim": Contestations of National Identity?', *Journal of Ethnic and Migration Studies* 34(3): 389–409. doi: 10.1080/13691830701880210.

Kamali, Mohamed Hashim. 2008. *Shari'ah Law: An Introduction*. Oxford: Oneworld Publishing, 2008.

King, Ebony. 2013. 'Conversion to Islam: The Motivations and Experiences of Women in Australia', Honours dissertation, Griffith University.

Köse, Ali. 1996. *Conversion to Islam: A Study of Native British Converts*. London: Kegan Paul International.

Lapidus, Ira. 2002. *A History of Islamic Societies*. Cambridge: Cambridge University Press.

Lopez, Kay and Danny Willis. 2004. 'Descriptive Versus Interpretive Phenomenology: Their Contributions to Nursing Knowledge', *Qualitative Health Research* 14(5): 726–35. doi: 10.1177/1049732304263638.

McGinty, Anna Mansson. 2006. *Becoming Muslim: Western Women's Conversion to Islam*. New York: Palgrave MacMillan.

McGinty, Anna Mansson. 2007. 'Formation of alternative femininities through Islam: Feminist approaches among Muslim converts in Sweden', *Women's Studies International Forum* 30: 474–85. doi: 10.1016/j.wsif.2007.09.004.

Moosavi, Leon. 2015. 'The Racialization of Muslim Converts in Britain and their Experiences of Islamophobia', *Critical Sociology* 41(1): 41—56. doi: 10.1177/0896920513504601.

Onnudottir, Helena, Bryan Turner, Bryan and Adam Possamai, Adam 2013. *Religious Change and Indigenous Peoples: The Making of Religious Identities*. Farnham, UK: Ashgate Publishing.

Rambo, Lewis. 1993. *Understanding Religious Conversion*. New Haven: Yale University Press, 1993.

Rane, Halim. 2010. *Islam and Contemporary Civilization: Evolving Ideas, Transforming Relations*. Melbourne: Melbourne University Press, 2010.

Rane, Halim, Nora Amath, and Nezar Faris. 2015. 'Multiculturalism and the Integration of Multigenerational Muslim Communities in Queensland, Australia', *Journal of Muslim Minority Affairs* 35(4): 503–19. doi: 10.1080/13602004.2015.1112121.

Rao, Aliya H. 2015. 'Gender and Cultivating the Moral Self in Islam: Muslim Converts in an American Mosque', *Sociology of Religion* 76 (4): 413–35. doi: 10.1093/socrel/srv030.

Rayment, Sean. 2006. 'Whites Being Lured into Islamic Terror', *The Telegraph*, 2 July. Available at: http://www.telegraph.co.uk/news/uknews/1522878/Whites-being-lured-into-Islamic-terror.html. Accessed on 1 October 2016.

Roald, Anne Sofie. 2006. 'The Shaping of a Scandinavian Islam: Converts and Gender Equal Opportunity'. In *Women Embracing Islam*, Karen van Nieuwkerk (ed.), pp. 48–70. Austin: University of Texas Press.

Soutar, Louise. 2010. 'British female converts to Islam: choosing Islam as a rejection of individualism', *Language and Intercultural Communication* 10(1): 3–16. doi: 10.1080/14708471003602355.

Stephenson, Peta. 2010. *Islam Dreaming: Indigenous Muslims in Australia*. Sydney: University of New South Wales Press, 2010.

———. 2011. 'Indigenous Australia's Pilgrimage to Islam', *Journal of Intercultural Studies* 3(2): 261–77. doi: 10.1080/07256868.2011.565737.

Suleiman, Yasir. 2016. *Narratives of Conversion to Islam in Britain: Male Perspectives.* Cambridge: University of Cambridge, 2016. Available at: http://www.cis.cam.ac.uk/wp-content/uploads/2016/01/Narratives-of-Conversion-Report-1.pdf. Accessed on 1 November 2016.

Turner, Karen. 2010. 'Contracts with Clauses: The Secret Politics of Being and Becoming Muslim in Australia'. In *Challenging Identities: Muslim Women in Australia*, Shahram Akbarzadeh (ed.), pp. 31–55. Melbourne: Melbourne University Press.

Van Nieuwkerk, Karen. 2006. 'Gender and Conversion to Islam in the West'. In *Women Embracing Islam: Gender and Conversion in the West*, Karen van Nieuwkerk (ed.), pp. 1–16. Austin: University of Texas Press.

Van Nieuwkerk, Karen. 2014. 'Conversion to Islam and the Construction of a Pious Self'. In *The Oxford Handbook of Religious Conversion*, Lewis R. Rambo and Charles E. Farhadian (eds), pp. 67–86. Oxford: Oxford University Press.

Woodlock, Rachel. 2010. 'Praying Where They Don't Belong: Female Muslim Converts and Access to Mosques in Melbourne, Australia', *Journal of Muslim Minority Affairs* 30(2): 265–78. doi: 10.1080/13602004.2010.494076.

Zebiri, Kate. 2008. *British Muslim Converts: Choosing Alternate Lives.* Oxford: Oneworld Publishing.

11

ENZO PACE

MOHAMMED KHALID RHAZZALI

Muslim Communities in a Catholic Country

The Case of Italy

The Muslim presence in Italy differs in many respects from most other European countries that have come to terms with migration from Muslim countries sincethe 1960s. In Italy, it is a relatively recent phenomenon. The first large groups originating from Tunisia began to arrive in Sicily at the beginning of the 1970. In the following decade, larger flows came from Morocco and Senegal with immigrants moving to nearly every region of the country. There was a limited number of immigrants coming from Somalia, Italy's ex-colony, prevalently linked to the internal political ordeals of that country and that cannot be compared with the waves of immigrants from former British and French settlements in Africa or Asia (Allievi and Dalla Zuanna 2016; Ambrosini 2008, 2010). The arrival of immigrants towards Italy intensified in 1990, when different driving forces and objectives became more multifaceted and numerous. Immigrations from the Maghreb and Sub-Saharan Africa increased over time. The number of Muslim immigrants attempting to reach Italy's coasts continued to grow as new immigrants began to arrive from the Balkans (Albania and later ex-Yugoslavia), and from South-East Asia (Bangladesh, India, and Pakistan).

According to estimates recently published by the *Fondazione Iniziative e Studi sulla Multietnicità* (ISMU 2016), there are approximately 1,423,900 Muslims residents in Italy, amounting to 2.34 per cent of the Italian population. In addition, the number of Muslims covers at least some tens of thousands of persons including Italian citizens who have converted, so-called naturalized persons and their children, and the children of mixed naturalized couples and of those who have converted (Allievi 2009; Cerchiaro 2015; Rhazzali 2013). The Moroccan component still holds the primate representing a third approximately of that figure (424,300), followed by immigrants from Albania (214,300), Bangladesh (99,700), Tunisia (94,400), Pakistan (94,400), Egypt (93,500), Senegal (84,500) and, finally, Macedonia (52,100). In 2016, the number of Muslims has fallen by nearly 200 thousand with respect to the figure registered in 2012, as many have returned to their homelands or have migrated to other European countries, given the economic crisis that the Italian society has been experiencing these past few years. In that sense, it is a phenomenon that does not regard only immigrants of Muslim culture.

Immigration is changing the Italian society sharply. In a country that is, aging the demographic composition of the Italian population is destined, with the passage of the generations, to become increasingly multicultural. It means both a high difference in lifestyles, family patterns, consumption, religious dietary, and an unprecedented plurality of religions. In a country of Catholic tradition, the religious landscape is changing profoundly. Due to the presence, which will gradually become more and more visible, not only of Muslims but of Orthodox, African, Asian and Latin American Pentecostals, Buddhist, Hindu, and Sikh (Pace 2013a), Italy is transforming from a mono-religious society to a pluralistic one. The political establishment is coping with the societal transformation with a limited capacity to manage this unexpected religious diversity. The status quo still enjoyed by the Catholic Church will gradually decrease. At the same time, political parties, accustomed to take into account the authoritative voice of the Catholic Church, will have to pay more attention to other voices, all those new religions that in the meantime have learned to speak in the public sphere.

The social framework in which new immigrants are trying to define their identity does not facilitate this task. Due to political conflicts about the migration, it has not been possible to overcome the legislative gap regarding formal recognition of citizenship as part of a real social inclusion programme that considers immigrants and their children a true resource (Ambrosini and Molina, 2004; Rhazzali 2008, 2010). The most significant difference between political parties is precisely the idea that the immigrant is *always* a foreigner and he can never be an Italian citizen, not even when it comes to children born in Italy. The fear of invasion by the aliens becomes for some parties the ideological core of their political struggle. Up to now, the Italian parliament has not yet modified the law n. 91, passed in 1991, stating that only children born in Italy whose parents are citizens can apply for citizenship.[1]

Despite their wide diffusion throughout the country, Muslims remain foreigners indefinitely positioned at the threshold of a world where they were often born and raised, studied, worked, and contributed to the growth of national Gross Domestic Product (GDP). However, Muslims in Italy, nevertheless, represent a relevant piece of the national picture. The wide spread of the religious community in all regions of the peninsula along with the new forms of cultural experience that the presence of Muslims at local level, contribute to highlighting the dimensions and features of the progressive root of Islam in Italy. Their religious and cultural experience is not merely an importation of a foreign religion into a Catholic country. At the contrary, the process of adaptation of Muslims to Italian society represents a peculiar way to being Italian Muslims (Allievi 2009; Frisina 2007, 2014). Economic and social reasons explain this process.

First, the Muslim presence has spread throughout Italy largely in accordance with the economic relevance of its cities and regions, and particularly in the industrial districts in Northern and Centre of the peninsula. It reflects the general tendency of employment-based immigration. The distribution tends to follow the geography of the labour market. As a result, despite significant numbers settling in southern Italy where work opportunities are in agriculture sector, vending, and tourism, Northern and Centre of Italy remain the main destination for the immigrants. The highest percent of Muslims in Italy are, according to

---

[1] Despite a positive public attitude and the political willingness by many parties (except that of the Northern League) to recognize Italian citizenship to children born in Italy of immigrant parents, the Italian parliament has not yet modified Law n. 91, passed in 1991, stating that citizenship is recognized to children born in Italy whose parents are citizens.

ISMU (2017) and Caritas (2016) report, in the Lombardy region 368,000 (equal to 26 per cent of the total number of Muslims living in Italy), followed by Emilia-Romagna (183,000), Veneto (142,000), and Piedmont (119,000), then by the Lazio 112,800 and Tuscany (104,400).

Second, the variety of their homelands and the diversification characterizing the migration flow has led Muslim migrants to find occupation in various manufacturing and commercial sectors. Their numbers in the service industry are also increasing as ethnic micro-entrepreneurial experiences (Bevilacqua, Rhazzali, and Saint-Blancat 2008) in the form of Kebab shops, phone centres, money transfer agencies, halal butchers, hairdressers and barbers, etc., sprout up and often blossom.

Third, Muslim communities appear to be spreading and becoming ever more visible in the large cities just as in townships and small villages. Its entrenchment is often characterized by intense experiences and strong forms of identification with the local context although in many cases there is a distinct willingness to move on if opportunity knocks. Beyond experiences in the small and large cities and despite some conflicts over mosques, immigrants often engage in fruitful forms of interaction with local residents where the mosques often constitute the only form of aggregation for those immigrants. The number of Muslims in large and small centres does not in any case exceed the threshold beyond which its strength would permit it to be incisive in local and national politics and thus to effectively express its own specific needs (Allievi 2010). Finally yet importantly, an important sign of change is the recent successes of some members of the new generation of Muslims: Khalid Chaouki was elected to the Italian Parliament; Sumaya Abdel Qader, became municipal councilwoman of the Milan's City. Both present themselves as Muslim protagonists on the political scene and founders of the Giovani Musulmani d'Italia (Young Muslims Association from Italy).

Mapping Out Mosques and Other Places of Worship (*Musallyat*)

The spreading of Muslim worship places reflects both the gradual intensifying visibility of Islam in Italy and its various theological and doctrinal orientations in Italy. Therefore, worship places belong to different Muslim organizations that have taken upon themselves to coordinate their activity.

Muslim places of worship that can truly be considered *masjid* (mosques) are only six, and can be found in Rome, Milano, Catania (now inactive) Palermo, Ravenna, and Colle Val d'Elsa (in Tuscany). A longer list could include unsuccessful attempts to establishing others, and that have been interrupted for political reasons. Other ritual places include *musallayat* (plural for *musallah*, literally praying-places), simple rooms used for basic religious services. They are usually temporary solutions to which Muslim community resorts to praying. This situation has led to the reconversion of garages, warehouses, basements, and or buildings, originally employed for commercial activities, into *musallayat*. They are constantly in danger of eviction or of receiving notification of lease suspension by local authorities, as they are not conceived by law as ritual places. The solidarity of lay and or religious associations that are sensitive to interreligious dialogue occasionally intervene to counterbalance the political obstacles and opposition of a part of the local people.

In some cases, the construction of a mosque or the demand to rent a place for a *musallah* require economic resources based on voluntary contributions on the part of the local Muslim communities. Moreover, economic aid comes from Muslim states, but the timing of arrival and the quantity are generally unpredictable making planning precarious and arduous.

For all these reasons, carrying out a census of what we will call mosque and *musallayat*, is not an easy endeavour. It is not simple to establish a distinct line between places that even with all material limits can be formally considered places of prayer and other spaces temporarily utilized like rooms in homes, places rented for a particular event by groups of Muslims. Except for the Great Mosque in Rome, designated by Italian architect Paolo Portoghesi, and inaugurated in 1995, thanks to an agreement between the Italian state and Saudi Arabia, all other prayer places, from a legal point of view, are the headquarters of single associations instituted with various social and cultural purposes.

The religious nature of the practices that take place therein remain a private choice of the associations. From the point of view of local, governmental, and state authorities, either it means the respectful attempts to collaborate or, as has often happened, mirroring restrictive interpretations of laws and rules, characterized by juridical controversies and rhetorical discussions, aiming to make the life of the mosque difficult if not impossible.

It is important to remind the relationships between the worship places we mapped and the regional and national Islamic organizations, which form a network. Making the research, we directly applied for their collaboration. In particular, UCOII (Union of the Islamic Communities and Organizations in Italy), CII (Italian Islamic Confederation), and COREIS (Italian Islamic Religious Community) provided the addresses of their respective places of worship. A network of *imam* and leaders of communities created during the research project helped us to verify achieved data. We came up with all the information concerning the addresses (including the postal code) of each worship place with a software package (TargetMap). The Minister of Scientific Research granted the research, coordinated by the Padua University along with five other Italian universities. We published the outputs of the survey in 2013 (Pace 2013b).

We analyse the collected figures together with information concerning how long the mosque had been open. We checked if some of these places were covered local and national papers. Then we explored the internet to identify other unregistered mosques, and through contact with city administrations and non-Muslim religious associations working locally, we were able to collect data about the existence of other places of prayer. We compared our data with two other investigations carried out in recent past: the first conducted by Allievi and Dassetto in 1992 (Allievi and Dassetto 1993), the second by Bombardieri between 2008 and 2011 (Bombardieri 2011). It is worthwhile, finally, to mention the 2007 report by CESIS (Executive Committee of Information and Security Services) realized by the Ministry of Interior in 2005 in cooperation with of the Department of Information Security (DIS) working on behalf of the president of the Council of Ministers.

According to the data, we were able to gather that there are 655 mosques and prayer centres in Italy. This figure is lower than the one reported by the CESIS in 2007 (774) and by Bombardieri (746). The discrepancy depends on the different criteria adopted by each investigator. With regard to the former, the report reflects security reasons. They tried to photograph as accurately as possible the presence of all places of Muslim aggregation, including cultural association or small Sufi groups that usually organize meetings in private apartment, in Italy. The second research, carried out few years later, confirmed the result of the precedent: the author has taken into account all types of aggregation among Muslims and not just those places destined to strictly religious

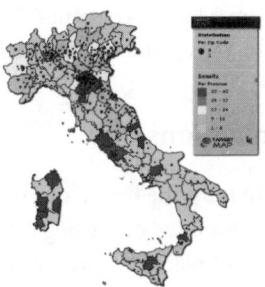

FIGURE 11.2   Distribution of Muslim places of worship by province
Source: Pace (2013b).
Note: This map is not to scale and does not represent authentic national and
international boundaries.

activities. Our methodological choice was quite different. Instead of
considering any kind of aggregation as a place of prayer, we took in consideration only those places really opened to prevalent religious practices
(prayer room, library and school for children, *madrasa*) and with at least
a minimum amount of publicity and endowed with a legal personality.

The geographic distribution of the mosques substantially reflects the
structure of the labour market and the industrialization model widespread with small and medium factories in the North and Central Italy.
An analysis of the distribution by province shows that there are more
mosques and prayer centres in large cities such as Milan (where the dimensions of the single *musallah* are more relevant than their numbers), Turin,
and Bologna, as well as in other provinces such as Bergamo, Brescia, and
Vicenza, characterized by a capillary distribution of manufacturing and
commercial activities. Northern Italy represents the area where there are
more mosques and *musallyat*. Moving down the peninsula, the number
tends to diminish except for in some areas in the Tuscany region such
as the Colle Val d'Elsa. This mosque built in accordance with the local
administration, both as a worship place and an Islamic Cultural centre.
In Rome, besides the Great Mosque, there is a large number of cultural
centres and places of prayer. The data regarding Sicily differs with respect
to the rest of the South because the presence of Muslims reflects the
traditional relationship of the island with its neighbours on the other
side of the Mediterranean Sea (Tunisia overall) rather than to the recent

immigration coming from Muslim countries. The largest concentration of Muslims is in Palermo, the capital of the Sicily.

The Islamic Organizations

In the history of Islam in Italy, the first association was USMI (Union of Italian Muslim Students) founded at the beginning of 1970s. They managed the first mosques and places of prayer, in relation with the local institutions on behalf of the faithful. Other networks have been taking form and endeavouring to coordinate and to promote negotiations at a national level with the Italian government.

Only a few studies analysed the religious practice of Muslims in Italy (Allam and Gritti 2001; Allievi 1999, 2010; Cerchiaro 2015; Frisina 2007; Pace and Frisina 2011; Piraino 2016; Rhazzali 2010, 2015; Saint-Blancat 1999, 2015). In particular, we do not know the real numbers of Muslims taking part in the cultural and religious activities in the mosques and prayer centres.

The main Muslim organizations have resolutely endeavoured to present themselves as centres of aggregation in the attempt to facilitate dialogue and negotiation with the Italian government. The goal is to gain public and juridical recognition of Islam as religion and to access to funds allotted to religious activity by the Italian state. One of the most relevant association is the UCOII—an umbrella organization founded in 1990 by former leaders of the USMI. It was already active in the 1970s and collaborating with several Islamic centres in the attempt to coordinate the complex reality of prayer centres and cultural associations of Muslims in Italy. Today 205 mosques and *musallayat* refer and adhere to the UCOII. Thanks to its efforts, the first drafts of an agreement between the Islamic communities and the Italian state were signed in February 2017. Its relationship with the public institutions has however always been arduous. In the past, some Italian politicians were suspiciously staring the UCOII for its closeness to the Muslim Brotherhood. The turnover of the leadership of the association in recent years favoured a new political direction. The Union of the Islamic Communities and Organizations in Italy, under the new leadership, is trying to accredit itself as an organization that represents *Italian* Islam and which, is therefore, no longer conditioned and driven by foreign states or transnational associations. *Italian* Islam means many things:

cooperation with public bodies, supporting interreligious dialogue with Catholic, Protestant and Jews communities, promoting at a managerial level of the association a new generation of Italian Muslims of foreign origins, and publicly assuming positions of firm condemnation of any form of terrorism and Islamic jihadist interpretation. Therefore, they are receiving more appreciation and recognition by public opinion and institutions as an actor who works for the social cohesion.

From 2009 to 2012 a federalization process has been leading many Islamic organizations to unite in regional federations and ultimately in the CII. The association runs 209 worship places. The confederation explicitly refers to the government of Morocco and to several of that country's cultural and religious institutions. The collaboration with the mother country presents some positive aspects, despite the fact that it tends to create a dependence of *Italian* Muslims from a foreign country, especially when it comes to new generations of Moroccan origin, but born and raised in Italy. The recent constitutional evolution and reforms in the Kingdom actually biases cultural and religious attitudes among the Muslim communities, Moroccan origins, towards a tolerant Islam. The reform of personal status or family code (*Mudawwana*), for instance, passed by the Moroccan Parliament in 2004, focused on the women rights and gender equality, overcome some traditional constraints of the *shari'a*. A second example is the establishment of a new training curriculum for imams and religious science scholars (*'ulama*), open to women (*murshidat*), with the explicit purpose of reopening the door to the interpretation (*ijtihad*) of sacred texts, culturally fighting against any form of fundamentalism. The regional federations that make up the CII were constituted through an arduous negotiation favouring involvement and participation of the members of Islamic centres. The Italian Islamic Confederation is facing many challenges in the immediate future to demonstrate its capacity to interpret its cultural and social role within the Italian and European context.

Since the second half of the 1990s, the CO.RE.IS (Italian Islamic Religious Community) plays a relevant role in the religious landscape. The association, founded in 1993 by an Italian who became Muslim, brings together mainly Italian converts to Islam. It has undertaken to strengthen dialogue and provide information on the Islamic civilization in Italy thus representing the religious interests of Muslims present in Italy and Europe. The organization focuses in particular on theological, philosophical and cultural studies and activities and interreligious dialogue, bridging between Muslims and public institutions.

A Religious Visibility without Public Recognition

The presence of Islam in Italy is a relatively recent phenomenon, mostly represented by the first generation of immigrants with their various political and cultural backgrounds—from Pakistan to Bangladesh, from Mashreq to Maghreb, from Iran to Sub-Saharan Africa. Since the early 1980s, Islam in Italy entered the public space through aggregation and associations that have always focused on protecting Muslim identity and the right to preserving their cultural diversity biased by religious belonging.

Despite the ever more evident efforts made by many Islamic organizations aiming to construct a Muslim experience fully rooted in the Italian social and cultural fabric, the deadlock over the recognition of Islam as an official religious entity does not seem to be heading to a success. The contribution of Italians who have converted to Islam and of the organizations of Sufi inspiration, which focus their attention on the philosophical and theological culture of Islam, falls indeed under this heading. The 'second generation' immigrants that many thought would take over leadership from their fathers do not seem to be assuming until now a specific role in the evolution of Islam in Italy.

Nevertheless, looking at local and provincial level, many volunteer mixed groups (Italians of different religious and cultural orientation and Muslims) promote active participation of younger Muslims in civil society's issues (environment, protection of human rights, hospitality for refugees, intercultural, and interreligious meetings). This type of social action leads the new Muslim generation to overcome the attitudes of their parents who looked at the motherland or cultivated sympathetic relations with some international organization, like Muslim League or Muslim Brotherhood or Iranian Mujtahid. Younger generation of Italian Muslims are developing forms of dialogue and cooperation, adapting them to the specificity of experiences taking place at a local level. In Milan, for example, acts the CAIM (Coordination of Islamic Association of Milan). In Vicenza there is the Islamic Council of Vicenza, as well as in Genova the CUMUL, the network of Community of Muslims from Liguria. They are becoming credible interlocutors of the public bodies and the local Catholic Church. Therefore, they received recognition by the public institutions for their work and activities on behalf of the Islamic communities. The local authorities appreciated a public declaration by Muslim communities regarding terroristic phenomenon as well as with their efforts to engage in interreligious dialogue.

A tenacious form of diffidence towards Muslims seems nevertheless to linger despite these positive notes. Muslims in Italy are looked upon suspiciously. This determines an ambiguous situation in which the mistrust against of Muslims persists in a large part of society. Muslims in Italy find themselves in an ambiguous situation: on one hand, they experience openness to dialogue and on the other, they feel that they are perceived as a threat. According to a recent survey conducted by the Pew Research Center (2015), in European Union the Italians are most critical of Muslims: 61 per cent have an unfavourable view in comparison with Poland (56 per cent), Spain (42 per cent), Germany (24 per cent), France (24 per cent) and UK (19 per cent). When asked the question: 'How many Muslims are in Italy?', 58 per cent of Italians answered that they are about 20 per cent of the population, while in fact they do not reach 3 per cent.

We face a return among Muslims to a sort of ethnic nationalism at the crossroads of the sense of religious/national belonging, mirrored with the resurgence of nationalistic spirits, on the one hand, and the desire to secession on the other among the Italians. It is not the outcome of a precise strategy neither on the part of Italian politics nor on the part of Muslim *home* countries. Nor can it be considered a reworking of the formula of Islam states or in other words the propensity of home states to consider fellow countrymen who have immigrated as an offshoot or part of a diaspora over which political control can be exerted. Instead, in the face of a standstill in the process of social inclusion and of the strong need to be able to construct and exhibit their religious identity and to facilitate their integration, Muslim immigrants are tending to organize on the basis of ethnic national considerations which has been giving rise to linguistically and culturally homogeneous groupings in which Islamic universalism becomes associated to claims for more specific cultural identities. Distinct places and centres of prayer have thus sprung up: Muslims from Morocco group with others from Morocco, Muslims from Bangladesh meet with others from Bangladesh, Muslims from Macedonia gather with others from that country. The phenomenon is particularly evident in small- and medium-size urban centres where a large proportion of Muslim immigrants have made their homes.

Homeland countries in some cases have been providing financial support to this communitarian tendency in the attempt to maintain a link with their fellow citizens. Therefore, they too favour, paradoxically, the social integration of Muslims in Italy. The trend has meanwhile been counterbalanced by the Islamic organizations already mentioned above (UCOII e COREIS) as well as transnational organizations (such as the traditionalist association *Tabligh* and Pakistan or Bangladesh Muslim Leagues), as well as entities working prevalently to provide humanitarian relief (Islamic Relief and Qatar Charity). All Muslim organizations are heterogeneous. They are competing among themselves in the battle for public recognition. Everyone claims to represent the 'true Islam' and to have more credit than the other associations publicly representing the Islam in Italy.

Over the last few years and because of solicitations on the part of various Islamic organizations, the Italian state has displayed its willingness to recognize the legal rights of the Muslims through a juridical instrument, the formal agreement (*Intesa*) as it has been with other minority groups (Jews, Buddhists, Hinduists, Greek Orthodox, and various Protestant Churches).

Since 2002 attempts made by three Italian governments to reach a concrete solution have had no success, strengthening public's conviction that the Islam case is exceptional, not comparable to that of other religions and thus requiring special actions entrusted to particular the political and juridical instruments (Allievi 2009, 2010). A new attempt has been launched in 2015. In part repeating and in part reworking the formulae used in the past, the Minister of Internal Affairs formed another council for relations with Italian Islam setting up two commissions. The first was composed of exponents of the principal national federations that coordinate the activities of places of prayer and the other, made up of the academics and scholars on contemporary Islam. The relevance of terrorism associated prevalently with the radical image of Islam is one of the reasons that convinced the government to reopen the negotiation with Muslim organizations. The need to change the ways and means of integrating the Islamic presence in Italian society has been dictated also by the awareness on the part of politicians that the question cannot be reduced simply to a problem of security linked to the threat of jihadist proselytism (Guolo 2015).

Finally, it is good to remind the role played by the Catholic Church in all these years as regard Islam. While attempts to recognize Islam by the Italian governments failed, the Catholic Church, in all its articulations (from bishops to parishioners, from volunteer groups engaged in care migrants and refugees to Caritas) was an important cultural and religious mediator. No government in Italy can ignore this active presence of the Catholic Church, and in some cases its social action can push a government to tackle and solve long-lost issues that are unresolved or removed from the political agenda.

Islam in a Catholic Country

Italian people continue to consider their country a relatively homogenous society in a religious sense. The social and linguistic customs marking Italian life continue to mirror a reflection of this collective self-awareness. Catholicism is the matrix that engenders that identity. The vast majority of Italians continue to define themselves as Catholics, and in keeping with that view, they are relatively faithful to the ritual forms prescribed by the Catholic Church (in particular with regard to attendance at Sunday Mass). On average, in comparison with other European countries (except for Ireland), Italy has the highest level of religious observance (24 per cent), and religious socialization still remains at high levels (80 per cent); at the same time trust in the church as an institution remains relatively high (above 60 per cent) (Cartocci 2011; Frisina, Garelli, and Pace 2012; Garelli 2011). Almost unanimously, Italians perceive themselves as Catholic, a perception that includes a plurality of ways of belonging to the Church associated to various forms of religious practice and flexibility in many areas of social and individual life. The formula that summarizes this variety of attitudes is the *unity in diversity*.

Italians continue to believe that Catholicism facilitates a unified perception of a situation that is increasingly differentiated in religious, ethical, and moral terms. The presence of the *other*, identified as the *Muslim* has contributed, in at least a part of the Italian population, to reinforcing the sense of shared cultural roots springing from Catholicism. This collective belief is shored up and fortified even today, although to a lesser degree with respect to the recent past, by the social bonds that individuals establish with various local institutions (parish churches, Catholic associations, volunteer groups, and so on), which exist at a grassroots level as manifestations of the Catholic church throughout the country.

We cannot ignore the tensions assaulting the ethnic and cultural identity of the Italian people, if such an identity has ever existed in a land of a thousand 'bell towers' (an idiomatic expression referring to the country's fragmented, individualistic local identities). If we were to overlook or misconstrue this tension, it would be impossible to comprehend why a majority of Italians today collectively identify with being Catholic. From this point of view, Catholicism of and for Italians (both believers and non-believers with different ideological viewpoints) is a generalized symbolic code that in some ways reduces the contingency and differentiation that actually exists in the society, particularly today as it faces a transformation from a single religion dominated society to a nation characterized by increasing religious diversity. All the elements mentioned above explain why the majority of Italians feel that Catholicism represents even today a shared value system contributing to a sense of belonging despite the secularization process, taking place in many fields of everyday life.

To understand the infrastructures that shape the religious public sphere in Italy and the function allotted to Islam in Italy, it is important to remind the juridical position of religions in Italian society particularly with respect to the dispositions established by Italy's new Constitution at the end of World War II. Table 11.1 outlines the pivotal role played by the Catholic Church and the legal position of other religious minorities in Italy.

Table 11.1 shows that in spite of many turning points in Italian history the privileged status enjoyed by the Catholic Church has endured. After the fall of Berlin Wall and the collapse of the Italian political system in 1992, the role recognized to the Catholic Church was politically supported by a right-wing Government operating between 2001 and 2006 (Berlusconi's second and third administrations) and between 2008 and 2011 (Berlusconi's fourth government). The Northern League, a right-wing regionalist, founded in 1989 by Umberto Bossi, played an important role in that government. The new party advocated secession of the north from the south, blocking all immigration in general and specifically Muslim immigrants to prevent the spread

TABLE 11.1 Changes in the relationships between the State, the Catholic Church, and religious minorities

1848 Carlo Alberto of Savoia Statute (Pre-unification Italian State)	The 1929 Concordat between the Fascist State and the Holy See	The Concordat was incorporated into the Republican Constitution	The 1984 revision of the Concordat (Centre-Left Government)	The 2001 political change
Catholicism was the religion of the State	Catholicism was the only religion of the State.	The principle of separation between State and Church was limited by recognition in the Constitution (art. 7) of the 1929 Concordat: Catholicism remained the religion of the State.	Abolishing the formula 'Catholicism is the religion of the State', it reaffirmed the centrality of the Catholicism in the national identity.	Since the 9/11 2001 many politicians (more from the right-wing, less from left) have encouraged the Catholic Church to play *de facto* the role of the religion of the State.
Other religious minorities (Waldensians, Jews and so on) were recognized by the State	The other religious minorities were recognized by the concordat *as cults admitted* by the State.	Religious freedom was guaranteed but minorities were tolerated.	According to the new revision there was an agreement (*intesa*) between the State and some specific religious minorities granting them similar financial benefits.	While the public sphere is exclusively occupied by the Catholic Church which has *de facto* been re-established. No agreement (*intesa*) with some religious minorities (Jehova's Witnesses, Buddhists and Muslims)

Source: Ferrari (2013).

of Islam. Anti-Islam rhetoric and gestures have in particular marked the party's rise and evolution (Guolo 2012; McDonnell 2016; Pace 1997). Following an identity crisis when Bossi stepped down, the party put on a new face and now, having abandoned the idea of secession; it openly aligns with Le Pen's National Front in France. Consequently, the anti *islamization* of Italy becomes a crucial point of the ideological discourse, in defence of the Catholic roots and against any form of cultural hybridization.

During the right-wing government, particularly after 9/11 Twin Towers attacks, Italy's policy on immigration was that of favouring the arrival of immigrants from Eastern European countries and discouraging entry of immigrants from so-called Muslim countries. In a public address in September 2000 presented to an audience made up of members of the Caritas/Migrantes, Cardinal Giacomo Biffi, the Bishop of Bologna (the capital of the Emilia-Romagna, traditionally a *red* region, ruled by the Communist and Socialist parties) pointedly listed those migrants whose integration is greatly facilitated because of their religious affiliation. At the top, those who come from Catholic (like Philippine or Latin America), and Christian (like Eastern Europe) countries. The second choice for the Cardinal would be Asian which, according to him, integrate quite easily. Muslims at the contrary are determined to remain substantially different from our values and rules, particularly their 'fundamentalist vision' (Biffi 2000) based on 'the perfect identification between religion and politics'. The Bishop told that his proposal would be a sustainable integration policy, not linked to xenophobia or religious discrimination.

Up until now, the Italian Parliament has been unable to pass a law on freedom of religion that officially does not exist in spite of the liberal sentences in the 1948 Constitution. Efforts to change the situation began 10 years ago, but have led to no real signs of progress. On the one hand, the new law would introduce equality of the various religious institutions and communities existing in Italy in the eyes of the State, on the other, it implies the end of the Catholic juridical primacy in Italy because there would be common rules for both the religion of the majority and for all the minority ones. Indeed both the Catholic Church (at least the Italian Bishops Conference-CEI) and the right-wing political parties (and some factions within the left-wing parties) would like to maintain the Concordat regime because it supports the following:

1. A series of privileges enjoyed by the Catholic Church (financial support by the State to Catholic schools, the centrality of the Catholic teaching in public schools);
2. Recognition of the Catholic Church as the public guardian of the collective memory and the national identity which would reduce the incumbent effect of religious pluralism that is beginning to shape the Italian landscape, especially with regard to a religion that is often portrayed as aggressive and intolerant (that is, Islam);
3. To confirm the historical compromise and agreement to divide *moral labour* between the State and the Church, an arrangement that integrates religion and politics (according to the *entente cordiale* model) in the attempt to maintain social order.

The Catholic Church has firmly opposed the text of the new law on the freedom of religion precisely because it would mean recognizing the equality of all religions in the eyes of the State. The Church then together with the political establishment continues to be interested in conserving the hierarchic state–church structure, a privileged axis that places other religious minorities in a lower, less privileged position. In fact, little is heard about other religious interpretations when moral issues such as euthanasia, abortion, gay unions are being debated. From this perspective, Islam represents the tolerated religion that the *wicat* (White Italian Catholic) may regard suspiciously, an attitude that limits its influence and position in the Italian society (Frisina and Pace 2011). Two examples can demonstrate this point of view. Firstly, Northern League launched the idea to hold popular referendums in municipalities where new places of worship for Muslims are being planned. Secondly, two regions, ruled by Northern League, passed laws that established many restrictions and permits for the new places of worship, introducing double standards for Catholics and Jews, on one hand, and the other new religious presences, on the other. Rules were more flexible for the former, more rigid for the latter. The target is to close many *musallayat* that do not match the general juridical criteria for worship places (safety exits, sufficient outdoor parking spaces, fire-fighting systems, and so on) and to limit the building new mosques (Allievi 2010).

In conclusion, Islam in Italy is not yet a public actor and does not have official status because it supposedly does not share the same values preserved by Catholicism despite efforts made by Catholic volunteer organizations to help immigrants, independently of their religious affiliation, to become integrated.

References

Allam, Magdi and Roberto Gritti. 2001. *Islam, Italia: chi sono e cosa pensano i musulmani che vivono tra noi.* Milano: Guerini.

Allievi, Stefano (ed.). 2009, *I musulmani e la società italiana. Percezioni reciproche, conflitti culturali e trasformazioni sociali.* Milano: FrancoAngeli.

———. 2010. *La guerra delle moschee. L'Europa e la sfida del pluralismo religioso.* Venezia: Marsilio.

Allievi, Stefano and Gianpiero Dalla Zuanna. 2016. *Tutto quello che non vi hanno mai detto sull'immigrazione.* Bari: Laterza.

Allievi, Stefano and Dassetto Felice. 1993. *Il ritorno dell'Islam. I musulmani in Italia.* Roma: Edizioni Lavoro.

Ambrosini, Maurizio. 2008. *Un'altra globalizzazione: la sfida delle migrazioni trans-nazionali.* Bologna: il Mulino.

———. 2010. *Richiesti e respinti: l'immigrazione in Italia, come e perché.* Milano: Il Saggiatore.

Ambrosini, Maurizio and Stefano Molina (eds). 2004. *Seconde generazioni. Un'introduzione al futuro dell'immigrazione in Italia.* Torino: Edizioni Fondazione Agnelli.

Bevilacqua, Paola, Khalid Rhazzali, Clantal Saint-Blancat. 2008. 'Il cibo come contaminazione fra diffidenza e attrazione'. In *Il cibo fra natura e identità*, Federico Neresini and Valentina Rettore (eds), pp. 67–77. Roma: Carocci.

Bombardieri, Maria. 2011. *Moschee d'Italia. Il diritto al culto. Il dibattito sociale e politico.* Bologna: EMI.

Biffi, Giacomo. 2000. *Nota Pastorale 14 settembre 2000.* Available at: www.chiesa. espressoonline.it. Accessed on 15 December 2017.

Cartocci, Roberto. 2011. *L'Italia cattolica.* Bologna: Il Mulino.

Caritas/Migrantes. 2016. *XXV Rapporto Immigrazione.* Roma: Tau.

Cerchiaro, Francesco. 2015. 'Christian-Muslim Couples in Veneto Region', *Social Compass* 62(1): 43–60.

McDonnell, Duncan. 2016. 'The Lega Nord: The New Saviour of Northern Italy'. In *Saving the People: How Populists Hijack Religion*, Nadia Marzouki, Duncan McDonnell, and Olivier Roy (eds), pp. 13–28. Oxford: Oxford University Press.

Ferrari, Alessandro. 2013. *La libertà religiosa in Italia.* Roma: Carocci.

Frisina, Annalisa. 2007. *Giovani musulmani d'Italia.* Roma: Carocci.

————. 2014. *Young Muslism Women's Public Self Representation: A New Generation of Italian Seeking Legitimacy*. In *The Changing Soul of Europe*, Inger Furseth, Enzo Pace, Per Petterson, and Helena Vilaça (eds), pp. 173–92. London: Routledge.

Frisina, Annalisa and Enzo Pace. 2011. *Italian Secularism Revisited: Muslim Claims in the Public Sphere*. In *Sociology of Islam: Secularism, Economy and Politics*, Tugrul Keskin (ed.), pp. 291–315. New York: Ithaca University Press.

Frisina, Annalisa, Franco Garelli, and Enzo Pace. 2012. 'Portrait du Catholicisme en Italie'. In *Portraits du Catholicisme: Une comparaison européenne*, Alfonso Perez-Agote (ed.), pp. 159–205. Rennes: Presses Universitaires de Rennes.

Garelli, Franco. 2011. *Religione all'italiana*. Bologna: Il Mulino.

Guolo, Renzo. 2012. *Chi impugna la croce? La Lega e la Chiesa*. Roma-Bari: Laterza.

————. 2015. *L'ultima utopia*. Milano: Guerini e Associati.

ISMU. 2016. *XXII Rapporto sulle migrazioni*, Milano: Franco Angeli.

————. 2017. *Ventiduesimo rapporto sulle migrazioni*. Milano: Franco Angeli.

Pace, Enzo. 1997. 'La questione nazionale fra Lega e Chiesa cattolica', *Il Mulino* 5: 857–64.

————. 2013a. 'Achilles and the Tortoise. A Society Monopolized by Catholicism Faced with an Unexpected Religious Pluralism', *Social Compass* 3: 315–31.

Pace, Enzo (ed.). 2013b. *Le religioni nell'Italia cha cambia: mappe e bussole*. Roma: Carocci.

Pew Research Center. 2015. *Global Attitudes Survey*. Washington DC: Pew Research Center.

Piraino, Francesco. 2016. 'Between Real and Virtual. Sufi Communities in Western Societies', *Social Compass* 63(1): 93–108.

Rhazzali, Mohammed Khalid. 2010. 'Il sintomo delle seconde generazioni', *Esodo* 1: 47–51.

————. 2013. 'I musulmani e i loro luoghi di culto'. In *Le religioni nell'Italia che cambia: mappe e bussole*, Enzo Pace (ed.), pp. 47–72. Roma: Carocci.

————. 2014. 'Halal "made in Italy"'. Genèse, acteurs et enjeux'. In *Les sens du Halal: le halal comme espace symbolique*, Florence Bergeaud-Blackler (ed.), pp. 207–27. Paris: Editions CNRS.

Saint-Blancat Chantal (ed.). 1999. *L'Islam in Italia, una presenza plurale*. Edizioni Lavoro, Roma.

Saint-Blancat, Chantal. 2015. 'Italy'. In *The Oxford Handbook of European Islam*, Jocelyne Césari (ed.), pp. 265–310. Oxford: Oxford University Press.

Index

acculturation 8, 40. *see also*
Interactive Acculturation Model
(IAM)
Anglo-Australian University
students' acculturation
orientations and attitudes
92–103
Berry's model of 40
Anglo-Muslim relations in Australia 8
contact strategies to promote
acculturation 93–103
negative perceptions 92–93
Arabization 206
assimilation 40, 80, 84, 177–78, 203–4
associationist hypothesis 70
Australian-Muslims 91–92
construction of 124–25
Australian Muslim students, study of
attitudes of 7, 15
about religion 29
images or symbols related to
Australian 23–25
least liked about non-Muslim
Australians 26–29
most liked about non-Muslim
Australians 25–26
Muslim students' knowledge of
Christianity 30
need for multiculturalism 33–35
students' knowledge and attitudes
to Australia 30–32

students' perception of dual
Islamic and 'Australian'
identities 7, 15, 20–23
survey method and sample
characteristics 19–20
towards Christians 31
Australian Security Intelligence
Organisation (ASIO) 117, 119

Battle of Broken Hill (1915) 116n5
bonding and bridging 191–93

Canadian 9/11, Project Samossa 70n5
Canadian academia
future of Islam in open societies
76
Islamic faith and violence,
correlation between 77–78
Islamist inspired home-grown
terrorism 77, 79–80
orthodox understanding of Islam
76
radicalization factors 78–79
Canadian Muslims 69n2
Canadian perception of Muslims and
Islam 8, 69
anti-Muslim sentiments and
anti-Islam feelings 74
associationist views and theses
80–84
of Canadian academia 75–80

mass media, role in influencing 74–75
securitization of Muslims and Islam 84–85
security and counterterrorism 71–75
  in terms of relations between Muslims and non-Muslims 72
  terrorism-related risk perceptions 73–74, 74n9
Christendom 1
Christians
  negative attitudes towards 4
  self-identification of Christian minorities in Muslims countries 17
The Clash of Civilizations 2
Clyne, Irene 16
common good, notion of 179–81
conversion 10, 216–17
  in Australian context 218–19
  self-other relations, impact on 217–18
  Western converts, impact on 218
conversion to Islam, Australian context, study
  experiences 233–34
  interpretations and 'expressions' of Islam 223–27
  methodology 219–20
  motivations for 220–22
  social implications and effects 227–33
Council of American-Islamic Relations (CAIR) 130
Countering Violent Extremism (CVE) 81–84
Credlin, Peta 39

Direct and Indirect (distal) contact strategies 93, 99–104

Dual Identity Electronic Contact (DIEC) strategy 102–3

extended contact 100

faith-based statistics in Canada 69n1
French Quebec Identity 83n14

global jihadism 9, 156–59, 165–69
  forms of jihad 167–68
  kinds of *jihad fi sabilillah* 166–67
Gulf war, 1990–1 129

identity, concept of
  group or collective identity 130
  Muslim identity 130
  social identity 130–31
integration 40
Interactive Acculturation Model (IAM) 93
  acculturation orientations, desirable 96–98
  experiences 95–98
  features of 94–95
Iranian Revolution of 1978–9 2, 129, 156
Islam
  in Australia 16
  in Catholic country 249–54
  Kabyles perception of 212–13
  mainstream Australian perception of 56
  media representation of 138–45
  negative portrayal of 2
Islamic State of Iraq and the Levant (ISIL) 129
Islamic terrorism 80, 116
Islamic violence 41
Islamist extremism in Canada 80–81
Islamophobia 177

in Czech Republic 210–12
experience of 122
Islamophobic incidents and
'Muslim question' 129–30,
151–53
Islam-West relations 1, 156–57
embracing of modernization and
national development 161–62
impact of colonialism 1–2, 157–61
Muslim radicalization and 169–73
Italy
adaptation of Muslims to Italian
society 239
conversion to Islam 246
immigration impact in 238
Islamic organizations in 244–46
legal rights of Muslims 248
Mosques and *musallyat* centres in
240–44
Muslim immigrants in 237–40
Muslim participation in social
actions 246–47
recognition of citizenship 238–39
recognition of Islam 246, 249

Jewish religious radicals 111

Kabyles in Algeria
Algerian national identity *vs*
identity of 205–8
polarization between Arabs and
Kabyles 202–8
Kabyles in Czech Republic 10, 197–98
characteristics of migration
209–10
identity 208–9, 212–13
Islamophobia and 210–12
perception of Islam 212–13
religious practice of 198–202

Lebanese Muslim criminal gangs 118

mainstream Australian perception of
Muslims and Islam, study of 7–8,
39
about Christian Palestinian
migrants 56–58
about Iran 58
cultural and historical differences
between Christians and
Muslims 61–64
gender differences 51–53
images or symbols related to
Muslims 44–46
knowledgeable about Muslim and
Islam and 56
least liked about Muslims 48–50
most liked about Muslims 46–47
opinions of those with Muslim
friends and those without
55–56
proportion of correct responses
56–61
religious affiliation and 53–54, 63
statements relating to 'Muslims'
58–61
survey method and sample
characteristics 43–44
mainstream community *vs* Muslims
39–40
Manji, Irshad 76
Manne, Robert 5, 35
marginalization 40
moderate Muslims 5
Muslim asylum seekers 118
Muslim exceptionalism in Canadian
immigrant policy 69–70, 85
Muslim identity in Australia
attitudes of Muslims towards
Australia 18
students' perception of dual
Islamic and 'Australian'
identities 7, 15

'Muslim question' 84–85, 129
  adaptation strategy to cope with
    150–51
  in context of contemporary
    incidents 131–33
  identity formation and 136–49
  Islamophobic incidents and 129–30
  media representation of Islam and
    Muslims 138–42
  racialization, post 9/11 145–49
  as strategy to combat
    homegrown terrorism and
    Islamophobia 151–53
  use of excessive force by law
    enforcement agencies 149
Muslim radicalism/radicalization
    8–9, 108–13, 156–59
  goal of Muslim radicals 111
  Islam-West relations and 169–73
  meaning 163–65
  in Nigeria 113
  political aspect of 171
  problems with 113
  as rage against Western
    globalization 170–71
  as solution to crisis of modernity
    112
  Western political discourse of 112
Muslims
  in Catholic country 10, 238–54
  in Dutch Society 9, 177–91
  in Europe 177, 180–81
  media representation of 138–45
  negative views of 2–4
Muslim schools in Australia 16
  curriculum content in 16
Muslim world 1, 9. *see also* global
  jihadism; Muslim radicalism/
  radicalization
  popular uprisings against
    European "benefactors" 171

Western impositions and denials,
    impact 169–72
  young middle class Muslims
    162–63

Netherlands, the, Muslims in 177–78
  participation in charitable work
    186–87
  participatory practices and
    conceptions 183–86
  societal engagement 186–91
  Turkish Muslims 185
New Australians 38
non-violent radicalists 113
Not in my name 177

'other'/'othering'/'Risky Other'
    114–18
  counterterrorism and countering
    violent extremism strategies
    118–24
  operational function of 115
  restriction of use of public spaces
    115–16

participation society 180

Reader, Ian 75
religion in Dutch society 181–82
religious activities 186
religious conversion 217. *see also*
  conversion
religious radicalism 110–11

Salman Rushdie affair, 1989 129
secularism 17
securitization
  in Canada 84–85
  direct or indirect consequences of
    121–22
  effect on citizenship 122

as political technique of framing
policy questions 123
as a preventive measure 118–24
as regulatory tool or strategy 122
social exclusion of Muslims and
118–24
separation 40
social exclusion of Muslims 8,
114–18
employment rate, effect on 121
Islamophobia, experience of 122
securitization and 118–24
sense of alienation 121

terrorist attacks 2, 69n3, 112, 117–18,
129, 156
Ottawa and Saint-Jean-sur-
Richelieu 73
transnational governmentality 122

vicarious contact 100

Western Europe, anti-Muslim and
anti-Jewish opinion in 3–4
Wij Blijven Hier (We Stay Here) 178

young middle class Muslims 162–63
young Muslims' identity (Australia
and US), study of 9
adaptation strategy to cope with
'Muslim question' 153
bicultural self-identity 150
endorsement as Muslim, journey
136–38
media representation of Islam and
Muslims 142–45
'Muslim question' and identity
formation 136–49
religiosity and civic behaviour
138–42
research methodology 133–35
survey method and sample
characteristics 134–35

Editors and Contributors

Editors

Jan A. Ali (PhD) is a religious sociologist specializing in Islam. He is a senior lecturer in Islam and Modernity at the School of Humanities and Communication Arts, University of Western Sydney. His main sociological focus is the study of existential Islam. Currently, Jan is working on three separate research projects. His first project is a study of different aspects of Muslim terrorism particularly its causes and consequences. In his second project Jan is looking at Rohingyas in Australia, and the third project is a collaboration with Professor Shahadat Hosse in examining the redefinition and reconfiguration of Global City of Sydney.

Abe W. Ata graduated in social psychology from the American University of Beirut and was soon nominated as a delegate to the United Nations World Youth Assembly in New York. He gained his doctorate at the University of Melbourne in 1980 and has since been teaching and researching at several Australian, American, Jordanian, West Bank, and Danish universities. Currently, Abe is working at Deakin University and is adjunct professor at Swinburne University. His publications span 124 journal articles, 18 books, and 23 entries in the *Encyclopaedia of Australian Religions* (2009), *Encyclopaedia of the Australian People* (2001), and the *Encyclopaedia of Melbourne* (2005). Several of his books were nominated for the Prime Minister's Book Awards including, *International Education and Cultural-Linguistic Experiences of International Students in Australia* (2015). He was also nominated as the Australian of the Year in 2011 and 2015.

Contributors

Hisham M. Abu-Rayya received his PhD in social-developmental psychology at the University of Cambridge, England, in 2005. Since then, Professor Abu-Rayya is the recipient of research fellowships for outstanding young researchers, such as the University of Sydney (Australia) Postdoc Research fellowship and Maof fellowship at the University of Haifa. He also won the highly competitive research grants such as the Australian Research Council Project Discovery Grant and Israeli Science Foundation Grant. Abu-Rayya's teaches at the University of Haifa, Israel, and is also an adjunct professor at La Trobe University, Australia. Abu-Rayya is particularly interested in cross-cultural transitions/acculturation, religiosity, and adjustment; inter-group relations and prejudice reduction; and mixed-cultural marriages, identity, and adaptation. His research is published in high impact social and cultural psychology journals.

Drew Cottle (PhD) teaches history and politics at Western Sydney University, Australia, with a deepening interest in international relations of the Middle East. His most recent publication is a co-authored book, *Syria: The Hegemonic Flash Point between Iran and Saudi Arabia* (2017).

Ali Ghanbarpour-Dizboni is associate professor at the Department of Political Science, Royal Military College of Canada, and a current federal SSHRC grant holder. His area of expertise is international relations and comparative politics. He has published numerous peer-reviewed books, chapters, and articles, some of which include: 'Muslim Discourses in Canada and Quebec', *Australian Religion Studies Review* (2008); *Islam and War* (2011); 'Internal Dynamics of Civilizational Dialogue', *Towards Dignity of Difference* (2012); 'Does Canada Have Strategic Subaltern', *Infinity Journal* (2016); 'Terrorist Resourcing in Canada', *Journal of Money Laundering* (upcoming), and *Hermeneutics of Military Operations in Afghanistan* (2017). He is a frequent commentator for the French- and English-speaking media on current national and international affairs.

Tereza Hyánková is a social anthropologist at the University of Pardubice, Czech Republic. She obtained her PhD at Charles University, Prague, undertook the internship at the University of

Aix-en-Provence-Marseille, France, and was a visiting lecturer at Bryn Mawr College, USA. Her research has dealt mainly with the Kabyle migrants. She has conducted fieldwork in France, Algeria, and the Czech Republic. Her main interests are Kabyle migration, ethnicity and nationalism theories, post-colonialism, and post-communism. In 2015 she published a monograph *From Algeria to the Future: Kabyle Migration to the Czech Republic.*

Nahid A. Kabir (PhD), is adjunct professor and visiting researcher at Prince Alwaleed bin Talal Center for Muslim-Christian Understanding, Edmund A. Walsh School of Foreign Service, Georgetown University, Washington DC, USA. She is also an adjunct senior research fellow at the School of Education, University of South Australia, Australia. Nahid Kabir was a visiting fellow at the Centre for Middle Eastern Studies, Harvard University, USA, in 2009–2011. He is the author of *Muslims in Australia: Immigration, Race Relations and Cultural History* (2005); *Young British Muslims: Identity, Culture, Politics and the Media* (2012); *Young American Muslims: Dynamics of Identity* (2014); and *Muslim Americans: Debating the Notions of American and Un-American* (2017).

Christian Leuprecht is a professor and a Matthew Flinders Fellow in the College of Business, Government and Law, Flinders University of South Australia and professor of political science at the Royal Military College of Canada. In 2016 he was elected a member of the New College of the Royal Society of Canada. He is the recipient of RMCC's Research Excellence Award. He is president of the International Sociological Association's Research Committee 01: Armed Forces and Conflict Resolution. He is senior fellow at the Macdonald Laurier Institute and cross-appointed to the Department of Political Studies and the School of Policy Studies at Queen's University where he is also a fellow of the Institute of Intergovernmental Relations and the Queen's Centre for International and Defence Policy. An expert on security and defense, political demography, and comparative federalism and multilevel governance, he is regularly called as an expert witness to testify before committees of parliament.

Paul Mitchell is a postgraduate student at the Australian National University's Centre for Arab and Islamic Studies. His research interests include religious conversion, the Israel-Palestine conflict, and rentier dynamics in contemporary Middle Eastern politics.

Enzo Pace is professor of sociology of religion at the University of Padua, Italy. Past-President of the International Society for the Sociology of Religion (ISSR) and visiting professor at the EHESS-Sorbonne, he is also a co-editor of the *Annual Review of the Sociology of Religion* (Brill). His recent publications on religious pluralism are: 'Charisma as Transnational Enterprise', *Religion, Nation and Transnationalism in Multiple Modernities* (2017); *Religious Pluralism. Framing Religious Diversity in the Contemporary World* (co-editor 2015); *The Changing Soul of Europe* (co-editor 2014); *Mapping Religion and Spirituality in Post-Secular World* (co-editor 2012); *Religion as Communication* (2011).

Halim Rane (PhD) is an associate professor of Islam-West relations at Griffith University. In 2015, he received the prestigious 'Australian University Teacher of the Year' award. Associate Professor Rane's research focuses on Islamic thought, political Islam, Islamist extremism, and Muslim communities in Australia. He is the author of numerous articles and books on Islamic and Muslim issues including: *Media Framing of the Muslim World: Conflicts, Crises and Contexts* (co-authored with J. Ewart and J. Martinkus 2014); *Making Australian Foreign Policy on Israel-Palestine: Media Coverage, Public Opinion and Interest Groups* (co-authored with E. Han 2013); *Islam and Contemporary Civilisation: Evolving Ideas, Transforming Relations* (2010); and *Reconstructing Jihad amid Competing International Norms* (2009).

Mohammed Khalid Rhazzali is postdoc research associate at the Department of Philosophy, Sociology, Education, and Applied Psychology, University of Padua, Italy; PhD in sociology from the University of Padua and CADIS-EHESS, Paris; visiting researcher at CRASC (Centre de recherche d'anthropologie culturelle e sociale, Oran University) and at IRMC (Institut de recherche sur le Maghreb contemporain, Tunis). Recent publications include: 'Quels destins pour l'islam en Europe? Identités et formes d'in/exclusion des musulmans en Italie' (2017); *Imusulmaninelcontestoeuropeo. In S. Allievi, R. Guolo, K. Rhazzali (eds), *Sociologia dell'islam contemporaneo* (2017); *Comunicazione interculturale e sfera pubblica* (2015); *L'islam in carcere* (2010).

Thijl Sunier is a professor of cultural anthropology and holds the chair of 'Islam in European Societies' (VU Amsterdam). He has conducted research on inter-ethnic relations, Turkish youth, and transnational Islamic movements in Europe and comparative research among Turkish youth in France, Germany, Great Britain, and the Netherlands. He has written several reports on Islam in the Netherlands commissioned by the Dutch government. Currently, he conducts a research project on Islamic authority, leadership, and knowledge production in Europe. He is involved in research on critique on religion and he is part of a European consortium to set up a project on Islam in the digital age. His latest English book (with Nico Landman) is *Transnational Turkish Islam* (2015). He is chairman of the board of the Netherlands Inter-University School for Islamic Studies (NISIS) and Executive Editor of the *Journal of Muslims in Europe* (JOME/Brill).